CLASSIFIED

Compiled by David B. Frost
and from McFarland

John F. Kennedy in Quotations:
A Topical Dictionary, with Sources (2013)

Ronald Reagan in Quotations:
A Topical Dictionary, with Sources,
of the Presidential Years (2012)

CLASSIFIED

A History of Secrecy in the
United States Government

David B. Frost

McFarland & Company, Inc., Publishers
Jefferson, North Carolina

LIBRARY OF CONGRESS CATALOGUING-IN-PUBLICATION DATA

Names: Frost, David B., 1945– author.
Title: Classified : a history of secrecy in the United States government /
  David B. Frost.
Description: Jefferson, North Carolina : McFarland & Company, Inc.,
  Publishers, 2017. | Includes bibliographical references and index.
Identifiers: LCCN 2017021777 | ISBN 9781476664002 (softcover : alkaline
  paper) ∞
Subjects: LCSH: Official secrets—United States—History. | Government
  information—United States—History. | Transparency in government—
  United States—History. | United States—Politics and government. |
  National security—United States—History.
Classification: LCC JK468.S4 F76 2017 | DDC 352.3/79—dc23
LC record available at https://lccn.loc.gov/2017021777

BRITISH LIBRARY CATALOGUING DATA ARE AVAILABLE

ISBN (print) 978-1-4766-6400-2
ISBN (ebook) 978-1-4766-2951-3

Front cover photograph of U.S. Capitol Building © 2017 iStock

Printed in the United States of America

McFarland & Company, Inc., Publishers
  Box 611, Jefferson, North Carolina 28640
  www.mcfarlandpub.com

For Hannah, Noah, Ethan,
Colleen and Kaylee

Table of Contents

Preface

Secrecy historically has been seen as the act of someone who has something sinful to hide. Thomas Jefferson once counseled his young grandson that "when tempted to do anything in secret, ask yourself if you would do it in public. If you would not, be sure it is wrong." Despite the accepted wisdom of Jefferson's advice, however, secrecy is not always wrong, either in our personal lives or in the life of government. Secrecy has its place. Often it is necessary.

When the framers gathered together in Philadelphia in the summer of 1787, their deliberations were shrouded in secrecy. The doors to Pennsylvania's State House were locked shut. Armed sentinels stood guard inside and out, and each of the fifty-five delegates was sworn to secrecy by the convention's presiding officer, George Washington. The American people were allowed no role in the shaping of their country's new national charter, nor were they even allowed to know of the alternatives their representatives were considering. Yet if their deliberations had been open to the public, it is far from certain that the Constitution would have been adopted. Indeed, the Constitution's principle architect, James Madison, had little doubt that the secrecy surrounding the Convention's work was necessary "to save both the convention and the community from a thousand of erroneous and perhaps mischievous reports."

Classified: A History of Secrecy in the United States Government is not about secrets. It is instead about the role that secrecy has played in American governance for more than 240 years, beginning with the earliest days of the First Continental Congress in 1774, to the president's executive privilege of withholding information from Congress and the American people, to World War II's Manhattan Project, to today's

1

highly complex and often controversial classification procedures for safeguarding national security and other sensitive information. It is a book about the tension between the ideal of openness in government and the real-world need for secrecy and the political accommodations that have been made over the years for each.

1

Secrecy and the Continental Congress

The doors shall be kept shut during the times of business and all members shall consider themselves under the strongest obligations of honor to keep the proceedings secret until the majority shall direct them to be made public.—Patrick Henry, September 6, 1774

On September 5, 1774, forty-five delegates from twelve of the thirteen colonies gathered at Carpenter's Hall in Philadelphia.[1] North Carolina's three delegates would arrive later, as would an additional eight delegates from the colonies that were already represented. Only Georgia, which was then lobbying England for assistance in dealing with a series of Indian uprisings along its western frontier, declined to send delegates to this First Continental Congress.

The initial call for a "Congress of American States" appeared in an open letter, entitled "Observation," written by Samuel Adams and published in the *Boston Gazette* on September 27, 1773. On May 23 of the following year, New York City's Committee of Fifty-One, a group of pro–English merchants who nonetheless objected to Britain's often-brutal trade policies, joined with Massachusetts in calling for the Congress: "Upon these reasons we conclude that a Congress of Deputies from all the Colonies in general is of the utmost moment; [and] that it ought to be assembled without delay."[2] Support for the meeting spread quickly throughout the colonies. Less than three months later the Congress was called into session.

The purpose of this First Continental Congress was to formulate a unified response to the passage of the Coercive Acts of 1774, a series of punitive statutes that the British Parliament enacted earlier in the

3

year in response to what many in the English political class saw as a growing and intolerable pattern of resistance to British rule. The tipping point for the British occurred the preceding December when the local branch of the Sons of Liberty, a group of Massachusetts patriots who were outraged by the Tea Act, thinly disguised themselves as Mohawk Indians, boarded three British merchant ships, and proceeded to dump more than 300 chests of East India Company tea into Boston Harbor.

Although nearly all of the Congress' deliberations over the next seven weeks would be cloaked in secrecy, the colonies had made no attempt to conceal their decision to convene the Congress nor had they made any effort to mask the identities of the fifty-six delegates who had been selected to attend it. Some of the delegates were elected by the people directly, some by their colony's legislative assembly, and others by appointment of their local committee of correspondence. Correspondence committees had been organized in most of the colonies for the purpose of reporting on British policies that were seen as unfair and then disseminating the information not only among themselves but also throughout the rural areas where many of the colonists lived. Regardless of the method of selection, the majority of delegates were selected in full view of both the public and English officials. Although the Massachusetts assembly did choose its delegates behind closed doors, the purpose of the meeting was hardly a secret; indeed, the secretary to Thomas Gage, the British Governor-General, stationed himself outside the chamber and, pounding on the door, loudly proclaimed that the assembly had been officially suspended. No special effort was made either to conceal the delegates' journey to Philadelphia. When John Adams and the other delegates from Massachusetts began their three-week journey from Braintree to Philadelphia on August 10, more than fifty of their supporters gave them a rousing send-off, all in plain view of British troops. Cheering men, women, and children crowded the doorways. The delegates' procession to Philadelphia often took on a celebratory, if not defiant air. "As the [Massachusetts] delegation passed through Connecticut," John Adams recorded in his diary, "every town rang its bells and shot off its cannons."[3]

Although the events preceding the Congress had been mostly open to the public, a markedly different approach to transparency would be taken once the Congress convened. Virtually nothing of the delegates' deliberations would be revealed to the public. The doors to Carpenter's Hall would be closed, the delegates would be sworn to strict secrecy, and the official journals of their deliberations would be closely edited. Later, once war with England became inevitable, all matters relating to the war effort would be recorded in separate, secret journals.

The Delegates' Oath of Secrecy

The delegates gathered informally on Sunday evening, September 4, in Philadelphia's City (or Smith's) Tavern, some two blocks from Carpenter's Hall. The delegates agreed that the first order of business the following day would be the adoption of the rules of conduct they would observe while in session and the election of a presiding officer. The formal seating of the delegates took most of that next day, however. Each delegate's credentials had to be presented, read, and then approved, leaving only enough time for the election of Virginia's Peyton Randolph as President (an honored though largely ceremonial position) and Pennsylvania's Charles Thomson, who was not a delegate, as Secretary.

On the following day, Tuesday, September 6, the delegates turned their attention to the rules of conduct. Among the first rules adopted was one proposed by Patrick Henry of Virginia providing that "the doors be kept shut during the time of business, and that all members consider themselves under the strongest obligations of honor, to keep the proceedings secret until the majority shall direct them to be made public."[4] Although the First Continental Congress was not a government in any technical sense of the word, the adoption of Henry's resolution marks the first instance of America's political leaders acting collectively to transact the people's business in secret.

On its face the delegates' pledge of secrecy was at odds with the principles of popular sovereignty and the rule of law, principles to which the delegates were broadly committed and which would later lie at the heart of their new country's constitution. Despite the delegates' philosophical commitment to those principles, the secrecy resolution they adopted ran contrary to both. The public would have no ability to assess accurately what the delegates would be doing behind their closed doors (essential to the notion of popular sovereignty), nor would they be able to judge the fairness and regularity of the decision-making procedures the delegates would be following (essential to the rule of law). Although the delegates' decision to conduct the people's business in secret was certainly not unprecedented, it was nonetheless out of step with the public's growing interest in greater openness in government.

The idea that government is essentially an esoteric business that is better left to those who are practiced in its arts continued to be embraced by many of America's politically leaders in 1774. Even so, that view no longer dominated political thinking the way it once did. The centuries-old acceptance of secrecy in government, historically based on the presumed inerrancy of the ruling monarch, was beginning to give way to a presumption in favor of greater openness in government—a presumption rooted in the notion of popular sovereignty and its corollary proposition that the dissemination of information about the government's actions should be the norm, rather than the exception. The relationship between members of the public and their government was undergoing a profound change. The people were no longer mere subjects; they were becoming citizens. And because of their new-found citizen status, the people were becoming the primary, if not the sole, source of legitimate political authority. Governments were thus being seen more as the people's servants, and less as their masters. This movement toward popular sovereignty was increasingly defining the limits of lawful government and its powers. And among the consequences of that movement was the belief that those who argue for secrecy in governmental affairs should be prepared to offer a proper justification for withholding important information from the people.

The proceedings of Parliament had historically been kept secret from the British public. The votes and speeches in Parliament were all secret, and any member who violated that rule of secrecy was liable to citation for contempt. Indeed, the House of Commons in early February 1641 even expelled one of its own members, Sir Edward Dering, and imprisoned him briefly in the Tower for publishing three of his own speeches. As late as 1747 the editor of *The Gentleman's Magazine*, Edward Cave, was arrested and brought before the House of Lords for having reported on one of its proceedings. Cave was fined and required to petition for forgiveness while kneeling at the bar of the Lords. Cave promised to cease printing the parliamentary debates, but resumed publishing them five years later. Parliament's insistence on secrecy began to change in 1771 during the reign of King George III, though, when the

House of Commons lifted the ban on the press' coverage of House proceedings.

The American colonies had generally followed suit and, in a few cases, had even surged ahead of the British. To be sure, the colonial senates and councils—whose members were typically appointed by the colonial governor who, in turn, served at the monarch's pleasure—continued to bar the public from their sessions. These councils functioned much as an American counterpart to the British House of Lords, approving new laws that were usually originated in the colony's legislative assembly and typically treating any instructions from the Crown as controlling their actions. Nevertheless, more and more Americans were expecting their government to operate in the open.

Many of the Congressional delegates had served in their state's legislative assembly and had therefore been elected by the people. Because those assemblies were generally expected to carry out the wishes of the people, they tended to go about much of their business in the open, not in secret as Henry's resolution required. Those assemblies often published journals of their proceedings and sometimes even admitted the public to their sessions. In Massachusetts, for instance, the proceedings of the colonial legislature had been published since 1685. The Massachusetts General Court was also the first legislative body in America to open its doors to the public, yielding in 1766 to the public's demand for greater access to the assembly's debates. Of the constitutions that were adopted by the colonies during the Revolutionary War, two, New York and Pennsylvania, explicitly called for their legislative bodies to be open to the public as a matter of course. The New York Constitution of 1777 provided that "the doors of both the senate and the assembly shall at all times be kept open to all persons, except when the welfare of the State shall require their debates be kept secret."[5] The Pennsylvania Constitution of 1776 similarly provided that "[t]he doors of the general assembly shall be and remain open for the admission of all persons who behave decently, except only when the welfare of this state may require the doors be shut."[6] Both constitutions also required their legislatures to publish their official journals on a regular basis.

Despite the trend toward greater openness in government, the doors of Carpenter's Hall were closed to the public and would remain so throughout the life of the Congress. Although Congress' official journal gives no key to the delegates' reasoning in adopting its closed-door policy—the journal reports only that Henry's secrecy resolution was passed unanimously—the letters and diaries of several of the delegates indicate that their decision to meet in secret was the product of two considerations: first, Congress' need to move with dispatch; and second, and perhaps even more important, the need to maintain the appearance of American solidarity.

A great deal of work lay ahead of the delegates and, given the rapid pace at which events were unfolding—events which John Adams described as being fraught with "great difficulty and distress"—approaching that work with a sense of urgency was no doubt warranted. Opening up the delegates' day-to-day deliberations to public view, much less to public involvement, would certainly have slowed things down. Caesar Rodney, a delegate from Delaware, expressed that concern in a letter to his younger brother, explaining that keeping Congress' proceedings secret until a resolution was adopted authorizing their publication was necessary "to avoid needless disputations out of doors."[7] Despite the value that broad public participation might have brought to the process, the delegates assigned a higher priority to efficient decision-making.

The delegates also understood that maintaining the confidentiality of their deliberations was essential if the colonies were to be seen by the British as standing firmly united in their demand for a change in British policy. Indeed, it was the appearance, if not the fact, of institutional coherence that was one of the chief advantages that Great Britain was seen as enjoying in its dealings with the colonies. The importance of presenting a unified front to the British was underscored in a letter written in June 1773 by Thomas Cushing, Jr., Speaker of the Massachusetts House of Representatives to Peyton Randolph, Speaker of the Virginia House of Burgesses: "Those who have aimed to enslave us, like a band of brothers," Cushing wrote, "have ever been united in their councils and their conduct. To this they owe their success. Are they not in this regard worthy [of] imitation? Here it is praiseworthy to be instructed even by an enemy."[8]

Cushing overstated the degree of unity that actually existed among the British. More than a few members of Parliament felt some measure of sympathy for the American colonies. William Pitt, 1st Earl of Chatham, an honored statesman who had twice served as the leader of the British cabinet, came out of retirement to warn the House of Lords that "we shall one day be forced to undue these violent acts of oppression." The wiser course for England, Lord Chatham counseled, would be to "retract while we can, not when we must."[9] In the House of Commons, Edmund Burke, one of the leading political thinkers of his time, urged England to give the American colonies a greater role in managing their own internal affairs. The situation that England was then facing, Burke explained, happens to "all nations who have an extensive empire…. In large bodies, the circulation of power must be less vigorous at the extremities. Nature has said it…. The Sultan gets as much power as he can, [but] governs with a loose reign that he may govern at all. This is the immutable condition, the eternal law, of an extensive and detached empire."[10]

Regardless of the degree of unity on the British side, it was all but inevitable that serious rifts would develop on the American side. The economic and political views that held sway in the commercial centers of the north and the agricultural centers of the south were markedly different. The aspirations of the colonists who lived along the eastern seaboard were not the same as those of the colonists who were working to build new lives along the western frontier. In many ways, the American colonies enjoyed a closer relationship with Great Britain than they did with each other. Indeed, at the personal level, most of the delegates had never met. John Adams is reported to have asked when hearing about a speech that Colonel George Washington had made before the Virginia legislature, "[w]ho is Colonel Washington and what was his speech?"[11] Many of the delegates had never travelled beyond the boundaries of their own colony. John Adams himself had never set foot out of New England. Even religious beliefs could divide the delegates at times, leading at one point to a dispute over the religious affiliation of the clergy who would be called upon to offer morning prayer. As the First Continental Congress began, there was little history of successful trust or cooperation upon which the delegates could build.

It was true, of course, that each of the colonies had experienced the harshness of English rule at one time or another. That much, at least, they had in common. The British historian, John Adolphus, later wrote that "the same grievances although not felt by all, were complained of by all; and the same remedy, without apparent previous communication, was generally recurred to, with the only difference of more or less violence according to the genius of the people, or the temper of the favorite leaders."[12] It was that question—whether the colonies were prepared to take up arms to achieve their objectives—that would be the ultimate question the delegates would be called upon to answer.

Despite the colonies' grievances against British colonial policy, the First Continental Congress was not a congress on a march to war, nor was there anything approaching a consensus among the delegates that achieving their goals would necessarily entail a break with Great Britain. While the delegates had been instructed by their respective colonies to seek a redress of the colonies' grievances, none of them had been instructed to pursue full independence. Indeed, most of the delegates, such as those from New Hampshire, for example, had only been sent to Philadelphia to "restore that peace, harmony, and mutual confidence which once happily subsisted between the parent and her colonies."[13] And although the delegates enjoyed considerable discretion in the measures they were authorized to take, it was assumed by those who had appointed them that those measures would be "lawful and prudent measures."[14]

As circumscribed as the delegates' instructions may have been, the individual views of the delegates spanned a wide range of options. Samuel Adams, one of the earliest and most zealous advocates of colonial independence, had little doubt that a clean break with England was the only sure path to liberty. When urged by England's General Gage to make peace with the King, Adams replied, "I have long since made my peace with the King of Kings," adding that "[n]o personal consideration shall induce me to abandon the righteous cause of my country."[15] A more centrist approach was advocated by Philip Galloway, a loyalist delegate from Pennsylvania, who favored keeping the colonies in the British Empire. While labeled by some a "halfway" patriot, Galloway assured his fellow delegates that he was as much a friend of liberty as any, but that "the most proper Plan for cementing the two countries together" lies not in separation, but in granting "America the same Rights and Privileges as are enjoyed by the Subjects in Britain."[16] Philip Livingston, a delegate from New York, stood at the other extreme, deriding the very notion of American independence as "vain, empty, shallow, and ridiculous," warning that if "England should turn us adrift, we should go instantly to war among ourselves."[17]

In view of the economic, political, and philosophical differences that existed among the delegates and the colonies they represented, the decision to contain within the walls of Carpenter's Hall the divisions that were certain to arise among them proved to be a prudent one. William P. Massy, an English historian and Member of Parliament, later wrote that "[it] is probable that [without the secrecy resolution] this famous assembly would have separated without having arrived at any result, and certainly without having exhibited to their constituents and to England that formidable display of union, discretion and firmness which excited so much admiration and respect."[18]

Swearing an oath of secrecy is one thing: keeping it, of course, is something else. As Benjamin Franklin quipped in *Poor Richard's Almanack*, "[t]hree may keep a secret, if two of them are dead." Yet despite the truth of Franklin's witticism and the absence of any penalty for its violation, the delegates for the most part honored their secrecy oath, even withholding information about the work of Congress from those closest to them. John Adams wrote to his wife, Abigail, that "[t]he proceedings of the Congress, are all a profound Secret,"[19] partly explaining to her in an earlier letter that "the times are such, as render it imprudent to write freely."[20] In another letter written by Adams to fellow Bostonian Elbridge Gerry, Adams acknowledged the necessity of the secrecy rules, but expressed his regret that they prevented him from seeking the counsel of others. "I am under such restrictions, injunctions, and engagements of secrecy respecting everything which passes in Congress," Adams wrote, "that I cannot communicate my own thoughts freely to my friends, so far as is necessary to ask for their opinion concerning questions which many understand much better than I do. This, however, is an inconvenience which must be submitted to for the sake of superior advantages."[21] Connecticut delegate Silas Deane affirmed his commitment to the secrecy oath as well, writing to his wife, Elizabeth, that "our proceedings for various reasons will be kept secret, so that on that head shall say nothing until we break up; for though we may publish to the whole world the whole, it would be improper to do it prematurely."[22] Samuel Adams likewise wrote that "[t]he Subject Matter of their Debates I am restrained upon Honor from disclosing at present."[23]

By the time the First Continental Congress adjourned on October 26, the delegates had succeeded in adopting a "Declaration and Resolves"—a declaration of colonial rights and grievances—and a Statement of Continental Association—a written commitment by the twelve represented colonies to cease the bulk of their commercial dealings with England until an acceptable change could be achieved in British colonial policy. The Congress also voted to meet again on May 10, 1775, in the event their grievances were not adequately redressed. After adopting these measures, the delegates to the First Continental Congress returned to their homes.

Congress' Declaration and Resolves received a cool but not unexpected reception when they were presented to the English Parliament. By that time—mid–April 1775—the battles at Lexington and Concord had already been fought. The siege of Boston by the British had also begun. Throughout English society, moreover, there was a growing disdain for the American people and their pretensions to equal standing as British citizens.[24] Less than a month later, Parliament declared the Massachusetts Bay Colony to be in a state of rebellion. Parliament also affirmed its resolve to enforce "the laws and constitution of Great Britain" and called upon the King "to take the most effectual measures to enforce due obedience to the laws and authority of the supreme legislature."[25] Any hope for a peaceful reconciliation seemed all but gone.

The Second Continental Congress was called into session on May 10, 1775, this time at the Pennsylvania State House in Philadelphia, the colonial seat for the Province of Pennsylvania. This Second Congress, like the First, had been granted no explicit authority to govern. Yet it was this Second Continental Congress that would function over the next fourteen years as the *de facto* national government of what would eventually become the United States of America.

Delegates from twelve of the thirteen colonies were in attendance when the Second Continental Congress was called to order, including many of the same men who attended the First Congress. Over the next two weeks, additional delegates would take their seats, including such notable new arrivals as Benjamin Franklin from Pennsylvania and John Hancock from Massachusetts. Georgia, which did not participate in the First Congress, initially declined to send delegates to the Congress, but at a Second Provincial Congress held in Savannah on July 4, 1775, Georgia adopted the provisions of the Continental Association and elected the five delegates who would represent it in Congress. Peyton Randolph and Charles Thomson were returned to their respective offices of President and Secretary. When Randolph was called back to Virginia in late May to preside over the House of Burgesses, Thomas Jefferson was selected to replace him in the Virginia delegation. On

May 24, 1775, John Hancock was named President, a position he would hold until October 29, 1777.[26]

Among the first decisions taken by the Second Continental Congress was the adoption of a secrecy resolution that was nearly identical to the one that had been adopted by the earlier Congress. This second resolution, adopted on May 11, again placed the delegates "under the strongest obligations of honor to keep the proceedings secret."[27] As was the case before, there was no penalty attached to its violation. The Second Continental Congress also took the additional precaution of requiring those who were not delegates, but whose involvement with Congress gave them access to Congress' private deliberations, to swear an oath of secrecy as well. When Secretary Thompson was given permission to employ a clerk, Timothy Matlack, it was conditioned upon Matlack "having first taken an oath ... to keep secret the transactions of Congress that may be entrusted to him, or may come to his knowledge."[28] A much broader secrecy policy was put into place the following year, on June 12, 1776, requiring all employees of the new government to swear that they would not "directly or indirectly divulge any manner or thing which shall come to [their] knowledge." This new secrecy oath was first required of the employees of the Board of War and Ordinance, a special standing committee that had been created by Congress to oversee the administration of the Continental Army.[29]

By the time the Second Congress convened, little hope remained for a peaceful reconciliation with Great Britain. Those British leaders who had earlier advocated making some concessions to the colonies were dwindling in number. On the American side, a growing number of citizens were coming to the view that the liberty they sought could not be achieved without the use of force. At one point, Congress wrote to "The Oppressed Inhabitants of Canada" declaring, "[w]e, for our parts, are determined to live free, or not at all."[30] On May 15, less than a week after it had convened, the Second Continental Congress voted to put the American colonies into a "state of military defense." A month later, George Washington, who had already begun wearing his colonel's uniform to Congressional sessions, received his commission as Commander in Chief of the Continental Army.

Any prospects there may have been for a peaceful reconciliation with England suffered a final blow on August 23, 1775, when King George issued a Royal Proclamation declaring Virginia to be in "open and avowed Rebellion." The King commanded all British officers and loyal subjects to "transmit to one of our principal Secretaries of State, or other proper officer, due and full information of all persons who shall be found carrying on correspondence with, or in any manner or degree aiding or abetting the persons now in open arms and rebellion against our Government."[31]

The escalating tension with England gave rise to a heightened need for secrecy, which, together with suspicions that some members of Congress may have violated their oath of secrecy, led Congress to adopt a second secrecy resolution, this time one with severe penalties attached to its violation. This second resolution, adopted on November 9, 1775, declared that "if any member shall violate this agreement he shall be expelled this Congress and deemed an enemy to the liberties of America & liable to be treated as such, & that every member signify his consent to this agreement by signing the same."[32] Eighty-seven delegates signed the new pledge: thirty-nine on November 9 and the reminder when and as they reported to Congress.

Throughout the nearly fifteen years that the Continental Congress was in session (September 5, 1774, through March 2, 1789), Congress accomplished much. It declared America's independence from England, it established a new national government, organized an army, and engaged in a bloody and costly war of more than six years' duration— all of which it achieved without the public ever being allowed a first-hand look at the Congressional deliberations leading up to those decisions.

Congressional Journals

Despite their decision to meet behind closed doors, the delegates did not intend for their deliberations to be withheld from the public permanently. The secrecy resolutions adopted by the First and Second Continental Congresses both made provision for their proceedings to be made public, although only at such times as "the majority shall direct." Even so, however, the record that was eventually released to the public captured only a part what took place behind Congress' closed doors. Much remained a secret.

On October 22, 1774, just before adjourning, the First Continental Congress directed that "the Journal of the proceedings of the Congress, as now corrected, be sent to the press and printed."[33] This practice of "correcting" the journal continued into the Second Congress. On July 25, 1775, Congress appointed a committee consisting of John Adams, Richard Henry Lee, and John Rutledge "to revise the Journal of the Congress and prepare it for the press."[34] Even with the committee's revisions, though, not all of the proceedings appear to have been made public initially. Some were evidently withheld. On November 30, 1775, Congress authorized the further publication of its journals and directed the same committee "to examine whether it will be proper yet to publish any of those parts omitted in the journal of the last session."[35] Later that year, on December 14, Congress adopted standing rule providing that "every morning the minutes of the preceding day be read [and] as corrected, be transcribed in order to be sent to the press."[36]

Congress' journals were subject to more than just routine editing. Secretary Thomson decided early on to record the final vote only on those proposals that were actually adopted. Motions that were made, but not adopted, were not recorded in Thomson's journal. "With respect to the taking of minutes, [w]hat Congress adopted," Thomson explained, "I committed to writing; with what they rejected, I had nothing further to do."[37] John Adams later wrote in his autobiography that "[n]o record was made of them by the Secretary unless the motion prevailed and was reported to Congress."[38] "This arrangement," Adams noted rather sarcastically, "was convenient for the party in opposition ... who by this means evaded the appearance on the Journals, of any subject they disliked."[39] Thomson's journal also excluded all floor debates, even on those measures that were adopted.

Secretary Thomson's decision to record only the affirmative actions of Congress was influenced by a speech that Patrick Henry made shortly after the First Continental Congress was convened. In that speech, Henry drew a parallel between the uncertain times in which the colonies then found themselves and a man who was engulfed in difficult circumstances, but, being unsure of which course to take, called upon his friends for advice. "One would propose one thing and another a different one," Henry said, "whilst perhaps a third would think of something better suited to his unhappy circumstances, which he would embrace, and think no more of the rejected schemes with which he would have nothing further to do."[40] Henry's reasoning made sense to Thomson, who later explained that "I thought this was a very good instruction with respect to the taking of minutes."[41] Although Thomson's approach to minute keeping was initially his decision alone, Congress took no action to change it. It thus became Congress' official policy as well.

Even those matters that ought to have been included in the Thomson's official journal were not always recorded. Controversial proposals, such Joseph Galloway's "Plan of a Proposed Union between Great Britain and the Colonies,"[42] were omitted from the journal if their public disclosure might be seen, even potentially, as evidencing a lack of unity among the colonies. Galloway's plan called for a sharing of power over the colonies' internal affairs by a Grand Council whose members would be selected by the colonies' respective assemblies—essentially a colonial counterpart to the English Parliament—and a President General to be appointed by the King, who would serve as chief administrator. Galloway's plan failed to win approval on first reading, although by only a single vote.[43] Because of the closeness of the vote, the delegates ordered that it be held over for further consideration. Galloway's plan was duly entered by Thomson into the official minutes. The plan was never given that further consideration, however, and on October 22, the last day of the session, the pro-independence radicals succeeded in expunging Galloway's plan from Congress' journal. Although their identities were never discovered, there was little doubt in Galloway's mind that Samuel Adams had engineered the defeat of his plan. "He eats little," Galloway said of Adams, "drinks little, sleeps little, thinks much, and is most decisive and indefatigable in the pursuit of his objects."[44] The Royal Governor in New Jersey, William Franklin, later reported to the Earl of Dartmouth, England's Secretary of State for the colonies, that "[t]hey not only refused to resume the consideration of it [Galloway's plan], but directed both the Plan and Order [referring it for further consideration] be erased from their minutes so that not a vestige of it might appear there."[45] Although many Americans might well have supported Galloway's plan, they were unaware that he had even proposed it.

Secret Committees

In the fall of 1775, the American colonies had yet to declare their independence from England, a step they would not take until the following summer. Nonetheless, the Second Continental Congress began preparing for war by establishing two "secret" committees: the "Secret Committee" and the "Committee of Secret Correspondence." Both committees were charged with carrying out a number of governmental functions that are ordinarily the responsibility of a government's executive branch—principally national defense and foreign relations. In the absence of an executive branch, those responsibilities, as well as the responsibilities of government generally, fell to Congress. The role of secrecy became even more pronounced.

The Secret Committee was established on September 18, 1775.[46] Its mission was to procure and then distribute the various war materials that the Colonial Army would need, initially including gunpowder, brass field pieces, and muskets. The funds that were necessary to make the purchases were typically raised by shipping American goods to Europe for sale there. Because the Royal Navy had put a blockade in place, most of the American shipments in both directions were arranged through intermediaries sailing under foreign flags. The agents who worked with the Secret Committee were expected to maintain the highest level of secrecy in carrying out their assignments. William Bingham, a wealthy Pennsylvanian who would later serve in the United States Senate, for instance, was dispatched to Martinique by the Committee to purchase "Ten Thousand good Musquets, well fitted with Bayonets." Bingham was reminded in the written instructions he was given of his duty "to observe the strictest Secrecy and not to discover any Part of the Business you are Sent upon to any Persons, but those to whom you are under an absolute Necessity of communicating it."[47]

The Committee of Correspondence was established ten weeks later, on November 29, 1775. The Correspondence Committee's role was to communicate with colonial agents in Britain and with "our friends in ... other parts of the world"[48] in an effort to secure their diplomatic and financial support for the colonies' war effort. Because of the clandestine nature of the Committee's activities, its members began adding the word "secret" to the Committee's name. The Committee soon became known officially as the Committee of Secret Correspondence. The Committee's diplomatic duties continued to grow and later, on April 17, 1777, Congress officially renamed it the Committee for Foreign Affairs.

Ensuring the confidentiality of the two committees' activities was paramount. In order to ensure that confidentiality, Congress directed that the Committees' activities be recorded in "Secret Journals." These journals were kept separate and apart from the public journals in which the decisions of Congress concerning other, less sensitive matters were recorded. On May 10, 1776, when Congress requested the Committee of Secret Correspondence to "lay their proceedings before Congress," the Committee was directed to exclude "the names of the persons they have employed, or with whom they have corresponded."[49] The Committee deployed undercover agents overseas and it was understood that disclosing their identities would compromise their missions. The names of those agents were thus recorded in the Secret Journals. Throughout the war, the degree of secrecy to be accorded the correspondence that was sent to and from Congress by its envoys in Europe was determined on a case-by-case basis. On May 3, 1784, however, after the war had ended, the Confederation Congress adopted a motion by Thomas Jefferson providing that "all letters from the ministers of these United States in Europe, be considered, at all times, as under an injunction of secrecy, except as to such parts of them as Congress shall, by special permission, allow to be published or communicated."[50] The adoption of Jefferson's motion likely represents the first application of the "born classified" principle in the United States.

Preventing Great Britain from obtaining war-related and other sensitive information necessarily meant that the American public be kept in the dark as well. And while the people's representatives in Congress normally had access to confidential information, the activities of the Committee of Secret Correspondence were often an exception. Information about the Committee's work was routinely withheld from those other members of Congress who were not also members of the Committee. Arthur Lee, a Virginian and American patriot who had studied law and medicine in Great Britain, agreed to serve as the Committee's secret agent in London where he was then living. Lee submitted a report to the Committee in late September 1776 announcing France's willingness to provide arms and ammunition to the Continental Army. Upon receipt of Lee's report, the Committee, led by Benjamin Franklin and Robert Morris, concluded that, "considering the nature and importance of it, we agree in opinion, that it is our indispensable duty to keep it secret, even from Congress.... We find by fatal experience," the Committee explained, "that Congress consists of too many members to keep secrets."[51] Indeed, no less a patriot than Thomas Paine, author of *Common Sense*, was later discharged from his position as secretary to the Committee after he publicly disclosed the news about France's willingness to aid the Americans.[52]

As Congress ramped up its efforts to justify and gain support for the war effort, public demand for greater openness in Congress began to mount. Calling upon the American people to make the sacrifices that war entails—the per capita death rate during the Revolutionary War was greater than it was during World Wars I and II—while at the same time withholding from them the deliberations that underlay the decisions that Congress was making—became increasingly untenable. Thus in 1777, Congress initiated the periodic publication of its official journal. Weekly publication became the general rule in 1779. Weekly publication continued only to the end of the year, however, because "[t]he expense was great, and the purpose of the publication could have hardly been attained, as the distribution was on a small scale, and, in truth, the general interest in what Congress did was not strong."[53] The Secret Journals remained secret.

Even with the end of the war in September 1783, and with it all of the past reasons for keeping the journals secret, Congress continued to withhold them from public view. It was not until February 2, 1820, nearly half a century later, that a resolution was introduced by George Strothers from Virginia calling for the publication of the Secret Journals. "The theory of our government," Strothers said, "stands on the virtue and intelligence of the people; and its practice should be that public men should be judged by their acts; that the tree should be judged by its fruit and [it is now time] to see the fruit, that [the people] might judge the tree. Would any honest man," Strothers asked, "desire a veil to be drawn over his acts to hide his conduct from the public eye? [I] conceive not."[54] Although there was some opposition to Strothers' resolution, mainly because of the cost of publication, Congress adopted the resolution on April 21, 1820, authorizing the publication of the Secret Journals "together with all Papers and Documents connected with that Journal, and all other Papers and Documents heretofore considered confidential, of the old Congress."[55]

2

The Coming of a
New Constitution

*It now rests with the Confederated powers, by the line of conduct
they mean to adopt, to make this country happy and respectable;
or let it sink into littleness; worse perhaps, into Anarchy and
confusion.*—George Washington, July 8, 1783

The Failure of the Articles of Confederation

The colonies' formal Declaration of Independence of July 4, 1776,
made it imperative that some form of central, governing authority be
put in place. Coordinating the war effort, securing foreign recognition,
and creating a sense of national identity all required the formation of
a national government—an American government. The task of drafting
a plan for that national government was assigned to a Congressional
committee headed by Delaware's John Dickinson. Despite the importance of Dickinson's work to the American people, his committee met
in closed session without the involvement or even knowledge of the
public. The product of his committee's work was a series of proposals
that ultimately formed the basis of the Articles of Confederation and
Perpetual Union—an agreement among the thirteen founding states
that established the United States of America as a confederation of
sovereign states—"a firm league of friendship with each other."[1]

The Articles of Confederation were formally adopted by Congress
on November 15, 1777. Two days later, the Articles were sent to the
states for ratification. The unanimous approval of all thirteen states
was required. On December 16, 1777, Virginia became the first state to
ratify the new national charter. Other states ratified the Articles during

the early months of 1778. By the time Congress reconvened in June of 1778, only Maryland, Delaware, and New Jersey had failed to give their approval to it. The smaller states were unwilling to ratify the Articles unless the other, larger states agreed to abandon their claims to western lands. New Jersey and Delaware eventually agreed to the Articles, with New Jersey ratifying the document on November 26, 1778, and Delaware on February 12, 1779. Maryland remained the lone holdout. Irritated by Maryland's recalcitrance, several of the state legislatures adopted resolutions calling for the formation of a national government, but without the state of Maryland. Other states, such as North Carolina, supported the Articles but maintained that leaving Maryland out of the new union would only lead to a weak, divided country, one that would be open to future foreign intervention and manipulation. As the dispute between Maryland and the other colonies continued, British forces began launching raids on Maryland communities along the Chesapeake Bay. Maryland officials asked for naval assistance from France, but were urged by the French to ratify the Articles and then look to its sister states for assistance. France's lukewarm response to Maryland's call for assistance, together with Virginia's agreement to relinquish its western land claims, led the Maryland legislature to ratify the Articles of Confederation on March 1, 1781. Thomas Rodney recorded in his diary that "the Completion of this grand Union & Confederation was announced by Firing thirteen Cannon on the Hill" in Philadelphia.[2]

Although the purpose of the Articles was to establish a national government, the Articles made no provision for either an executive or judicial branch. The national government consisted solely of a unicameral legislature, a body in which each state delegation had one vote. Important decisions—and there were relatively few given the limited scope of the Articles' authority—required a super-majority vote of a least nine of the states. The weakness of the Articles, however, was not unintentional. With the decision to break with England having been made only eighteen months earlier, few Americans were willing to accept the creation of a central authority with any real power. The collective sense of national unity and purpose that a functioning central authority requires had not developed at that point. The prevailing attitude among most Americans was that governmental power should be exercised at home, rather than by an assembly of strangers meeting in some distant location, whether in London or Philadelphia. "Independence," Thomas Jefferson would later write, "can be trusted nowhere but with the people."[3] The Articles thus gave the Congress only limited powers, expressly declaring that "[e]ach state retains its sovereignty, freedom, and independence, and every Power, Jurisdiction and right which is not by this confederation expressly delegated."[4]

The inability of the new central government was particularly pronounced in matters of consequences. Congress had no ability to raise revenue without the states' assistance, nor was it empowered to enforce treaty obligations or pay the war debts the country owed to foreign creditors, estimated by Alexander Hamilton to be on the order of $52 million. Not surprisingly, the weakness of the Articles was not without consequence. America's inability to abide by the obligations of the Treaty of Paris, for instance, furnished the British with a convenient excuse for retaining their northwestern forts, a serious impediment to America's westward expansion. It was not only the serious problems, though, that were facing the Confederation that would lead to a political crisis during the mid–1780s. Perhaps even more troublesome was the inability of Congress to do anything to resolve them. Nonetheless, even with its serious shortcomings, the Articles did serve the vitally important functions of legitimizing Congress' action in directing the war and engaging in diplomacy with Europe. Upon the adoption of the Articles, the Second Continental Congress officially became the Congress of the Confederation.

Despite the Articles' failure to provide a workable model for national governance, it did nudge Congress toward a greater degree of openness, albeit only slightly, by establishing the fundamental principle that matters coming before Congress are matters of public record. Unlike the journals of the earlier Continental Congresses that were to be published only upon the specific direction of Congress, the Articles of Confederation created a presumption in favor of publication by directing that "Congress ... shall publish the journal of their proceedings monthly."[5] Publication of those journals was thus made mandatory, rather than discretionary, although like its predecessors, the public record called for by the Articles would contain less than a full account of Congress' proceedings. Specifically exempted were "such parts thereof relating to treaties, alliances or military operations, as in their judgment require secrecy." Even the "transcripts of said journals" that were periodically sent to the state legislatures omitted any matter that had been left out of the public journal on the ground of secrecy.[6] Those excepted parts were recorded in Congress' Secret Journals. Nonetheless, the Articles' publication requirement did mark a significant step toward greater openness in government.

In July 1783, following Congress' ratification of the preliminary peace treaty with Great Britain, the Rev. William Gordon, who was then compiling a history of the American Revolution, inquired of George Washington what course he expected the United States to take. Washington replied that "[i]t now rests with the Confederated Powers, by the line of conduct they mean to adopt, to make this country happy and respectable; or to let it sink into littleness; worse perhaps, into Anarchy and Confusion."[7] While America had not sunk as low as Washington had feared, the functioning of the new government was far from successful. Most of the important functions of the national government depended for their success on the voluntary cooperation of the states. The national government could do little on its own: it had no power to collect taxes, provide for national defense, pay the public debt, or address the ongoing trade issues that were not only straining relations among the states, but that were also hindering the development of a functioning national economy. Thomas Jefferson wrote to George Washington earlier that "on all great questions, not only a unanimity of States, but of members, is necessary; a unanimity which can never be obtained on any matter of importance."[8] By the middle 1780s, Congress had essentially ceased governing. Although George Washington may not have been the most advanced political thinker of his day, he was a keen student of practical politics, and Washington knew that if government was to function, then those who are charged with the responsibility of governing must be given sufficient authority to do so. In Washington's view, "unless adequate powers are given to Congress ... we shall soon moulder into dust and become contemptible in the eyes of Europe."[9]

The worsening commercial relations among the states were among the most vexing issues facing the new country. Each state was at liberty to impose its own tariffs and trade regulations. "The interfering and un-neighborly regulations of some States," wrote Alexander Hamilton, "have given just cause of umbrage and complaint to others ... [which] if not restrained by a national control [will only lead to] injurious impediments to the intercourse between the different parts of the Confederacy."[10] Strained relations among the states inevitably followed. One writer in Boston's *Massachusetts Sentinel* commented on the consequences of the dissention among the states this way: "[i]n times of war we were bound together by a principle of fear; that principle is gone. We are no longer United States because we are not under any firm and energetic compact. The breath of jealousy has blown the cobweb of our Confederation asunder. Every link of the chain of union is separated from its companion. We live, it is true, under the appearances of friendship, but we secretly hate and envy and endeavor to thwart the interest of each other."[11] Firm action had to be taken.

The Annapolis Convention

By 1786, the deteriorating economic conditions in the United States had become a matter of national concern. In January of that year, the Virginia Legislature, at the urging of James Madison, adopted a resolution inviting the other states to attend a special meeting to be held in September in Annapolis, Maryland.[12] The stated purpose of the meeting was "to take into consideration the trade of the United States; to examine the relative situations and trade of the States; to consider how far a uniform system in their commercial regulations may be necessary to their common interest and their permanent harmony." Virginia also proposed that the states prepare a broader report for Congress detailing other necessary amendments to the Articles.

The Annapolis Convention—officially the "Meeting of Commissioners to Remedy Defects of the Federal Government"—began on September 11, 1786, at Mann's Tavern. John Dickinson of Delaware was elected chairman. There had been no attempt to conceal the calling of the meeting or its purpose. The public was not granted admittance, however, nor was a detailed record kept of the Convention's proceedings. A written notation was made of when the Convention convened and adjourned each day, but little else. Indeed, the Convention apparently found it unnecessary to appoint a secretary to keep the record. America's political leaders were again meeting in secret.

Despite the importance of the issues to be addressed at the Annapolis Convention, the meeting was poorly attended. Only twelve delegates attended, representing just five of the thirteen states (New York, New Jersey, Pennsylvania, Delaware, and Virginia). Four additional states (New Hampshire, Massachusetts, Rhode Island, and North Carolina) appointed delegates, but none arrived in time for the meeting. Maryland, Connecticut, South Carolina, and Georgia took no steps at all to participate in the Convention.

The delegates to the Annapolis Convention were authorized by their respective legislatures "to take into consideration the trade and Commerce of the United States ... [and] to consider how far a uniform system in their commercial interest ... might be necessary."[13] The delegates' instructions generally went no further. Only New Jersey had authorized its delegates "to consider ... other important matters [that] might be necessary to the common interest and permanent harmony of the several states."[14]

Many of the Annapolis delegates, seven of whom had served in the Continental Army, were concerned about matters other than trade and commerce. Because of their service in the Army, many traveled throughout the colonies and had gained a broader insight into the challenges facing the states as a whole. Their travel and experience in the Army had exposed them to other shortcomings in the system of the federal government that were just as significant, if not more so, than a breakdown in interstate commerce. Given "the circumstance of so partial and defective a representation," however, the Annapolis delegates "did not conceive it advisable to proceed on the business of their mission ... [and therefore] determined to rise" without addressing any of the matters which had brought them together.[15] The Convention lasted only three days.

In a letter written to Noah Webster some eighteen years later, James Madison, who had been a delegate to the Annapolis Convention, reported that early in the session the delegates' "[c]onsultation took another turn [toward] a more radical reform than the Commissioners had been authorized to undertake." As the Convention noted in its final report to the states, even the regulation of trade "is of such comprehensive extent ... that to give it efficacy ... may require a correspondent adjustment of other parts of the Federal System." It was thus agreed that the Convention would recommend to the states another "meeting ... of Commissrs. with authority to digest & propose a new & effectual system of Govt. for the Union."[16] Led by New York's Alexander Hamilton, the Convention's delegates prepared a report for the states "express[ing] their earnest and unanimous wish that speedy measures be taken to effect a general meeting of the states in a future convention" to be held in Philadelphia beginning on "the second Monday in May next." The purpose of the meeting was "to take into consideration the Situation of the United States [and] to devise such further provisions as shall appear to them necessary to render the constitution ... adequate to the exigencies of the union." On September 14, 1786, the Annapolis Convention's report—*Proceedings and Report of the Commissioners of Annapolis, 11–14 September 1786*—was signed by Chairman Dickinson and then delivered to Congress and to the legislatures of the five states whose delegates participated in the Convention.

In calling for a special convention of the states, the Annapolis Convention departed radically from the prescribed order in which amendments to the Articles of Confederation were to be considered. Article XIII of the Articles expressly provided that no alteration could be made to the Articles "unless such alteration [first] be agreed to in a Congress of the United States; and [then] be afterwards confirmed by the legislature of every State." Given the explicit requirements of Article XIII, the delegates' instructions typically provided that any revision to the Articles that might be proposed at the Annapolis Convention was first to be reported "to the United States in Congress assembled" and then to the states. The only justification offered by the Annapolis delegates for recommending a special convention of the states, rather than referring the matter to Congress first, was that "in the latter body, it might be too much interrupted by the ordinary business before them, and would, besides, be deprived of the valuable counsel of sundry individuals who were [not members] of that assembly."[17]

Although the Annapolis Convention failed to achieve any of the objectives that had been set out for it, it did serve to spark a broader discussion among the states about the need to revise the Articles of Confederation more generally.[18] Many of the men who played prominent roles in the American Revolution were now convinced that dramatic and immediate action was imperative. In a letter to James Madison written not long after the Annapolis Convention adjourned, George Washington laid out his case for a new and stronger central government: "The consequences of a lax, or inefficient government, are too obvious to be dwelt on—Thirteen sovereignties pulling against each other and all tugging the federal head, will soon bring ruin to the whole."[19] In another letter written by Washington to Henry Knox—who would later become the first Secretary of War—Washington acknowledged the procedural irregularity of the proposed convention, but nonetheless stood firm in his conviction that bold action was required: "The legality of this convention I do not mean to discus, nor how problematical the issue of it may be. That powers are wanting, none can deny. Through what medium they are to be derived will ... engage public attention. That which takes the shortest course to obtain them will ... be found best. Otherwise, like a house on fire, whilst the regular mode of extinguishing it is contended for, the building is reduced to ashes."[20] Noah Webster, who would later become a leading supporter of the new constitution, was no less worried about the weakness of the central government, writing that "[s]o long as any individual state has the power to defeat the measures of the other twelve, our pretended union is but a name, our confederation a cobweb."[21]

The Annapolis Convention unquestionably played a critical role in the movement to reform America's system of governance. It would be inaccurate, though, to draw a straight line between the meeting in Annapolis and the Constitutional Convention that would be convened in Philadelphia some eight months later. The Annapolis Convention did issue the first formal call for reform, and for that reason its role was obviously important; but it was the growing discontent with the economy and government's seeming inability to govern that was the driving force for change. Shays' Rebellion, the first major armed rebellion in the post–Revolutionary War period, provided the necessary sense of urgency.

Shays' Rebellion

The inability of the Confederation Congress to exert effective control over the county's affairs was dramatized from late summer 1786 through February 1787 when a group of struggling farmers, led by former Continental army Captain Daniel Shays, took up arms and attempted to seize the federal arsenal in Springfield, Massachusetts. The nation had fallen into a severe economic recession with rampant inflation and unstable currencies. Economic conditions in central and western Massachusetts were especially dire. Farmers who were unable to pay their debts were having their farms seized by local sheriffs, while others were simply put in prison. Although a limited measure of tax and debtor relief had been provided by the state, the Massachusetts legislature stead- fastly refused to grant the insurgents' key demand that the state begin printing paper money.[22]

Shays' Rebellion never seriously threatened the stability of either Massachusetts or the national government. The rebellion was put down in a matter of months by an armed militia organized by the Governor, James Bowdoin, and funded by eastern merchants. Nevertheless, the Rebellion did highlight in a stark terms the bleak economic conditions that existed in the states and the overall inability of the national govern- ment either to improve those conditions or, in the case of Shay's Rebel- lion, to maintain civil order. Many of America's leaders were alarmed by the event.[23] As an object lesson, the Rebellion shocked many men into action who had been only mildly receptive to the idea of a consti- tutional convention. Stephen Higginson, a Massachusetts delegate to the Continental Congress, noted the change in attitude in a letter to Henry Knox: "I have never [seen] so great a change in the public mind, on any occasion, as has lately appeared."[24]

Shortly after the rebellion began, George Washington wrote to Henry Knox expressing his great surprise at the breakdown in civil order. "[I]f three years ago any person had told me that at this day, I should see such a formidable rebellion against the laws & constitutions of our own making as now appears I should have thought him a bed- lamite—a fit subject for a mad house." If the government "shrinks, or is unable to enforce its laws," Washington continued, "anarchy & con- fusion must prevail."[25] In another letter written in December 1786 to General David Humphreys, an aide de camp to Washington during the War, Washington exclaimed, "[w]hat, my gracious God, is man that he should [show] such inconsistency and perfidiousness in his conduct? It is but the other day that we were shedding our blood to obtain the Constitutions under which we now live; Constitutions of our own choice and making; and now we are unsheathing the sword to overturn them."[26]

No recounting of the factors leading to the Constitutional Con- vention would be complete without acknowledging the pivotal role played by the press in building public support for the Convention. By highlighting the economic and fiscal problems that were plaguing the country, a consensus began to emerge among ordinary citizens that overhauling the nation's system of governance was required. One newspaper in Massachusetts wrote that "[t]his state has made reiterated and strenuous exertions to restore that firmness, confidence, and greatness which distinguished a united America from 1774 to 1782, but to little purpose: It is therefore time to form a new and stronger union."[27] A few editors went even further, warning that unless the central government was strengthened, an invasion by a foreign power might even take place. As one writer in Massachusetts asked, "[f]or what is there now to prevent our subjection by a foreign power, but their contempt for the acquisition?"[28] By early February 1787, six of the states had already appointed delegates to the convention called for by the Annapolis delegates.

On February 21, 1787, Congress adopted a motion by the Massachusetts delegation calling for the appointing of state delegates to a new convention. After first citing the Articles' provision allowing "for [the] making [of] alterations therein by the assent of Congress ... and ... the legislatures of the several states," Congress adopted a resolution calling for a convention of the states "to devise such further provisions as shall appear to them necessary to render the constitution of the Federal Government adequate to the exigencies of the Union."[29] Congress was careful to make clear, though, that the convention was being called "for the sole and express purpose of revising the Articles ... and reporting to Congress and the several legislatures such alterations and revisions therein as shall when be agreed to in Congress and confirmed by the states."[30] Any proposed revision to the Articles would first have to be agreed to by Congress and then sent to the states for their confirmation. Following that call, six additional states appointed delegates. While it is probable that several of those states would have appointed delegates in any event, Congress' decision to sanction the convention added an important degree of legitimacy to what otherwise would have been seen by many as an extralegal meeting of the states.

3

The Federal
Constitutional Convention

*It is expected our doors will be shut and communications upon
the business at the convention be forbidden. This I think, myself,
a proper precaution to prevent mistakes and misrepresentations
until the business shall have been completed.*—James Mason,
June 1, 1787

The Delegates Gather in Philadelphia

The Federal Convention—later to be known as the Constitutional
Convention—met in Philadelphia in the same Pennsylvania State House
(today's Independence Hall) where other delegates had declared America's
independence from England some eleven years earlier. Although
the building was adequate for the delegates' purposes, it was not the
picturesque scene that is typically depicted on today's post cards.

Construction on the State House began in 1732, and although the
Pennsylvania Assembly began meeting there in 1735, the structure was
not finally completed until 1748. During the British occupation of
Philadelphia, from September 1777 through June 1778, the first floor
of the building was used as a barracks for British soldiers. The second
floor was taken over and converted into a hospital ward for American
prisoners. It was on that floor where the Convention delegates would
meet. Signs of wear and tear from the British occupation were evident
everywhere. The building's steeple had begun to rot and in 1781 had to
be removed. By 1787, the State House was not in a state of good repair.
The neighborhood was not among Philadelphia's finest, either. Across
the street from the State House was the four-story Walnut Street Jail.
Prisoners called out at passers-by for alms and cursed at those who

failed to oblige them. The only improvement that was made for the benefit of the delegates was that the cobblestone street in front of the State House had been covered with loose earth so that the noise of passing carriage traffic would not disturb the delegates' deliberations inside.

Philadelphia itself was the foremost city in America in 1787. It was a place of culture and accomplishment. Its streets were full of people of diverse national origin. Restaurants, taverns, and boarding houses were plentiful. Businessmen prospered. There was another side to Philadelphia, though, one that revealed the hard life that many Philadelphians lived. More than half of Philadelphia's population of 40,000 lived in or on the edge of poverty. Prostitution and disease were widespread. The heat that September was especially oppressive, the worst in nearly forty years. This was the city that would become America's "cradle of independence."

The delegates' living accommodations, while not always affording the same degree of comfort to which many of them were accustomed, were nonetheless acceptable. George Mason, a wealthy planter from Virginia, wrote to his oldest son, George Mason, Jr., describing his living arrangement. "In this city, living is cheap. We are at the Old India Queen [Tavern] in Fourth Street [where four other delegates also stayed], where we are very well accommodated, have a good room to ourselves, and are charged only twenty-five Pennsylvania currency per day, including our servants and horses, exclusive of ... liquor and extra charges; so that I shall be able to defray my expenses with my public allowance, and more than that, I do not wish."[1] George Washington initially stayed at Mrs. Mary House's boarding house, but later moved to Robert Morris's mansion a few doors down the street. It was the finest private residence in the city.

Only eight delegates from two states, Virginia and Pennsylvania, arrived by May 14, the day the Convention was scheduled to begin. Though clearly disappointed, Madison tried to put the best face he could on the delegates' lack of punctuality. Writing to Thomas Jefferson, then the Ambassador to France, Madison admitted that "[t]here is less punctuality in the outset than was to be wished," but assured Jefferson that "the late bad weather has been the principal cause,"[2] not any lack of interest. George Washington was less forgiving, writing to his nephew, George Augustine Washington, that the other delegates' tardiness "is highly vexatious to those who are idly and expensively spending their time here."[3] Washington also wrote to fellow Virginian Arthur Lee that "these delays greatly impede public measures and serve to sour the temper of the punctual members who do not like to idle away their time."[4] It was not for another eleven days, until May 25, that a quorum of seven states was finally achieved.

During the seventy-nine days the Convention was in session,[5] the delegates would depart radically from the specific instructions that Congress had given them. The delegates did not merely propose "alterations" to the Articles of Confederation, as they had been authorized to do, but undertook instead to draft an entirely new Constitution to replace the Articles in their entirety. So dramatic was the delegates' change in course that several of the new constitution's principal architects would likely not have been sent to Philadelphia if those who had appointed them had known the course the Convention would ultimately take.

Twenty-nine delegates from twelve of the thirteen states initially attended the Convention. Only Rhode Island (disparagingly referred to by many as "Rogue Island") declined (by a two-thirds vote against) to send delegates. Two years later, Rhode Island's decision would be described by the First United States Congress as evincing "a spirit sufficiently hostile to every species of reform, to prevent the election of Deputies on an occasion so generally deemed momentous."[6] Although New York and Pennsylvania were often accused of pursuing their own self-interests at the expense of others—"How long," one news writer asked, "is Massachusetts to suffer the paltry politics, weak jealousy, or local interests of New York and Pennsylvania?"—when it came to fixing blame for the ineffectiveness of the Confederation, many Americans singled out one state above all others—Rhode Island. David Daggett, a leading Federalist from Connecticut who would later be elected to the United States Senate, made no attempt to disguise his contempt for Rhode Island. In a public oration on July 4, 1787, Daggett is reported to have said that "Rhode Island has acted a part which would cause the savages of the wilderness to blush. Fraud and injustice there stalk openly.... That little State is an unruly member of the political body, and is a reproach and byword among all her acquaintances."[7] James Madison also regretted that not all of the states were represented, but was quick to downplay the significance of Rhode Island's absence: "[i]f her [Rhode Island's] deputies should bring with them the complexion of the State, their company will not add much to our pleasure, or to the progress of the business."[8] Not all Rhode Islanders, though, were hostile to the Convention. In a letter written to Virginia's Lieutenant Governor, Beverly Randolph, Edmund Randolph reported that "a respectable minority in Rhode Island are solicitous that their State should participate in the Convention."[9]

Fifty-five of the seventy-four delegates who were chosen to serve as delegates would actually attend the Convention, although daily attendance was rarely more than forty. Nineteen other delegates either declined the appointment or, for one reason or another, failed to attend the Convention.[10] The delegates who did attend represented a crosssection of 18th century American leadership. Almost every one of the fifty-five delegates was a major political figure in his state. Forty-one were or had been members of the Continental Congress, and two, Washington and Madison, would later serve as president of the United States. Five attended the Annapolis Convention. Thirty-four of the delegates had studied law. Seven had served as the chief executive of their state. Eight signed the Declaration of Independence, and twenty-one fought in the Revolutionary War. Although the delegates fairly represented the political class in America in 1787, though, they did not represent a cross-section of America more generally. Their ranks included no women, free blacks, or other racial minorities. White males who were insufficiently "propertied" were excluded as well. As one historian observed, it was a "Convention of the well-bred, the well-fed, the wellread, and the well-wed."[11]

The makeup of the Convention was hardly surprising. The American colonies were still far from being democratic either in their governance or in their political outlook. Indeed, the very word "democracy" carried with it pejorative overtones, summoning up images of disorder, government by the unworthy, and even mob rule. Although the right to vote varied among the thirteen colonies, voting eligibility was typically limited to white male property owners twenty-one years of age or older. Most of those who were eligible to vote not only accepted the restrictions on voting, but also opposed any broadening of the franchise. John Adams wrote several years earlier that no good could come from enfranchising more Americans: "It is dangerous to open so fruitful a source of controversy and altercation as would be opened by attempting to alter the qualifications of voters; there will be no end to it. New claims will arise; women will demand the vote; lads from 12 to 21 will think their rights not enough attended to; and every man who has not a farthing, will demand an equal voice with any other, in all acts of state. It tends to confound and destroy all distinctions, and prostrate all ranks to one common level."[12] This elitist attitude no doubt explains much of the ease with which the decision was made to close off the Convention's proceedings to the public.

Despite the similarity of their backgrounds, the delegates often came with different instructions, usually depending on whether their state was a small or large one. "The members of the convention," Luther Martin observed, "came under different powers; the greatest number, I believe, under powers nearly the same as this state [Maryland]." The delegates from the small state of Delaware, for example, "were expressly instructed to agree to no system which should take away from the equality of suffrage [for the small states] secured by the original Articles of Confederation."[13]

Although the men who gathered in Philadelphia had much in common—their wealth, education, and generally privileged backgrounds—they were not of a single political mind. As was the case with the delegates to the Continental Congress, each delegate to the Constitutional Convention brought with him his own ideas, experiences, prejudices, and political leanings. So diverse was the assembly that on the last day of the Convention, Benjamin Franklin remarked that "[it] therefore astonishes me ... to find this system [of government] approaching so near to perfection as it does."[14] Despite the sharp differences that often separated them, though, the delegates were broadly committed to the principle of political liberty. All were devoted to establishing a constitutional republic that would be founded on the primacy of the individual's rights—a government that would be operated by and with the consent of the governed. When they disagreed—and disagreed they often did—it was more often than not about how best to put that guiding principle into effect.

George Washington was nominated by Pennsylvania's Robert Morris to preside over the new Convention. Washington's election was unanimous. Washington was a revered national hero whose presence did much to enhance the Convention's status and legitimacy. When Washington arrived in Philadelphia on May 13, the event was reported the next day in the *Pennsylvania Packet*: "Yesterday His Excellency General Washington ... arrived here. He was met at some distance and escorted into the city by the troops of horse, and saluted at his entrance by the artillery. The joy of the people on the coming of this great and good man was shown by their acclamations and the ringing of bells."[15]

Washington was not eager at first to participate in the Convention. He had done his part in America's war for independence and, at this point, wanted nothing more than to live out his remaining days (Washington was then 55) at his beloved home at Mount Vernon. Washington wrote to Edmund Randolph in March of 1787 explaining that he was also worried that his attendance would give "too much cause to charge my conduct with inconsistency, in again appearing on a public theatre after a public declaration to the contrary; and because it will, I fear, have a tendency to sweep me back into the tide of public affairs, when retirement and ease is so essentially necessary for, and is so much desired by me." Despite his wish to remain in retirement, Washington was finally persuaded to return to the service of his country. "As my friends, with a degree of solicitude which is unusual, seem to wish my attendance on this occasion, I have come to a resolution to go."[16] Even then, Washington was not at all certain that the Convention would prove to be successful, reportedly telling Pennsylvania's Gouverneur Morris that "[i]t is too probable that no plan we propose will be adopted. Perhaps another dreadful conflict is to be sustained. The event is in the hand of God."[17]

As presiding officer, Washington would rarely take part in floor debates. Only five times did Washington cast a vote, and then only because without his vote the Virginia delegation would have been evenly divided. Outside the meeting hall, Washington was far more engaged with his fellow delegates, but rather than pressing his own views, Washington's approach was usually marked by compromise and a willingness to set aside his own opinions on a given subject if doing so would allow a consensus to be reached.

Major William Jackson, a war veteran from South Carolina who had applied to Washington for the position of Secretary, was selected to fill that post. Jackson's journal would include minutes of both the full Convention and the Convention when sitting as a Committee of the Whole. But like Thomson before him, Jackson recorded none of the floor debates or other routine proceedings. His official journal would show only formal motions and roll call votes tabulated by state (but not by delegate). Only the delegates themselves, moreover, had access to the Convention's official journal.[18]

Although the journal was withheld from public inspection during the Convention (and, as it turned out, for many years thereafter), the delegates did take steps to ensure that the official record of their actions would be reasonably accurate—unlike the heavily edited journals of the earlier Continental Congresses. While that step toward greater openness reflected the majority sentiment of the Convention, it did not enjoy universal support among all the delegates. A few of them preferred to continue the former practice of "preparing" the journal before releasing it to the public. A motion to that effect was made by Charles Pinckney of South Carolina, proposing that a committee be named to "superintend the minutes." Pinckney's motion garnered some support, but was ultimately defeated. Those opposing it, led by Gouverneur Morris, carried the day by arguing that "the proceeding of the Convention belonged to the Secretary as the impartial officer," cautioning that "[a] committee might have an interest & bias in moulding the entry according to their opinions and wishes."[19] The minutes of the Convention's proceedings remained as taken by Secretary Jackson.

Secrecy During the Convention

Secrecy had been one of the distinguishing characteristics of the Continental Congress. It was now even more so. From the very outset, the delegates operated under the strictest rules of secrecy. When in session, they met behind closed doors and drapery covered windows.[20] Armed sentinels stood guard both inside and outside the State House. Extraordinary measures were sometimes taken to maintain secrecy. Benjamin Franklin was notoriously given to talking too much about the Convention's work and, because of that propensity, a "discrete member" of the Convention would often attend Franklin's dinner parties and steer the conversation in a different direction whenever Franklin appeared to be on the verge of saying too much about the Convention's work.

Although the delegates were not required to take a personal oath of secrecy, as had been the requirement in the Continental Congress,

General Washington impressed upon the delegates that "[n]othing spoken or written here can be revealed to anyone—not even your family—until we have adjourned permanently. Gossip or misunderstanding," Washington warned, "can easily ruin all the hard work we shall have to do this summer." It was not until the last day of the Convention, after the new Constitution had been approved and signed, that Washington's "[i]njunction of secrecy was taken off."

There was little doubt among the delegates about the seriousness of General Washington in his demand for secrecy. William Pierce, a delegate from Georgia, reported that "[e]arly in the sessions, an unnamed delegate dropped a copy [outside the meeting room] of the propositions [the Virginia plan] which were before the Convention for consideration, and it was picked up by another of the delegates [Thomas Mifflin of Connecticut] and handed to General Washington. Washington said nothing about it until after the debates of the day were over. Just before raising the question of adjournment, Washington arose from his seat and reprimanded the member for his carelessness. 'I must entreat gentlemen to be more careful, lest our transactions get into the newspapers, and disturb the public repose by premature speculations. I know not whose paper it is, but there it is (throwing it down on the table), let him who owns it take it.' At the same time, he bowed, picked up his hat, and quitted the room with a dignity so severe that every person seemed alarmed.... It is something remarkable that no person ever owned the paper.'"[21]

Washington's insistence on secrecy was formally codified by a committee that had been appointed "to prepare standing rules & orders." Two of the rules brought forward by the committee on May 29 were expressly aimed at ensuring the confidentiality of the Convention's deliberations: first, "[t]hat nothing spoken in the House be printed, or otherwise published or communicated without leave"; and second, "[t]hat no copy be taken of any entry on the Journal during the sitting of the House without leave of the House."[22] Both rules were adopted on the motion of South Carolina delegate Pierce Butler. Butler explained to his fellow delegates that the rules were necessary in order to guard "against licentious publications of their proceedings."[23] Luther Martin later summarized the secrecy rules in his report to the Maryland House of Delegates as prohibiting "[m]embers ... even from taking copies of resolutions on which the Convention was deliberating, or extracts of any kind from the Journals, without formally moving for and obtaining permission by a vote of the Convention for that purpose."[24] Washington noted the adoption of the rules in his personal diary, but only briefly and without elaboration: "Established Rules agreeably to the plan brought in by the Committee for the government of the Convention.... No com.[munication] without doors."[25] Although not all of the delegates may have fully grasped the significance of the secrecy rule, its adoption was the most critical decision of a procedural nature that the Convention would make.

The Convention's secrecy rules were justified on two grounds. First, as had also been the reasoning in the First Continental Congress, keeping the deliberations confidential would stimulate thoughtful and frank debate by holding outside constituents at arm's length, thereby preventing the public from pressuring the delegates into entrenched positions. James Madison wrote some years later that "[h]ad the members committed themselves publicly at first, they would have afterwards supposed consistency required them to retain their ground, whereas by secret discussion, no man felt himself obliged to retain his opinions any longer than he was satisfied of their propriety and truth and was open to argument."[26] Alexander Hamilton, writing under the pseudonym *Amicus* in Philadelphia's *National Gazette*, expressed the view that without the guarantee of confidentiality provided for by the rules "[e]ach infallible declaimer, taking his own idea as the perfect standard, would have railed without measure or mercy at every member of the convention who had gone a single line beyond his standard."[27] By releasing to the public only their finished work, the delegates were able to propose freethinking, even radical ideas without fearing or pandering to "any gallery save that of posterity, one that usually brings out the best in men."[28] James Madison even believed that no Constitution would have been adopted at the Convention if the debates had been open to the public. In Madison's judgment, the secrecy rules were necessary to "save both the Convention and the Community from a thousand of erroneous and perhaps mischievous reports."[29] Madison did admit, though, that "I feel a great mortification in the disappointment it obliges me to throw on the curiosity of my friends."[30] Madison acknowledged that curiosity in a letter to Thomas Jefferson: "[t]he public mind is very impatient for the event, and various reports are circulating which tend to inflame curiosity."[31]

The second justification for the Convention's secrecy rules was set out by George Mason of Virginia, today regarded as one of the earliest advocates of civil liberties. In a letter to his son written two days before the rules were adopted, Mason reported that "[i]t is expected our doors will be shut and communications upon the business at the convention be forbidden during its sitting. This, I think, myself, a proper precaution to prevent mistakes and misrepresentation until the business shall have been completed, when the whole may have a very different complexion from that in which the several crude and indigested parts might, in their first shape, appear if submitted to the public eye."[32] North Carolina delegate Alexander Martin shared Mason's view, writing to his state's governor that "[t]his caution was thought prudent, least unfavorable Representations might be made by imprudent printers of the many crude matters & things which in their unfinished state might make an undue impression on the too credulous and unthinking Mobility."[33]

There is no doubt a temptation to see the delegates' decision to meet in secret as evidencing a certain undemocratic bias. After all, the delegates' work was arguably a matter of life and death for their new country. But while the delegates saw themselves as acting on behalf of the people, they were unwilling to allow the people to observe, much less have a voice in, the important work they were doing. The Convention, however, was not a legislative body. Its delegates were not sent to Philadelphia to give voice to the will of the people, but rather to draft a new constitution for subsequent presentation to the people's representatives in Congress and in the states. The will of the people was thus not being ignored; its consideration was simply being deferred. Seen from that perspective, the decision to meet in closed session is perhaps not as undemocratic as it might appear at first blush. Moreover, the delegates did not hold up the Convention as the ideal model for how the new government should carry out its work. Indeed, contrary to the procedures they followed in the Convention, the delegates were careful to build into the new constitutional framework they were creating the fundamental principle that government should be based upon laws that are made with the informed consent of the governed.

Even those who were not delegates to the Convention and who were therefore kept in the dark by the Convention's secrecy rules generally conceded the need for secrecy. Nathan Dane, a Massachusetts delegate to Congress which was then sitting in New York, wrote to fellow Congressman Rufus King, who was a delegate to the Constitutional Convention in Philadelphia, reporting that he understood the "propriety of the Convention order restraining its members from communicating its doings, tho' I feel a strong desire and curiosity to know how it proceeds. I think the public never ought to see anything but the final report of the Convention—the digested result only, of their deliberations and enquiries. Whether the plans of the Southern, Eastern or Middle States succeed, never, in my opinion, ought to be known."[34] Edward Carrington of Virginia, who was also a member of Congress, saw the risk in providing information to the public about the Convention's work in a piecemeal fashion. Carrington wrote to James Madison that "[h]aving matured your opinions and given them a collective form, they will be fairly presented to the public and stand their own advocates, but caught by detachments and while indeed immature, they would be actually the victims of ignorance and misrepresentations."[35] Edmund Pendleton, the Chancellor of Virginia also voiced his support for the Convention's policy of secrecy, explaining that it "was not only beneficial in that it occasioned the Ebuliations of Fire, Fancy & Party amongst the Members to evaporate in the room of their Session ... but it also prevented ... pre-determined Gentlemen, from making mangled details of the work, and by misrepresentation to Form a prejudice against it amongst the Citizens." The secrecy surrounding the delegates allowed "their work to be submitted to the Public in its perfect State...."[36]

The Convention delegates appear for the most part to have taken the secrecy rules seriously. Surprisingly little about the Convention's daily work was revealed to the outside world, either in the delegates' correspondence or in their casual conversations outside the State House. Even Richard Henry Lee, a good friend and longtime associate of many of the delegates was left in the dark. The only information Lee was able to send home after a stopover in Philadelphia while on his way to Congress in New York was that "I found the Convention at Philadelphia was very busy and very secret."[37] George Washington steadfastly heeded his own admonition. His personal diaries contained much about the weather or where he dined that evening, but nothing of a substantive nature about the work of the Convention itself. Washington's journal entries concerning the Convention consisted simply of either "In Convention" or "Attended Convention." James Madison, the delegate whose personal notes contain the most detailed account of the Convention's day-to-day activities[38] faithfully adhered to the secrecy rule, even withholding information about the Convention from both family and friend. Madison's cousin, the Rev. James Madison, president of the College of William and Mary, once complained to Madison about the news blackout. "If you cannot tell us what you are doing," Madison's cousin wrote, "you might at least give us some information of what you are not doing. This would perhaps be sufficient to satisfy present Impatience."[39] There is no evidence that Madison ever satisfied his cousin's request. Madison, who was the last delegate to die, went so far as to direct that his Convention notes not be published until after his death. Prior to the publication of Madison's Notes in 1840, most of the information about the Convention came from the notes that had been kept by Robert Yates, an anti–Federalist delegate from New York. Yates' notes, which most historians consider to be of "next importance," covered the period May 25 through July 10, 1787. They were published posthumously in 1821.

Perhaps the most remarkable observation to be made about the secrecy rules is not that they were so readily adopted by the Convention delegates, but that they were so scrupulously observed. Although there was surely the occasional breach, the Convention's secrecy rules enjoyed broad support both within and outside the Convention. Madison reported to Jefferson that he was unaware of "any discontent … at the concealment."[40] Madison was mostly correct: the rules did enjoy more than their share of support, though there were some notable exceptions. Luther Martin, a Convention delegate from Maryland, objected to the extreme secrecy surrounding the Convention because it prevented the delegates from seeking the counsel of others who were not also delegates. In a speech before the Maryland House of Representatives, Martin lamented the fact that "[s]o far did this rule extend that we were thoroughly prevented from corresponding with gentlemen in the different states upon the subjects under our discussion—a circumstance, sir, which I confess I greatly regretted. I had no idea," Martin added "that all the wisdom, integrity and virtue of this State or of others, were centered in the Convention. I wished to have corresponded freely and confidentially with eminent characters in my own and other states—not implicitly to be dictated by them, but to give their sentiments due weight and consideration."[41] The same criticism would be made later by the anti–Federalist essayist, *A Plebeian*, during the state ratification convention in New York: the Convention's proceedings "were kept an impenetrable secret ... [giving] no opportunity ... for other well informed men to offer their sentiments upon the subject."[42]

Thomas Jefferson, who was then serving as Foreign Minister in Paris, more broadly objected to the rules' suppression of information. In a letter to John Adams, who was serving as Foreign Minister to England, Jefferson wrote that "I am sorry they began their deliberations by so abominable a precedent as that of tying the tongues of their members. Nothing can justify this example but the innocence of their intentions and ignorance of the value of public discussions."[43] Jefferson voiced the same complaint to Madison who attempted to justify the rule on the ground that "[i]t was thought expedient to secure unbiased discussion within doors, and to prevent misconceptions and misconstructions without, to establish some rules ... which will for no short time restrain even a confidential communication of our proceeding."[44] Later Madison did promise Jefferson that "as soon as I am at liberty, I will endeavor to make amends for my silence."[45] There is no record that Madison ever did.

Despite the delegates' overall honoring of the secrecy rule, a few of them did run afoul of it, although usually unwittingly. After Georgia delegate William Pierce left the Convention and returned to Congress, believing that he was no longer bound by the secrecy rule, he told several fellow congressmen a part of what had been taking place behind the Convention's closed doors. Two of New York's delegates left the Convention in early July and, believing that the secrecy rule no longer applied to delegates who did not expect to return to Philadelphia, reported to New York Governor George Clinton that a radically different constitution was being secretly written behind the State House's closed doors.[46] Delegate Nicholas Gilman of New Hampshire, who arrived in the Convention two months late (and thus was not present for Washington's stern admonition), evidently saw the rules as permitting a measure of flexibility. Gilman wrote that "[a]s secrecy is not otherwise enjoined than as prudence may dictate to each individual—in a letter to my brother John.... I gave him (for the satisfaction of two or three who will not make it public) a hint respecting the general principles of the plan of national Government, that will probably be handed out—which will not be submitted to the Legislatures but after the approbation of Congress to an assembly or assemblies of Representatives recommended by the several Legislatures, to be expressly chosen by the people to consider & decide thereon."[47] Massachusetts Convention delegate Nathaniel Gorham wrote to Nathan Dane in Congress saying that "I do not know that I am at liberty to mention what the Convention has done—but to you in confidence I can say that they have agreed I believe unanimously that there ought to be a National Legislature, Executive, & Judiciary,"[48] while North Carolina delegate William Blount conveyed bits of information about the Convention to his brother back home.[49] In a few other cases, word of the delegates' work also got out, but most often because of a careless slip of the lip. Even with those occasional breaches, though, the great majority of delegates disclosed almost nothing about the Convention's work.

The public was not alone in being kept in the dark. By silencing the delegates, the Convention's secrecy rules also effectively silenced the press, preventing it from playing any formative role in shaping public attitudes about the direction the Convention was or should be taking. Other than what little could be gleaned from noting the coming and going of the delegates, there was little substantive reporting on the Convention's activities. The *Pennsylvania Herald* carried an opinion piece on June 2, 1787, expressing its irritation at being kept in the dark about a matter of such obvious and great national importance: "Such circumspection and secrecy [so] mark their proceedings ... that the members find it difficult to acquire the habit of communication even among themselves, and are so cautious in defeating the curiosity of the public that all debate is suspended on the entrance of their officers." The *Pennsylvania Packet* also faulted the delegates' decision to exclude the people from the process: "[a]t this awful moment, when a council is convened to decide the fate of the Confederation, would it not be dangerous and impolitic to divert or destroy that great channel which serves at once to gratify the curiosity and collect the voice of the people?" Other newspapers, however, expressed greater confidence in the Convention and its work. On July 28, 1787, the *Pennsylvania Herald* wrote that "it is hoped from the universal confidence reposed in this delegation, that the minds of the people throughout the United States are prepared to receive with respect, and to try with a fortitude and perseverance, the plan which will be offered to them by men distinguished for their wisdom and patriotism."

Although newspapers were eager for more information about the

Convention, most, like the *Pennsylvania Herald*, were willing to "admit the propriety of excluding an indiscriminate attendance upon the discussions of this deliberate council." At one point, the *Massachusetts Sentinel* attempted to calm the public's suspicions that something nefarious was taking place behind the State House's closed doors. "Ye men of America, banish from your bosoms the demons, suspicions and distrust, which has so long been working your destruction. Be assured, the men ye have delegated to work out, if possible, your national salvation are the men in whom ye may confide." Even so, it was still a widely shared hope, as one newspaper editorialized, "that the privacy of their transactions will be an additional notice for dispatch, as the anxiety of the people must be necessarily increased, by every appearance of mystery in conducting this important business."[50] At the end of the Convention, one newspaper, the *Pennsylvania Journal and Weekly Advertiser* even expressed a measure of admiration for the delegates' faithful adherence to the rules: "the profound secrecy being observed by members who composed it, which at least has done honor to their fidelity, as we believe that scarcely another example can be advanced of the same caution among so large a number of persons."[51]

Despite the strict secrecy surrounding the Convention, Philadelphia's newspapers were occasionally able to report bits of information about what was taking place behind the State House doors, though only once did the Convention delegates find it necessary to issue what today would amount to a press release. On August 18, 1787, the *New York Daily Advertiser* published an article reporting that the Convention was considering establishing a monarchy to be headed by Frederick Augustus, the Bishop of Osnaburg and the second son of King George III. The report was traced to a political letter that had been circulated in Connecticut suggesting that such a plan was being considered. Alexander Hamilton was certain that the whole matter "ha[d] been fabricated to excite jealousies against the convention, with a view to an opposition to their recommendations."[52] Nevertheless, in light of all that Americans had gone through to gain their independence from a British monarch, even the mere rumor that another monarch might be put in his place left the Convention delegates with little alternative to breaking their silence. The delegates thus unofficially authorized the publication of a statement in the *Pennsylvania Herald* assuring the public that "tho we cannot, affirmatively, tell you what we are doing; we can, negatively, tell you what we are not doing—we never once thought of a king."[53] Even with the occasional lapse in abiding by the secrecy rule, only the broadest outline of the new constitution was known outside the Pennsylvania State House. With the exception of printers who were granted access to the Convention's working papers, only the delegates themselves knew the complete details of what was to become America's new national charter.

The Convention Grapples with the Secrecy Issue

Beginning with the First Continental Congress and continuing through the Congress of the Confederation—a period of some fourteen years—sessions of Congress were closed to the public. The legislative enactments of those Congresses were usually reported to the public at some point, but very little otherwise was shared with the public about the alternatives that Congress had considered but not adopted, or about the compromises and tradeoffs that were often made in order to secure the necessary votes for those proposals that were adopted. In many respects, the average American, particularly those living outside the northeast population centers of New York, Boston, and Philadelphia, knew little more about the internal workings of Congress than they had previously known about the internal workings of Parliament.

Despite the trend toward greater openness that was developing among state governments, the delegates to the Constitutional Convention did little to address the roles that openness and secrecy were to play in the new national government. Although the Constitution did require Congress to publish a record of its proceedings, it was largely left to the discretion of Congress itself to decide what that record was to include. And while the constitutions of several of the states made provision for open legislative sessions, the question of whether the public should be admitted to sessions of Congress was not addressed at all, nor was the question of the extent to which the executive branch should be allowed to carry on its work in secret.

On July 24, 1787, the Convention appointed five of its members to a Committee of Detail, chaired by South Carolina's John Rutledge. The Committee's charge was to assemble all of the points that had been debated, and in many cases agreed to over the preceding two months, and then integrate them into a single document. That document, in effect a draft constitution, would then be used by the delegates as a basis for final debate. As was the case with many of the draft constitution's provisions, the Committee turned first to the Articles of Confederation as a starting point for addressing the question of secrecy.

With the exception of those proceedings that pertained to "treaties, alliances or military operations, as in their judgment require secrecy," the Articles of Confederation required that Congressional proceedings be recorded and published monthly. The distribution of those journals, however, was limited to "the legislatures of the several States." Thus, irrespective of whether the Articles provided a satisfactory method of disseminating information about the work of Congress to the states, it was evident that they could not serve as workable model for the new Constitution. At least in the House of Representatives, the people, and not the states, were now the primary constituency.

The Committee's final report to the Convention was submitted on August 6, 1787. The draft constitution they prepared had been given to the prominent Philadelphia printers, John Dunlap and David Claypoole. The two were also the proprietors of the *Pennsylvania Packet* newspaper. Dunlap and Claypoole were asked to print only enough copies for the use of the delegates and otherwise to keep the details of the draft to themselves. The two printers were also required to take an oath of secrecy: "We and each of us do swear that we will deliver all the copies of 'the articles of confederation' which we will print together with the copy sheet to the Secretary of Congress and that we will not disclose directly or indirectly the contents of the said confederation." There is no evidence that Dunlap and Claypoole failed to honor their oath.

The Committee's report recommended that Congress be given substantially less discretion in the publication of its journals than had been provided for in the Articles. Article 6, Section 7 of the Committee's draft constitution provided that "[t]he House of Representatives, and the Senate, when it shall be acting in a legislative capacity, shall keep a journal of their proceedings, and shall, from time to time, publish them." The Committee's draft thus gave the House of Representatives no power of secrecy at all, and then divided the Senate's proceedings into "legislative" functions, which would be recorded in its public journal, and "executive" functions (such as its deliberations in the area of foreign policy), which would not. Those executive matters would be recorded in the Senate's secret executive journal.

After the Committee of Detail's draft was submitted to the full Convention, it was referred to the Committee of Style and Arrangement, a five-member committee headed by Alexander Hamilton. Hamilton's committee was appointed on September 8 and was given the task of distilling the August 6 draft down from twenty-three articles to seven, and then organizing it into a single document that could be presented to the Convention for final consideration. Several of the changes that were made by the Committee of Style and Arrangement, however, went beyond mere organization and style. In particular, the Committee changed the August 6 secrecy provision to grant the House and the Senate the same broad authority to exclude matters from their journals. The final document that the Committee of Style presented to the full Convention on September 12 provided that "[e]ach house shall keep a journal of its proceedings, and from time to time publish the same, excepting such parts as may in their judgment require secrecy...." Precisely what those "parts" might encompass was not addressed, nor was any guidance given about what the term "from time to time" might mean.

Despite the work that had been done by the two committees, the Convention was unable to settle on a publicity provision that was acceptable to everyone. At one point the Convention even considered a proposal by Connecticut's Oliver Ellsworth's to drop the journal requirement altogether. Ellsworth saw little need for the requirement, arguing that public pressure alone would be sufficient to force Congress to publish a record of its proceeding. "The Legislature will not fail to publish their proceedings," Ellsworth said, because "the people will not fail to call for it if it should be improperly omitted."[54] James Madison recorded in his notes that another member of the Committee of Detail, Pennsylvania's James Wilson, took the floor against Ellsworth's proposal, arguing that "[t]he people have a right to know what their agents are doing or have done, and it should not be in the option of the Legislature to conceal their proceedings." Wilson also warned the Convention that because "this is a clause in the existing Confederation [requiring that the official journals be published] the not retaining it would furnish the adversaries of the reform with a pretext by which weak and suspicious minds may be easily misled."[55] Ellsworth's proposal met with unanimous disapproval.

Because Congress, unlike the executive branch, was subject to a general obligation to report its activities to the public, it alone required an explicit power to act in secret when circumstances warranted it. Even though there was broad agreement that some provision must be made for ensuring the confidentiality of sensitive matters that came before Congress—that never had been the issue—the delegates were unable to agree on a secrecy provision that enjoyed majority support. Perhaps out of frustration or simply because of the need to move on to other matters, the Convention finally decided to adopt a slightly reworded version of the Committee of Style and Arrangement's September 12 draft. That draft provided that both houses of Congress were to publish a journal of their proceedings, but left the question of secrecy to the discretion of each chamber: "The House of Representatives, and the Senate, shall keep a journal of their proceedings, and shall, from time to time, publish them, except such parts thereof as in their judgment require secrecy."[56] It is this provision that is now in the Constitution. It is also the only place in the Constitution where the word "secrecy" is used.

The frequency with which Congress was to publish its journals was not the only publication issue the Convention delegates were called upon to resolve. Virginia's George Mason, among others, remained concerned about the seemingly unlimited discretion that Congress had to exclude matters from its public journals. Mason believed that, if nothing else, Congress ought to be directly accountable to the people on tax and spending matters; that the public should at least be provided a complete detailing of the government's "receipts and expenditures." Thus, in a last-minute attempt to narrow Congress' discretion in the area of public finance, Mason moved that a new Section 9 be added to Article 1, requiring (in Clause 7) "that an account of the public expenditures should be annually published." In Mason's view, the new clause, later to be known as the Statement and Account Clause, was necessary not just as a matter of openness, but also as a necessary check on Congress' power of the purse. Mason's proposal was not without precedent. Article IX of the Articles of Confederation included a similar requirement that Congress "transmit every half-year to the respective states an account of the sums so borrowed and emitted."

Other delegates, while agreeing with the principle underlying Mason's proposal, expressed doubt about whether the accounting requirement was even workable. During the initial debate on Mason's proposal, Gouverneur Morris expressed his opinion that such an accounting would "be impossible in many cases," while Rufus King thought that it would be "impracticable" to account for "every minute shilling."[57] After all, they pointed out, the Articles' half-year financial reporting requirement had proved to be unworkable. James Madison embraced the greater accountability called for in Mason's proposal and, in an effort to resolve the frequency issue, moved to strike the word "annually" from the clause and substitute for it the more flexible term "from time to time." Madison's reasoning was that the phrase "from time to time ... would enjoin the duty of frequent publications," yet leave enough to the discretion of the Legislature. "Require too much," Madison warned, "and the difficulty will beget a habit of doing nothing."[58] After a brief debate, the Convention unanimously adopted Mason's proposal, as amended by Madison.[59] The new Clause 7 thus directed that "a regular Statement and Account of Receipts and Expenditures of all Public Money shall be published from time to time." Unlike the Journal Clause, though, the Statement and Account Clause contains no provision allowing sensitive information to be omitted. The text of the clause is unqualified: the obligation to publish information concerning applies to all public funds, regardless of the purpose for which they are being spent. No categorical distinction is made among the types of spending, nor is an exception made to the disclosure obligation when public funds are spent for military or other national security purposes. Nevertheless, the practice of excluding confidential expenditures from the statement soon became a matter of routine practice. The justification is straightforward: if there are activities that may be omitted from Congress' journals because of their sensitive nature, then the funds that Congress authorizes for those activities should be protected from public disclosure as well.

Congress attempted during its first session to amend the Constitution to require Congress to publish the statement of expenditures "at least once in every year." The proposal was again defeated.[60] The matter would be addressed again, but not by way of a Constitutional amendment. On September 2, 1789, Congress created the Department of Treasury, a permanent institution within the executive branch that was to be responsible for managing the national government's finances. Alexander Hamilton, who was Washington's chief aide during the Revolutionary

War, was named the Department's first Secretary. The act creating the new Department included a provision directing the Secretary "on the third day of every session of Congress, [to] lay before the Senate and the House of Representative, fair and accurate copies of all accounts," together with "a true and perfect account of the State of the Treasury."[61] The early reports were hardly illuminating, however. In his report of estimated receipts and expenditures for the fiscal year 1791–92, Secretary Hamilton reported expenditures by referring to the initial appropriation. Thus, to understand the report of expenditures the public was required to consult the associated appropriation. That first appropriation could hardly have been briefer: a single paragraph appropriating fixed sums "for defraying expenses of the civil list ... defraying expenses of the department of war ... discharging the warrants issued by the late board of treasury, and ... paying the pensions to invalids."[62]

During the Second Congress, Congress expanded its earlier legislation by adopting a resolution directing the Secretary of the Treasury to lay before Congress annually "an accurate statement and account of the receipts and expenditures of all public moneys ... distinguishing the annual receipts in each State or District, and from each officer therein; in which statements shall also be distinguished the expenditures which fall under each head of appropriation."[63] Elbridge Gerry explained the purpose of this additional legislation as being "necessary to forming a judgment respecting the propriety of additional taxes."[64] This statutory obligation is still in effect today, in substantially the same form: the Treasury Secretary is required to submit to Congress at the opening of each session "a report for the prior fiscal year on the total amount of public receipts and public expenditures listing receipts, when practicable, by ports, districts, and States and the expenditures by each appropriation." The Treasury Department discharges this obligation through the publication of its annual Combined Statement of Receipts, Outlays, and Balances. Those expenditures that are made for activities that are themselves withheld from public disclosure, however, are also concealed.

The Convention Wraps Up Its Work

When the Constitutional Convention began, the delegates' instructions were limited to developing a list of needed revisions to the Articles of Confederation. Shortly after the Convention began, though, Edmund Randolph, the head of the Virginia delegation, "laid the outline of a plan ... before the Convention." Because Virginia had played a leading role in calling for the Convention, it was widely expected that an introductory proposal would be offered by the Virginia delegation. That introductory proposal consisted of a series of fifteen resolutions that had been drafted by James Madison.

The so-called Virginia Plan went well beyond merely fine tuning the Articles. The plan called for fundamental revisions to the structure and powers of the national government and thus the relationship of that national government with the states and the people. So fundamental were the proposed changes that the Virginia Plan had the effect of scrapping the Articles of Confederation altogether and replacing it with a new constitution. Article VII of the Virginia Plan also lowered the bar for approval of the new constitution by providing that "[t]he ratification of the Conventions of nine states [and not all thirteen of the states as required by Article XIII of the Articles of Confederation] shall be sufficient for the Establishment of this constitution between the States so ratifying the Same." Eliminating the Articles' requirement of unanimity among the states also meant that the new constitution would have no application to any four or fewer states that failed to ratify it. Those states would become independent entities outside the union, a prospect that would later force Rhode Island grudgingly to approve it.

On September 12, 1787, the Convention's Committee of Style and Arrangement[65] presented the final draft of the new Constitution to the full Convention. On September 15, following two days' review, an agreement was reached on the document's final wording. Maryland delegate James McHenry recorded the next step in his daily journal: "Ordered [the Constitution] to be engrossed and 500 copies struck. Adjourned until Monday the 17th."[66] George Washington's journal entry for September 15 confirms McHenry's: "Adjourned till Monday that the Constitution ... might be engrossed—and a number of copies struck off."[67]

On September 17, the delegates met for the final time to sign the new Constitution. Benjamin Franklin had prepared a speech for the occasion, the "Sunrise Speech,"[68] but because of his frailty, (Franklin was then 83) the speech was delivered by his close friend and fellow Pennsylvanian James Wilson. Franklin appealed for unity in his speech, telling his fellow delegates that "I think it will astonish our enemies who are waiting with confidence to hear that our councils are confounded like those other builders of Babel; and that our States are on the point of separation, only to meet hereafter for the purpose of cutting one another's throat." Although Franklin urged his fellow delegates to maintain the confidentiality of their proceedings, copies of Franklin's speech became widely available within a matter of weeks. One of the leakers was Franklin himself, who sent "a Copy of that little Speech" to fellow delegate Nathan Gorham, telling him that the speech "Is at your Disposition."[69] The speech quickly found its way to a printer and thereafter to a host of newspapers.

George Washington was the first of the delegates to sign the new Constitution. Of the fifty-five delegates who attended the Convention, thirty-nine signed it.[70] George Read, of Delaware, signed on behalf of fellow Delawarean John Dickinson. Dickinson fully supported the Constitution, but was away from Philadelphia on the day of signing. Several of the non-signing delegates had already departed Philadelphia. Others refused to sign either because they did not approve of it or, like New York's Robert Yates and John Lansing, Jr., because they did not regard their instructions as permitting them to participate in the creation of a new constitution. The departure of the two New York delegates had a significant procedural effect. It left Alexander Hamilton as the sole delegate remaining from New York. Because there was not a quorum of New York delegates present, Hamilton was unable to vote on questions before the Convention because he could not alone represent New York's delegation. As a consequence, New York effectively had no formal voice in the proceedings after July 10. George Mason and Edmund Randolph of Virginia and Elbridge Gerry of Massachusetts stayed to the end of the Convention, but were unwilling to sign the Constitution, all three believing that the new Constitution failed to provide adequate protection of individual liberties. Despite the lack of complete unanimity among the delegates, though, a majority of each state's delegates who were then present (New York was technically not present) did vote for ratification.[71] Article VII of the Constitution, the final Article, was thus able to recite that the Constitution was approved "in Convention by the unanimous consent of the States present, the seventeenth of September, &c. In witness whereof, we have hereunto subscribed our names." Alexander Hamilton signed the document as a witness.

Following the adjournment of the Convention, the delegates gathered for a farewell banquet at City Tavern, where, according to George Washington, they "dined together and took cordial leave of each other." And cordial it was. The Tavern's bill for the fifty-five attendees and their guests that night lists fifty-four bottles of Madeira, sixty of claret, twenty-seven of port, eight of hard cider, twelve of beer, and seven bowls of alcoholic punch. The delegates then returned to their homes to begin the task of organizing support for their particular point of view—most for, but some few against, the new Constitution. Washington "retired to [his lodgings] to meditate on the momentous work which had been executed."[72] On September 18, five hundred copies of the Constitution were struck at the print shop of Dunlap and Claypoole. The following day, September 19, 1787, the full text of the new Constitution was published in the *Pennsylvania Packet and Daily Advertiser*. Within a week, the new Constitution was printed in all of Philadelphia's eleven newspapers. Over the next several weeks, it was printed in its entirety in more than fifty newspapers across the country.

On the same day the Constitution was signed, September 17, the Convention adopted a resolution directing that a copy of it be "laid before the United States in Congress assembled." General Washington charged Secretary Jackson with delivering a copy of the new Constitution (most likely the September 12 draft) to Congress, which was then meeting in New York. Jackson left Philadelphia on the morning of the 18th and arrived in New York mid-afternoon the following day. On September 20, Jackson delivered a copy of the Constitution (engrossed on five sheets of vellum parchment by Jacob Shallus, an assistant clerk in the Pennsylvania Assembly), the resolution of the Convention, and Washington's transmittal letter to Arthur St. Clair, President of the Continental Congress. A week later, on September 28, Congress adopted a resolution accepting the Convention's resolutions and directing that the new Constitution "be transmitted to the several Legislatures in Order to be submitted to a convention of Delegates chosen in each state by the People thereof."[73] Copies of the Constitution were printed in lots of ten thousand and distributed widely across the country.

Congress' resolution of February 21, 1787, was very clear in providing that any amendments to the Articles that might be proposed by the Convention were to take effect only when "agreed to in Congress and confirmed by the states." But rather than submitting the proposed

Constitution to the Congress for approval first and then to the states for confirmation, the Convention took an entirely different path, choosing instead to call for separate ratifying conventions in each of the states.[74] By circumventing the state legislatures, those supporting the new Constitution hoped to shield it from the undermining amendments that many of the states, jealous of ceding greater authority to a new national government, would almost certainly have demanded. As Rufus King of Massachusetts warned, "[t]he Legislatures ... being [the ones] to lose power, will be most likely to raise objections."[75]

The delegates made little attempt to reconcile their actions either substantively or procedurally with the instructions that Congress had given them or with the express provisions of the Articles of Confederation upon which those instructions were based. Nathan Dane of Massachusetts brushed aside any question about the apparent extralegal nature of the state conventions by arguing (creatively, but not illogically) that Congress only had the authority to address proposed changes to the Articles of Confederation, not a wholesale replacement of them. Congress was therefore without power constitutionally to express "an opinion respecting a System of Government no way connected with [the Articles.] Given the importance of the subject," moreover, "and the respect they owe their constituents,"[76] Dane argued, the report of the Convention should be submitted first to the states for their consideration. In other words, Congress was without the authority either to amend or dismiss the work of the Constitutional Convention. Regardless of the soundness of Dane's argument, Congress' decision of September 28, 1787, to accept the Constitutional Convention's resolutions largely insulated the new charter from attack on the ground that the Convention delegates had overstepped their lawful authority.

The Convention's decision to submit the Constitution to state ratification conventions put into actual practice the concept of popular sovereignty that was embodied in the new Constitution. The document that emerged from the Convention in Philadelphia, according to James Madison, "was nothing more than a draft of a plan, nothing but a dead letter, until life and vitality were breathed into it by the voice of the people, speaking through the several State Conventions."[77] To Madison, the new Constitution would be "of no more consequence than the paper upon which it is written, unless it be stamped with the approbation of those to whom it is addressed."[78]

The state conventions gave the people an opportunity—for the first time—to learn directly about the provisions of their new Constitution. Proponents and opponents of the new Constitution alike were able to stand before the people and openly make their case. Additionally, and perhaps more important, because the state conventions were comprised of men who had been elected specifically and solely for the purpose of approving or disapproving the new national charter, a decision by them to ratify the new Constitution would confer upon it a stature and authority that it would not otherwise have enjoyed. The secrecy surrounding the Constitution's drafting, however, was not at an end. Much would remain a secret for more than a half century.

Secrecy After the Convention

James McHenry from Maryland wrote in his private journal on September 17, 1787, "Injunction of secrecy taken off."[79] Even with the formal lifting of the injunction, the Convention's secrecy rules remained in effect as a practical matter. Most of the delegates understood that continued secrecy concerning the Convention was essential to securing the Constitution's ratification. On the last day of the Convention, Benjamin Franklin urged the delegates to keep silent about their concerns with the proposed Constitution and any personal differences they might have had with each other. Franklin believed that maintaining the confidentiality of the Convention's proceedings would allow the final document to be seen as enjoying greater support than it actually did, thereby increasing its chances of being ratified. Any evidence of division among the delegates, Franklin argued on the last day of the Convention, would be seized upon and exploited by the opponents of ratification. As Franklin explained, "[t]he opinions I have about the [Constitution's] errors, I sacrifice to the common good. I have never whispered a syllable of them abroad. Within these walls they were born, and here they will die. If every one of us," Franklin warned, "were to report the Objections he had to it, and use his Influence to gain Partisan in support of them, we might prevent it being generally received, and thereby lose all the salutary Effects and great Advantages resulting naturally in our favor among foreign nations as well as among ourselves from our real or apparent unanimity."[80] Alexander Hamilton shared

Franklin's reasoning, later writing under the name *Amicus* that "[h]ad the deliberations been open while going on, the clamors of faction would have prevented any satisfactory result. Had they been afterwards disclosed, much food would have been afforded to inflammatory declamation. Propositions, made without due reflection, would have been handles for a profusion of ill-natured accusation."[81]

Although the injunction of secrecy was officially lifted, George Washington continued in his insistence on post–Convention secrecy. Even after the Constitution was approved and signed, Washington reminded Secretary Jackson that it was still necessary to maintain the confidentiality of the Convention's proceedings: "you have been observed to be constantly taking notes of what passed in the Convention during the discussions of the numerous propositions presented for consideration," Washington told Jackson, "but it would be wholly improper to publish them, and I must therefore desire you not to suffer them to be made public while you live." Jackson pledged to Washington that his request "should be sacredly observed."[82] Jackson kept his word.

Once the Convention adjourned, several of the delegates, contrary to Franklin's request, took printed copies of the new Constitution with them back to their state legislatures and on occasion revealed part of the debate that had taken place during the Convention. Anti-Federalist Luther Martin of Maryland was the most detailed in his disclosures. Martin later expanded on the report he gave to the Maryland legislature in a twelve-part newspaper series entitled "Genuine Information." The series was also published in the *Maryland Gazette* from late December 1787 through early February 1788. The series was subsequently reprinted in several newspapers in Massachusetts, New York, Pennsylvania, Virginia, and South Carolina. Martin's report was also printed in pamphlet form on April 12, 1788. The pamphlet was circulated nationwide. Martin was roundly condemned by the Federalists because of his detailed disclosure of the Convention's proceedings. The anti–Federalists praised Martin. The anti–Federalist essayist *Centinel* described him as an "illustrious patriot, a man who laid open the enclave, exposed the dark scene within, developed the mystery of the proceedings, and illustrated the machinations of ambition. His public spirit has drawn down upon him the rage of the conspirators, for daring to remove the veil of secrecy."[83]

On the last day of the Convention, several of the delegates, led by

Rufus King, proposed that the Convention's journals "be either destroyed or deposited in the custody of the President." King was worried that if the journals were made public "a bad use would be made of them by those who would wish to prevent the adoption of the Constitution." Instead of destroying the journals, though, the Convention voted to deposit them, together with other important Convention papers into Washington's care, "subject to the order of Congress, if ever formed under the Constitution."[84] General Washington retained custody of the journals and the other Convention documents for more than eight years, eventually depositing them with the Secretary of State, Thomas Pickering, on March 9, 1796. All but a few of the records were transferred to the Library of Congress over a period of years in the early 1900s. Between 1894 and 1905, the Bureau of Rolls and Library of State Department compiled *The Documentary History of the Constitution of the United States of America, 1786–1870*, a five-volume work that, along with other documents, collected nearly all of the known notes and records of the Constitutional Convention. In 1952, the Federal Convention's records were transferred to the National Archives, where they are now held as part of the official records of the Federal government.[85]

Surviving Records of the Convention

In a letter written to James Madison many years later, in October 1818, John Quincy Adams, then Secretary of State, catalogued the documents that had been received from President Washington: "a Volume in Manuscript containing the Journal of the proceedings of the Convention—a second Volume containing their proceedings in Committee of the whole—A third, containing lists of yeas and nays on various questions—and nine separate papers—Two of which are copies of Resolutions submitted by Mr. Randolph and discussed in Convention, one is a printed draft of the Constitution as reported, with manuscript minutes of amendments to it adopted after debate, and the rest are papers of little or no consequence. These are all the documents possessed by the Government, coming within the scope of the Resolution of Congress at their last Session."[86]

Secretary Adams' review of the Convention documents revealed that the record was incomplete. The Convention's official journal mysteriously closed with the session of Friday, September 14, 1787. The proceedings of Saturday the 15th and Monday the 17th the last day of the Convention, were not entered in the official journal. Secretary Adams thought "[t]he chasm [to be] remarkable, as the adjournment on the 14th leaves a debate unfinished and to be resumed." There was even a partial entry of the proceedings of Saturday the 15th, Adams noted, "which is crossed out, upon the book."[87] James Madison later attempted to fill in the gaps, delivering to Adams "such extracts from my notes relating to the last two days of the Convention as may fill the chasm in the Journals."[88] In addition to the missing two days' journal entries, Secretary Jackson had burned "all loose scraps of paper" at the end of the Convention, even though some of them may have been important, if not actually a part of the Convention's official record.[89] Whether Jackson did so because he thought them unworthy of preserving, or whether he was only attempting to honor the pledge he had made to General Washington is not known.

With the ratification of the new Constitution, there seemed little justification for maintaining the injunction of secrecy. The journals and other papers of the Convention were nevertheless withheld from public inspection for more than twenty-three years until 1819, when Secretary Adams, in conformity with Congressional resolutions passed the previous year (March 27, 1818) compiled, edited, and published them as the *Journals, Acts, and Proceedings, of the Convention ... Which Formed the Constitution of the United States of America.* Pursuant to the Congressional resolution, one thousand copies were printed, with "one copy being furnished to each member of the present Congress, and the residue remaining subject to the future disposition of Congress."

Observers in the years to follow, while perhaps understanding the reasoning behind the Convention delegates' decision to meet behind closed doors, found little to justify Secretary Jackson's decision to omit so much of the Convention's proceedings from the official journal. In 1827, prior to the publication of James Madison's *Notes of the Debates in the Federal Convention of 1787,* Jared Sparks, an American publisher and editor, biographer (of George Washington), as well as the president of Harvard College, expressed a view that was held by many: "On many accounts, it is deeply to be regretted that the debates of the grand Convention ... have not been preserved. The advantages that might have been derived from the arguments of the members were then lost to the public. The Journal, as recently published, is meager beyond description, and hardly fills a blank in history.... The expediency of a secret session of that body is more than problematical at this day.... Had the deliberations been public and reported daily in newspapers, we apprehend no evil, but much good, would have resulted."[90]

One of the Constitution's principal architects, James Madison, downplayed the significance of the limited nature of the Convention documents, particularly when interpreting the Constitution.[91] Madison believed that the records of the state ratification conventions furnished the best evidence of the framers original intent: "[w]hatever veneration might be entertained for the body of men who formed our Constitution, the sense of that body could never be regarded as the oracular guide in expounding the Constitution.... If we were to look, therefore, for the meaning of the instrument beyond the face of the instrument, we must look for it, not in the General Convention, which proposed, but in the State Conventions which accepted and ratified the Constitution."[92]

Although Sparks remained critical of Thomson's approach to record keeping, he did admit that because most of the delegates to the Constitution Convention were also delegates to the state ratification conventions, their presence in those state conventions "diminishes in some degree the magnitude of the loss that might have otherwise been sustained." "It is probable," Sparks wrote, "that these members shed around them all the light which they had acquired at the first convention and repeated the arguments there advanced and the views received by them." Sparks nonetheless held to his criticism that the absence of a complete record of what had been said and done at the Federal Convention caused the delegates to the state ratification conventions to be less informed than they might otherwise have been: "if those arguments had gone out to the people from the original fountain ... they would have had a better understanding of the principle of the Constitution, and [would have been] better prepared to accord with them when that instrument came to be acted upon by the states."[93]

Despite Sparks' expectation that the Convention's delegates would fill in the gaps in the Convention's records, the propriety of doing so was not free of controversy. In a floor debate in the House of Representatives in February 1791, James Madison made reference to the Convention's disapproval of chartering national banks. Elbridge Gerry criticized Madison for using his memory of the Convention debates as authority for subsequent political guidance. Madison agreed with Gerry that it was probably best not to divulge the details of the Convention's deliberations. Later in 1796, President Washington himself would be criticized by Madison for citing the Convention's proceedings in one of his messages to Congress. In justifying his interpretation of the Constitution's provisions for negotiating treaties, President Washington told Congress that "[h]aving been a member of the General Convention, and knowing the principles on which the Constitution was formed, I have ever entertained but one opinion on this subject ... that the power of making treaties is exclusively vested in the President."[94]

The new Constitution—the document "of, by, and for the people"—was created behind closed doors by a handful of political elites. The new national charter was created without either the involvement or guidance of the people. Indeed, Virginia's George Mason pointed out what everyone already knew: that "[t]his Constitution had been formed without the knowledge or idea of the people."[95] Not even the most ardent supporters of the Convention's policy of secrecy denied that truth. And although the policy of secrecy had drawn only mild criticism during the Federal Convention, it came perilously close to derailing the Constitution's ratification during the state conventions.

4

The Secrecy Issue
During the Ratification
Conventions

*The evil genius presided at its birth, it came forth under the veil
of secrecy, and its true features being carefully concealed, and
every deceptive art has been and is practicing to have this spurious brat received as the genuine offspring of heaven-born liberty.—Centinel (Samuel Bryan), November 30, 1787*

Secrecy as a Basis for Attacking the
New Constitution

From the autumn of 1787 through the summer of 1788, the new
Constitution took center stage in American politics. *A Plebeian*
reported in April 1788 that "[i]t has been the object of universal attention—it has been thought of by every reflecting man."[1] Even Congress'
resolution of February 21 calling for the ratification conventions was
a major news story. Thirty-nine newspapers published the resolution
in its entirety, while two others printed it in summary form.[2] In six
states (Pennsylvania, Connecticut, Massachusetts, Virginia, New York,
and North Carolina) the debates in the state conventions were published in newspapers in special book-length supplements. No political
story had ever generated as much ongoing attention. Debates among
the print press were virtually non-stop—through newspapers, broadsides, and pamphlets—and among the people themselves in town meetings, taverns, and even chance meetings on the street. Despite its absence
during the Federal Convention, popular sovereignty was now on full
display.

The ratification strategy employed by the Federalists—those who supported the new Constitution—centered on presenting it as a grand design, rather than as the patchwork of compromises that it largely was. The Federalists knew that if each provision in the Constitution was linked with the demands of a particular state or faction, the anti–Federalists would attempt to focus the debates on the concessions that had been made by each, rather than on the merits of the plan as a whole. North Carolina's William Davis made that point during his state's ratification convention: "[t]here was ... some real difficulty in conciliating a number of jarring interests, arising from the incidental but unalterable difference in the states in point of territory, situation, climate, and rival[ry] in commerce. It was not easy to reconcile such a multiplicity of discordant and clashing interests. Mutual concessions were necessary to come to any concurrence.... Had each state obstinately insisted on the security of its particular local advantages we should have never have come to a conclusion. Each, therefore, amicably and wisely relinquished its particular views."[3] In Davis' judgment, those compromises could not have been reached if the Convention's deliberations had been open to the public.

Running against the Federalist's strategy was the commonly held the belief that secrecy is the act of one who has something sinful to hide. As Thomas Jefferson once counseled his grandson, Francis Eppes: "Never suffer a thought to be harbored in your mind which you would not avow publicly. When tempted to do anything in secret, ask yourself if you would do it in public. If you would not, be sure it is wrong."[4] Although the Convention's secrecy rules had provoked only limited criticism while the Convention was in session, the Anti-Federalists seized upon the secrecy surrounding the Constitution's framing as sufficient reason alone for rejecting it. To the anti–Federalists, the wall of secrecy encircling the Convention at least "bears upon its face the color of suspicion."[5] Other criticisms went beyond mere suspicion, depicting the Convention as a "dark enclave" and the Constitution itself as "the handiwork of an aristocracy intent on subverting the rights and liberties of the people.[6]

Most of the newspapers of the day supported the Federalist cause. Of the roughly one hundred newspapers that were in publication during the ratification campaign of 1787–1788, "not more than a dozen ... could be classed as avowedly antifederal."[7] Anti-Federalist arguments were rarely printed and even less often reprinted by other publishers.[8] Most newspapers, especially those whose stories were reprinted by others, were located in America's urban centers. Those cities tended to be dominated by merchants who, as a class, favored a national system, believing that it would facilitate trade and commerce. Newspapers were less common in the more rural, interior areas where anti–Federalist support tended to be the strongest. Those newspapers favoring the Federalist position often played on public sentiment, notably the great esteem in which George Washington was held. The most widely reported story concerned his return trip from Philadelphia to Virginia. A bridge collapsed along the way, but Washington escaped unharmed. The tale that many newspapers carried implied that Washington's life had been saved by "the providential preservation of the valuable life of this great and good man, on his way home from the Convention."[9]

Most of the anti–Federalists wrote under pseudonyms. The conventional thinking at the time, especially in political matters, was that the public should be swayed by the strength of one's argument, rather than the identity of the speaker. *Brutus, Cato, Federal Farmer,* and *Centinel* were the best known of the anti–Federalists who wrote under a pseudonym. The Federalists had their anonymous supporters as well, the best known and most respected publication being *The Federalist* papers, a collection of eighty-five articles and essays, each signed by *Publius,* a pseudonym used by *The Federalist's* three authors: James Madison, Alexander Hamilton, and John Jay.

Although the anti–Federalists' primary objection to the new Constitution was its substance, particularly the reduced role of the states, their initial point of attack was not as much on its substance as it was on the secrecy that surrounded its creation. The most prolific and virulent of the Anti-Federalist essayists was Samuel Bryan who wrote under the pseudonym *Centinel. Centinel* charged that "[t]he evil genius of darkness presided at its birth, it came forth under the veil of mystery, and its true features being carefully concealed, and every deceptive art has been and is practicing to have this spurious brat received as the genuine offspring of heaven-born liberty."[10] On another occasion, *Centinel* personally attacked "[t]he authors of the new plan, [who] conscious that it would not stand the test of enlightened patriotism, tyrannically endeavoured to preclude all investigation. If their views were laudable, if they were honest, the contrary would have been their conduct, they would have invited the freest discussion."[11] Continuing the Convention's rules of secrecy even after the Convention ended drew the special ire of a former officer in the Continental Army who described "the unaccountable suppression of the journals [as] the highest insult that be offered to the majesty of the people."[12]

Patrick Henry was a staunch anti–Federalist who had declined an invitation to serve as a delegate to the Convention reportedly because he "smelt a rat"[13] (the "rat" being the movement toward a strong national government). Henry was convinced that if the Federal Convention had opened its sessions to the public, the delegates would have produced a much different Constitution, one reserving far more power to the states. Although Henry was the author of the motion calling for the doors of the First Continental Congress to be closed to the public, Henry now declared that no government should be allowed to "carry on the most wicked and pernicious schemes, under the veil of secrecy. The liberties of a people never were nor ever will be secure, when the transactions of their rulers may be concealed from them."[14]

Other political leaders attacked the Constitution on more substantive grounds. George Clinton, governor of New York, organized opposition to the Constitution in his state. Clinton's objection was that the states "will be so enfeebled as not to afford that effectual security to the rights and liberties of the people, against the undue and extensive powers vested in the general government."[15] James Monroe, who would later become the nation's fourth president, also opposed ratification. Monroe wanted a Constitution that provided for the direct election of senators as well as the president, and the inclusion of a strong bill of rights. Future president John Quincy Adams, who was then in law school, also opposed ratification of the Constitution, although he later expressed regret for his early anti–Federalist views, describing them as a "monumental" error.[16]

In light of the criticism that was leveled at the veil of secrecy that had surrounded the Constitutional Convention's work, the proponents of the new charter realized that the states' ratifying conventions could not also be closed to the public. Denying the public access to the conventions' deliberations would have too easily played into the hands of the Anti-Federalists. All of the states thus decided to open their conventions to the public. Some of the states even relocated their proceedings from the statehouse or other customary meeting place to a more spacious venue in order to accommodate the larger crowds. In several states, summaries of the convention debates were printed in local newspapers.

Opening up of the ratification conventions to the public proved to be a prudent, if not essential step in the ratification process. Even so, the road to ratification was hardly a smooth one. The First Congress, in later recounting the Constitution's history, accurately noted that the Constitution's "ultimate fate hung for some time in dubious and painful suspense."[17] Continuing the practice of secrecy into the state conventions would almost certainly have led to the Constitution's rejection.

In addition to opening the state conventions to the public, Congress' earlier decision to distribute copies of the Constitution across the country also played an important role in its ratification. If copies of the Constitution had not been so widely distributed, suspicions that the Federalists were attempting to overwhelm any opposition to the new charter through a strategy of secrecy and surprise would have enjoyed far more credence. The distribution of full and accurate copies of the Constitution made it difficult for the anti–Federalists to contend credibly that anyone had been deprived of an opportunity to be heard.

Beginning on December 7, 1787, five states (Delaware, Pennsylvania, New Jersey, Georgia, and Connecticut) ratified the Constitution in quick succession, all within roughly thirty days. Other states, most notable Massachusetts, initially withheld their approval of the new Constitution. Their principal objection was that it lacked a provision reserving un-delegated powers to the states (a reservation now provided for in the 10th Amendment). Massachusetts also complained that the new Constitution did not contain a provision expressly protecting basic individual rights, such as freedom of speech, religion, and the press (protections now provided for in the 1st Amendment). In February 1788, a compromise was reached under which Massachusetts and its allies agreed to ratify the Constitution upon the express assurance that the amendments they sought would be taken up as a matter of first business by the First Congress. The Constitution was thus narrowly ratified in Massachusetts on February 6, 1788, followed by Maryland on April 28 and South Carolina on May 23. On June 21, 1788, New Hampshire became the ninth state to ratify the document, thereby establishing the new Constitution as the official governing document of the United States. The ratification process had remarkably taken only ten months. Virginia ratified the Constitution on June 25, 1789, followed by New York on July 26, and North Carolina on November 21, 1789. Rhode Island, which had earlier defeated ratification in a popular referendum by a margin of ten to one, finally ratified the Constitution on May 29, 1790, largely because of the other states' threat to treat Rhode Island as a foreign country. Rhode Island was not the only state, though, to withhold its full endorsement of the new Constitution. Four of the states—Massachusetts, New Hampshire, Virginia, and New York— all ratified the Constitution, but with affirmative votes of less than fifty-five percent.

The new United States government came into existence with the convening of the First Congress on March 4, 1789, in New York City's Federal Hall. George Washington was elected America's first president on April 6, 1789, and was inaugurated on April 30. On February 2, 1790, the Supreme Court held its first session, marking the date when all three branches of the new government became fully functioning.

The Conventions Debate the Secrecy Question

The need to maintain secrecy in certain areas of government, particularly in foreign and military affairs, was never in question during the state conventions. As John Jay wrote in *The Federalist* No. 64, "[i]t seldom happens in the negotiation of treaties, of whatever nature, but that perfect secrecy and immediate dispatch are sometimes required."[18] Even George Mason, a leading proponent of openness in government, readily conceded during the Virginia convention that "[i]n matters relative to military operations, and foreign negotiations, secrecy was necessary sometimes."[19] The observation that General Washington made some years earlier concerning the need for secrecy in times of war still rang true among the state conventions' delegates. "For upon secrecy," Washington had declared, "success depends in most enterprises of the kind, and for want of it, they are generally defeated."[20] It is largely for that reason that the delegates to the Constitutional Convention made indirect provision for secrecy in matters of national security by naming the president Commander-in-Chief of the country's armed forces, and in foreign affairs by assigning him the leading role in directing the country's dealings with foreign governments. The president was placed under no Constitutional duty, however, to disclose information in either area. It was evidently assumed by the delegates that the president would withhold information from the public only in those circumstances in which he determined that secrecy was necessary. The president's primacy in foreign affairs was later codified during Washington's first term when, in July 1789, Congress created the Department of Foreign Affairs. Congress provided in that legislation that the Secretary of the new department "shall conduct the business of said department in such manner as the President ... shall from time to time order or instruct."[21]

Although there was broad agreement among the delegates to the Convention delegates that secrecy was oftentimes warranted, there was an equally broad agreement that secrecy was justified only in certain cases and then only within certain limits. Thus, although Alexander Hamilton, John Jay, and others had little difficulty in finding a place for secrecy in the new Constitution when it came to foreign policy and national defense, none of them could accept the proposition that secrecy would or should be the norm in other areas of government. Indeed, even in matters of foreign policy and national defense, many of the delegates were unwilling to agree that a policy of secrecy should be absolute. Striking the right balance between openness and secrecy had been the challenge.

Many of the delegates who participated in the state conventions saw the Constitution's requirement that Congress publish its journals "from time to time" as representing a major step toward greater openness in government. In some respects it was. While the journals of the Continental Congress were also to be published, their publication was required only at such times as "the majority shall direct." The records of the Constitutional Convention were also to be published, but again only "upon the direction of Congress." Under Article 1, Section 5 of the new Constitution, the so-called Journal Clause, however, the duty of each house of Congress to publish its official journal was made mandatory, other than when the need for secrecy dictated otherwise. Although there were no safeguards built into the provision that would prevent Congress from engaging in secrecy when secrecy was not warranted, those supporting the provision, like Alexander Hamilton, pointed to the safeguarding vigilance of the states as a sufficient safeguard: "[t]he executive and legislative bodies of each state will be so many sentinels over the persons employed in every department of the national administration; and it will be in their power ... to know the behavior of those who represent their constituents in the national councils, and [they] can readily communicate the same knowledge to the people."[22]

Despite Madison's assurances, many of the delegates found the language of the Journal Clause to be too indefinite and thus, despite the "vigilance of the states," too easy to evade. Exactly how frequent, they asked, is "from time to time?" What information about Congress' "proceedings" is to be recorded in the public journals? What may be omitted? Are proposals that are offered on the floor of Congress but not adopted also to be included? What about floor debates? And, of course, beyond the question of the journals, are the official sessions of Congress to be open to public view? None these or other questions about the role of secrecy in government were directly answered in the newly drafted Constitution.

James Madison attempted to defend the sufficiency of the Constitution's Journal Clause by assuring his fellow Virginians that their fears were unfounded. The Constitutional Convention had never intended, he said, that Congress' right to exclude from their journals "such parts as may in their judgment require secrecy" should ever be extended beyond military matters and foreign policy—those were the outer limits. All other matters were to be included in the public journal. The Journal Clause's secrecy provision should thus be given a restrictive reading. Madison also pointed out that "[t]he part [Section 5] which authorizes the government to withhold from the public what in their judgment may require secrecy is imitated from the [Articles of] confederation." That document similarly excluded from public disclosure "such parts [of the journal] thereof relating to treaties, alliances or military operations." The Journal Clause in the new Constitution therefore authorized no less secrecy than its counterpart in the Articles of Confederation. And because it made the publishing of Congressional journals mandatory, the Journal Clause represented a major step toward greater openness in government.

Patrick Henry was much less trusting than Madison, expressing grave doubts about Madison's assurances that the phrase "such parts as may in their judgment require secrecy" would be given a restrictive reading. Henry argued to his fellow Virginians that "[t]he proceedings in the northern conclave will be hidden from the yeomanry of this country. We are told that the yeas and nays shall be entered into the journals. This, sir, will avail nothing: it may be locked up in their chests forever from the people; for they are not to publish what parts they think require secrecy: they may think, and will think, the whole requires it."[23] Henry also took aim at the Constitution's Statement and Account Clause, arguing that under it "the national wealth is to be disposed of under the veil of secrecy, for the publication from time to time will amount to nothing, and they may conceal what they think requires secrecy."[24]

Despite the great respect that James Madison and John Jay enjoyed among their fellow Virginians, their assurances were insufficient to calm the misgivings of the majority of the Virginia convention delegates. The convention thus adopted an amendment (for eventual submission to Congress) that was intended to remove any question about the frequency with which the journals were to be published and the type of information that could be omitted from them. That Virginia amendment provided "[t]hat the journals of the proceedings of the Senate and House of Representatives shall be published at least once in every year, except such parts thereof, relating to treaties, alliances, or military operation, as, in their judgment, require secrecy." The effect of the Virginia amendment was to make certain the frequency of the journals' publication and to put into writing Madison's assurances about the type of information that Congress could exclude from them. The Virginia amendment was subsequently introduced during the Congress's first session, but on September 8, 1789, was defeated.[25]

The questions surrounding the Journal and Statement Clauses were not the only secrecy-related issues that arose during the state ratification conventions. Four of the conventions—North Carolina, Rhode Island, New York, and Virginia—also objected to the absence of a provision in the new Constitution requiring Congress to meet in open session. The states' legislative assemblies were generally open to the public at that point and many in the states saw no reason why the national legislature should not be open to the public as well. In order correct that deficiency, several of the states included in their proposed Constitutional amendments one providing that "both Houses of Congress shall always keep their doors open during their sessions, unless the business may, in their opinion, require secrecy."[26] Even though the proposed amendment reserved substantial discretion to Congress about when sessions could be closed to the public, the amendment at least expressed a clear policy preference for open sessions. The amendment, though, as well as a number of others, failed to win Congress' approval.

Francis Hopkinson, a Maryland delegate to the Convention, is reported to have remarked of the Constitutional Convention that "no sooner will the chicken be hatched but everyone will be plucking a feather." Hopkinson's prediction proved to be correct. The First Congress was presented with no fewer than one hundred different amendments, most of which had been agreed to by one or more of the states during their ratification conventions. The most pressing of the demands was for the bill of individual rights that had been promised to Massachusetts and its allies in exchange for their support of the Constitution.

James Madison did not question the merit of many of the proposed amendments, but foresaw too great a risk in opening up the new Constitution to a long list of potentially contentious amendments. Putting the new Constitution in place had been difficult enough. Madison's strategy was thus to have Congress move quickly to adopt what would be become the Bill of Rights and then simply ignore the other proposals, however meritorious they may have been. Nineteen amendments were introduced in the House to address the most widely supported of the states' concerns. The House approved seventeen of them. The Senate consolidated and trimmed the number of proposed amendments down to twelve. Those twelve were approved by a joint resolution of Congress on September 29, 1789. By December 15, 1791, the states had ratified ten of the twelve amendments, now known as the Bill of Rights. The other two of Madison's proposed amendments (concerning the number of constituents to be represented by each member of the House and the compensation of Congressmen) failed to secure the necessary votes of ten states. Among those falling victim to Madison's strategy were the open-session amendments that had been proposed by several of the states. Madison later wrote to Edmond Randolph explaining his strategy: "[i]t has been necessary in order to effect anything, to abbreviate debate, and exclude every proposition of a doubtful and unimportant nature.... Two or three contentious additions would even now prostrate the whole project."[27]

The new Constitution of the United States was now in place. The national government was up and running and, although the question of secrecy in government had been addressed both during the Constitutional Convention and later during the state ratification conventions, the issue was far from settled. Beginning with the First Congress and continuing even to today, balancing the need for secrecy in government with the fundamental principle that government should conduct the peoples' business in the open remains an ongoing source of controversy.

5

Congress Opens
Up Its Doors

Remember, my fellow citizens, that you are still freemen; let it
be impressed upon your minds that you depend not upon your
representatives but they depend upon you, and let this truth
ever be present to you, that secrecy in your representatives is a
worm which will prey and fatten upon the vitals of your lib-
erty.—Philip Freneau, February 1792

The First Demands for Open Congressional
Proceedings

Hostilities between Great Britain and the United States ended as a practical matter with the signing of preliminary articles of peace on November 30, 1782. The Treaty of Paris, which marked the official end of the War, was finalized the following year on September 3, 1783. Even with the end of the war, and with it all of the war-time justifications for maintaining a policy of meeting in secret, the Continental Congress continued to bar the public from its sessions. The practice at the state level, however, was already changing.

Several of the states, notably Pennsylvania and New York, were by then regularly admitting the public to their legislative sessions. Pennsylvania's Constitution provided that "[t]he doors of the house in which representatives of the freemen of this state shall sit in general assembly, shall be and remain open for the admission of all persons who behave decently, except only when the welfare of this state may require the doors to be shut."[1] The New York Constitution took the policy of openness a step further by requiring that the sessions of both chambers be open to the public: "the doors of both the senate and the assembly shall at all times be open to all persons, except when the welfare of the State shall require their debates be kept secret."[2] Even though the constitutions of the two states authorized their legislatures to meet in secret when secrecy was deemed necessary, their constitutions nonetheless established the principle that those who legislate on behalf of the people should do so in the open.

Despite the movement toward greater openness at the state level, the decision to grant the people direct access to the deliberations of their national legislature remained several years away. Much of Congress' unwillingness to open its doors to the public was a function of its relationship with the people. Unlike the state legislatures, the Confederation Congress did not see itself as a popular representative body, but instead as a grand council of states. Votes in Congress were taken by state, not on the basis of a state's population. As George Mason would later note during the Constitutional Convention, "[u]nder the Articles ... the Confederacy Congress represents the States, not the people of the States; their acts operate on the States, not the individuals."[3] Given that relationship with the states, most members of Congress believed that the information that Congress provided to the state legislatures was sufficient to discharge their duty to keep those whom they represented abreast of their activities. Any further distribution of that information to the people was the responsibility of the state legislature. Even in Congress, though, the tide was beginning to turn.

On April 30, 1783, less than three weeks after Congress declared an end to the war with Great Britain, Pennsylvania delegate James Wilson moved "[t]hat in the future the doors of Congress shall be open, unless otherwise ordered by a vote or by the rules of the house." In making his case for greater openness, Wilson argued that "it is of importance in every free country that the conduct of those to whom the direction of public affairs is committed, should be publicly known."[4] Many in Congress saw merit in Wilson's proposal—the people should have a right to know what their representatives are doing—but there was also a concern, even among those who supported Wilson's motion, that any public gallery that might be provided (Congress was then meeting in Philadelphia) would be dominated by Pennsylvanians. In order to address that concern, North Carolina's Hugh Williamson moved to defer consideration of Wilson's proposal until such time "as Congress shall have fixed on some place where they may propose to continue their residence, and where they may have some kind of jurisdiction without being exposed to the influence of any particular state." Wilson's proposal, though, even as amended, was defeated.[5] The doors of Congress remained firmly closed to the public. That policy would not be changed until six years later when the First Congress was called into session under the new Constitution.

The Constitution makes no explicit reference to secrecy, other than for the "Journal Clause" which allows each house of Congress to exclude from its official journal "such Parts as may in their Judgment require Secrecy." While it may have been expected that the House of Representatives at least would meet in open session, except when the requirements of secrecy demanded otherwise, the Constitution contains no requirement that it do so; nor does it explicitly authorize either chamber of Congress to meet in secret. The question of open sessions was simply not addressed during the Constitutional Convention, and while several states did press for an open-session amendment during their ratification conventions, that amendment was not adopted by the First Congress.

While it may not have been understood at the time, the Journal Clause of the Constitution does provide a basis, albeit an indirect one, for the House and Senate to close their sessions to the public. If the two chambers may exclude from their journals "such parts as may in their judgment require secrecy," then, *a fortiori*, they must also have the right to exclude the public from any proceeding in which those matters are being discussed. The power to meet in secret is thus an implied one to be exercised at the discretion of the House and Senate. The specific procedures that the House and Senate follow in either opening or closing their sessions to the public are to be adopted pursuant to Article 1, Section 5, Clause 2 of the Constitution, which provides that "Each House may determine the Rules of its Proceedings."

Despite the absence of a specific Constitutional provision requiring the Congress to meet in open session, the twenty-five-year veil of secrecy surrounding Congress began to be lifted, almost immediately in the House of Representatives and more slowly, but surely and inevitably, in the United States Senate as well. The course that each chamber followed in opening its doors to the public would closely mirror the relationship that each saw itself as having with the people.

New York City's Common Council adopted a resolution on September 17, 1788, granting the use of its city hall as the official meeting place for the new Federal government. Major Pierre-Charles L'Enfant, a young French architect and engineer who fought as a volunteer in the Revolutionary War was hired by the city to renovate and redesign Federal Hall. L'Enfant's redesign perfectly reflected the different approaches that the House and Senate would take to granting the public access to their deliberations.

The House of Representatives

The Constitution established the House of Representatives as the legislative body more closely connected with the people, and therefore the legislative body that would play the leading role in keeping the people informed about the work of Congress. Given its role as the "people's chamber," L'Enfant's design called for the House chamber to be located on the ground floor of Federal Hall—a location that was intended to bring the people and their elected representatives together in a more immediate way. In order to accommodate those who might want to watch the House in action, L'Enfant's design also called for the construction of a visitors' gallery. Unlike the occasional publication of a dry, oftentimes incomplete journal, the House's visitors' gallery would offer the public direct, real-time access to the deliberations of their elected representatives.

While not required by the Constitution, the House of Representatives began admitting the public to its sessions on April 1, 1789, the opening day of its first session (it took from March 4 to achieve a quorum). The House's decision to admit the public was evidently made without any debate being had or vote taken. As the only legislative body directly elected by the people, it was generally assumed that the House would conduct its business in open session. The House's decision to open its doors to the public was thus in perfect keeping with the Constitutional role of the new House. Representative Alexander White of Virginia noted that point, writing in his diary that "[t]he pleasure which our open Doors, and the knowledge of our Debate obtained by the means, has given the People, can hardly be conceived."[6] White's views reflected the sentiment of the great majority of House members.

The House's open-door policy went beyond merely allowing the public to view its proceedings from the visitor's gallery. Indeed, visiting guests were often introduced by House members to their colleagues and even given seats on the House floor. The policy of openness did not come without its negative side, though. One member complained that the number of visitors was so large at times that House members could barely make their way to the front of the chamber to present papers to the presiding officer. Frequently there was no place where members could confer with one another in private.[7] Although the House did close its visitor's gallery during the consideration of confidential matters or because of rowdy behavior in the gallery,[8] the doors to the House of Representatives remained generally open to the public. On only one occasion was a formal attempt made to amend that policy.

The seat of the federal government was moved to Washington, D.C., in June 1800 during the presidency of John Adams. The House began meeting in the Senate's wing of the capitol building while its own wing was under construction. On November 7, 1804, Representative Michael Leib from Pennsylvania "observed the narrow limits to which the members were confined by the reduced size of their chamber" and, in an effort to ease the overcrowding, moved "to rescind [the rule] which permitted members to introduce strangers." The following day, when Leib's motion was brought up for final vote, an amendment was offered which added an additional clause providing that "blacks and people of color, other than freemen, shall be excluded from the gallery." Black Americans had generally been granted access to the visitor's gallery since the House's opening session in 1789. Leib's proposal "gave rise to some conversation, after which ... upon a division of the House, appeared to have but one member in its favor." Leib's initial motion to "exclude all persons from the lobby except members of the Senate and Stenographers" went down to defeat as well.[9]

Despite the House's general policy of openness, the receipt of confidential communications from the president was a standing exception, even in cases when the content of the communication was already a matter of public record. In January 1792, President Washington sent a message to Congress requesting funds for a buildup of military arms. When the customary motion was made to clear the visitor's gallery, an objection was raised on the point that the request had already been reported in several newspapers. The objection was overruled on the ground that "although it might be very proper that [the message] should be read [in open session], yet, as it had been confidentially received from the Executive, there would be a manifest trespass on propriety and decorum in having it read with open galleries."[10] A month later, the House adopted a formal rule governing the handling of confidential messages from the president. The new standing rule provided that "the House shall be cleared of all persons, except the members and the Clerk, and so continue during the reading of such communication and during all debates and proceedings to be had thereon."[11] Those proceedings were recorded in the House's secret journal. In December 1793, however, the opposition-controlled Third Congress amended the rule by declaring its right to disclose the contents of presidential communications if it deemed that disclosure was appropriate.

The Senate

An entirely different approach to open sessions was taken by the United States Senate. When the Senate officially gathered in Federal Hall for its opening session on March 4, 1789 (it was not until April 6 that a quorum was achieved),[12] it was generally assumed that the Senate's proceedings—both legislative and executive—would be closed to the public. So certain was the expectation that the Senate would meet in private that L'Enfant's redesign of Federal Hall called for the Senate chamber to be tucked away safely on the second floor. Also, unlike his design for the House, L'Enfant's design for the "upper chamber" made no provision for a visitor's gallery.

The Senate's doors were closed not only to members of the public, but also, somewhat surprisingly, to members of the House of Representatives and other government officials as well.[13] Strangers were welcome in the House, but not even House members were welcome in the Senate. On April 7, the second day the Senate was in session, James Mathers was named doorkeeper, a position similar to the one he had held in the Continental Congress. The position of doorkeeper was a particularly important post for a legislative branch that intended to conduct all of its sessions in secret. Mathers' principal duty was to ensure that the Senate's doors remained closed during the six months the Senate was ordinarily in session. His orders reportedly were "No public; no House members." An exception was made for the president, however, pursuant to a recommendation made by a committee that had been appointed to consider "the mode of communication proper to be pursued between [the president] and the Senate in the formation of treaties, and making appointments to offices." The Senate agreed on August 21, 1789, that when the president meets the Senate in the Senate chamber, he "shall have a chair on the floor."[14] Otherwise, those who were not members of the Senate or one of its employees were not welcome.

The Senate's attitude toward admitting the public to its sessions was largely a reflection of its role under the Constitution. Unlike the House, whose members were elected by the people, members of the Senate were elected by the state legislatures. The direct election of Senators did not come about until the ratification of 17th amendment in 1913. Senators were typically expected to take "instruction" from their respective legislature, not directly from the people. Given their relationship with the state legislatures, most Senators did not view themselves as representing the people in any direct sense. That was the responsibility of the state legislatures. In addition, the Senate was made up mostly of elder statesman who saw their role as one of counseling the president on foreign policy and other "executive" matters. Closed sessions were seen as being entirely appropriate to that role. Opening the Senate's doors to the public was regarded by most Senators as being neither necessary nor appropriate to the fulfillment of their Constitutional duties. Moreover, by continuing a closed-door policy, the Senate was only following the practice of the Continental Congresses, which, like the new Senate, had represented the interests of the States, rather than the people. If the role of the Senate was not to change under the new Constitution, the reasoning went, then there was no obvious reason for the Senate's procedures and protocols to change either.

Like members of the earlier Congresses, Senators were expected to maintain the confidentiality of their deliberations, particularly when sitting in executive session. Among the first rules adopted by the Senate was one directing that "inviolable secrecy shall be observed with respect to all matters transacted in the Senate while the doors are shut, or as often as the same is enjoined by the Chair."[15] The Senate's rules were engrossed on parchment and displayed in a conspicuous place in the Senate chamber. When a Senator violated one of the rules "his name, together with the nature of his transgression, [was] written on a slip of paper and annexed to the bottom of the rules, there to remain until the Senate ... shall take order on the same."[16]

The Senate was different from the House of Representatives in another respect as well. Many Senators saw themselves as being part of a new American aristocracy. Indeed, much of the Senate's first month in session was taken up in a running dispute with the House over the question of "what styles or titles it will be proper to annex to the offices of President and Vice President ... if any other than those given in the constitution."[17] Many in the Senate believed that it was important for senior government officials to be given lofty titles so that they might command the proper level of esteem and respect from foreign nations. At one point, when the Senate was considering how the president should be addressed, John Adams, Washington's Vice President and Senate President, urged that the president be referred to "His Majesty" or "His Highness," titles which Thomas Jefferson, then serving as the American Minister to France, derided as being "superlatively ridiculous." The Senate committee to which the matter was referred for consideration was no less pretentious, recommending in its final report (submitted on May 14, 1789) that the president should be addressed as "His Highness, the President of the United States of America and Protector of their Liberties." In the end, the Senate, being "desirous of preserving harmony with the House ... [thought] it proper to act in conformity with the House." George Washington would simply be called President of the United States. Nonetheless, the dispute between the two chambers reveals the pretentiousness that permeated the new Senate—a pretentiousness that tended to spill over into the Senate's relationship with the American people.

While members of the House typically sought out and nurtured a close relationship with the people they represented, many in the Senate saw their office as actually demanding a separation from the pressure of public opinion. Senator Paine Wingate of New Hampshire, one of the staunchest supporters of the Senate's closed-door policy, expressed that sentiment, declaring that "I do not desire that the private conduct or public proceedings of this body should be exposed to the daily inspection of a populace." Wingate believed, as did many of his Senate colleagues, that a certain dignified aloofness would actually promote respect for the Senate: "to be a little more out of view," Wingate explained, "would conduce to its respectability in the opinion of the country."[18] John Adams shared Wingate's opinion that the Senate should maintain a proper distance from the people. Adams and his supporters were eager to project a heightened image of the Senate, and they believed that the mystique that secrecy was thought to promote was an essential part of that image. Allowing the public to peer over their shoulders while they worked was inconsistent with the projection of that lofty image. Exposing their deliberations to the public, most Senators believed, would only serve to detract from their status as the "upper house" of Congress.

Despite its closed-door policy, the Senate did from time to time make some concession to greater openness. Early in its first session, on May 19, 1789, the Senate accepted a report of a committee that had been appointed to consider the form and scope of the journals that the Senate would keep of it activities. The report recommended that 120 copies of the Senate's official journal be printed. One copy was to be provided to each Senator. The journal was to include a synopsis, but not a detailed account of the proceedings of the Senate when meeting in legislative session. The record of the Senate's deliberations when meeting in executive session was to be "entered and kept in separate and distinct [secret] books."[19] The committee also proposed that the journals, "previous to each publication [be] revised by a committee to be appointed from time to time for that purpose."[20] Soon afterwards, on June 2, the Senate agreed to a resolution that the House adopted on May 28 increasing the number of copies to 700, thereby allowing for copies of the legislative journals of both chambers to be distributed to the executive, legislative, and judicial departments of both the national and state governments.[21] The committee also recommended that six hundred copies of the Acts of the Congress be printed at the end of each legislative session. During the session, twenty-two copies of each legislative enactment were to be lodged with the President, along with the request that he transmit two copies of the act to each of the "supreme executives in the several states." The Senate made no provision, however, for the distribution of either its journal or the Acts of the Congress to the public at large.

Despite the Senate's claim that its official journal was sufficient to keep the people informed, the journal did not fully capture what was actually taking place behind the Senate's doors. Reading the Senate journal days or even weeks later was hardly a substitute for first-hand, day-to-day accounts of the Senate's activities. Moreover, even when the journal was accurate—which was not always the case—it only reported on how individual Senators voted on a particular matter, and even then only when one-fifth of the Senators requested that individual votes be published. Because none of the actual floor debates were included in the journal, the public remained largely in the dark about why a Senator had voted as he did.

Most Senators, even while defending the Senate's closed-door policy, took no serious issue with the public's right to know what the Senate was doing or how individual Senators voted on particular legislative proposals. Their position was simply that the periodic publication of the Senate's official journal was all that was required of them to fulfill their constitutional duty to keep the state legislatures, and through them the American public, reasonably abreast of their activities. Nothing more was necessary.

Many Senators were aware, of course, that their closed-door policy denied them the opportunity to show off their oratorical skills in public. There was certainly no shortage of orators in the Senate. On the other hand, the secrecy surrounding their deliberations also shielded them from the risk of stumbling, either individually or institutionally, in front of the public. Senator Paine Wingate noted that benefit in a private letter: "there are certain foibles which are inseparable from men and the bodies of men and perhaps considerable faults which had better be concealed from observation. How would all the little domestic transactions of even the best-regulated family appear if exposed to the world; and may this not apply to a larger body?"[22] Thus, despite the occasional call for greater openness, the Senate's policy of closing its proceedings to the public remained firmly in place.

Those Senators who supported the closed-door policy were quick to point out that barring the public from their sessions did not necessarily mean that their proceedings were entirely hidden from the public. Unlike earlier Congresses, Senators and House members were not required to take an oath of secrecy. Members of the House were generally at liberty to speak openly about House activities, unless a specific resolution was adopted requiring that some part of those proceedings be kept secret. Senators were also free to discuss legislative matters, which, it was thought, were the matters in which the public would typically have the greatest interest. Senators were still expected, however, to maintain the confidentiality of any matter that was taken up by the Senate while in executive session or in legislative session when ordered to do so by the presiding officer.

The Senate's closed-door policy did not come without a political cost. In the end, it was that cost that would force a change in the Senate's policy. The secrecy surrounding its sessions not unexpectedly gave rise to suspicions on the part of many Americans that the Senate was a dark and mysterious place where secrets plots were continually being hatched against the public good. The House of Representative stood in stark contrast. Its business was carried on in a generally open and seemingly aboveboard manner. Even more worrisome politically was the realization that many Americans, reading about the House debates in the local press, but rarely seeing any account of what the Senate was doing, were beginning to think of the "House of Representatives" and "Congress" as being one in the same, ignoring the Senate almost entirely. Members of the House were beginning to be seen as the real legislative leaders of the new government, causing some Senators to fear that their upper chamber was in danger of becoming the forgotten chamber.

A common, almost dismissive attitude toward the Senate and its elitist penchant for secrecy was expressed in an editorial carried in a Carlisle, Pennsylvania, newspaper: "It matters little to the public who presides in the Senate: They do not choose to let the public know anything about the reasons of their political conduct; the public may therefore trouble themselves little about them, except to watch them with a jealousy and try to get rid of them as soon as possible."[23] Even President Washington was perplexed by the Senate's refusal to open its doors: "Why they keep their doors closed when acting in a legislative capacity," Washington said, "I am unable to inform you."[24]

Honoré-Gabriel Riqueti, comte de Mirabeau, a French populist and one of the key leaders of the National Assembly that governed France during the early years of the French Revolution, was one of the most vocal critics of the Senate's policy of secrecy. Mirabeau wrote that "[t]he Peers of America distain to be seen by vulgar eyes; the music of their voices is harmony only for themselves, and must not vibrate in the ravished ears of an ungraceful and uncourtly multitudes."[25] By choosing the term "Peers of America" Mirabeau was equating the American Senate with the British House of Lords. Whether it was taken as such, Mirabeau undoubtedly intended for the comparison to be an insult. A correspondent who wrote under the pseudonym *Condorcet* (presumably taken from Nicolas de Condorcet, a French philosopher and political scientist) expressed the attitude of many Americans, writing that "[t]his Patrician stile, this concealment, this affectation of pre-eminence but illy accords with the spirit of republican government.... It augers an unfriendly disposition in a public body that wishes to masque its transactions—Upright intentions, and upright conduct are not afraid or ashamed of publicity."[26] Philip Freneau, a classmate of James Madison at Princeton and a bitter opponent of secrecy in government, was recruited by Madison and Thomas Jefferson in 1791 to head the anti–Federalist newspaper, *The National Gazette.* Freneau railed against the "aristocratic junto" in the Senate, writing that "[s]ecrecy is necessary to design and a masque to treachery; honesty shrinks not from the public." Freneau's attack on the Senate's closed-door policy was relentless, writing on another occasion in *The Gazette* that "the Senate supposes there is, and usurps the privileges of the House of Lords. Remember, my fellow citizens, that you are freemen; let it be impressed upon your minds that you depend not upon your representatives but they depend upon you, and let this truth be ever present to you, that secrecy in your representatives is a worm which will prey and fatten upon the vitals of your liberty."[27] Freneau's attacks found a receptive audience among many Americans. Although the Revolutionary War had been fought and won and a new Constitution adopted, there was still a great deal of suspicion among everyday Americans that the forces of aristocracy were alive and well, especially in the Senate.

The initial attempt to lift the Senate's veil of secrecy took place only six months after the First Congress was called into session. On December 16, 1789, the Virginia Assembly instructed its Senators (William Grayson and Richard Henry Lee) to use "their utmost endeavors" to open the Senate's doors to the public. A resolution to that effect was introduced by the two Senators on April 29, 1790. Their resolution provided "that the doors of the Senate be open when they are sitting in their legislative capacity, to the end, that such citizens of the United States as may choose to hear the debates of this House may have the opportunity of so doing."[28] The resolution would have opened the Senate's doors only part way, however. It still permitted the Senate to continue to meet in closed session when sitting in executive session and thus would have opened up only its legislative sessions to the public. Executive sessions would have remained private. Although no one spoke in opposition to the resolution, "it passed in the negative," mustering only three votes. Despite the defeat, the Virginia Assembly continued its campaign for more openness in the Senate, often writing to the other States and urging them to instruct their Senators to join in the demand for an open-door policy.

A second attempt to open the Senate's doors was made seven months later, on February 24, 1791. A motion was introduced by Virginia's James Monroe proposing a more carefully qualified standing rule that would not take effect until the first day of the next Congress. Monroe's motion called for the doors of the Senate chamber to be opened to the public, but only "whilst the Senate shall be sitting in a legislative capacity, except in such occasions as in their judgment may require secrecy." In order to accommodate the public, the motion also directed the Senate Secretary to request the Commissioners of Philadelphia "to cause a proper gallery to be erected for the accommodation of the audience." Monroe's motion demanded even less of a change in Senate practice than had the earlier resolution. The motion fully maintained the secrecy of executive sessions and opened the Senate's legislative sessions to the public only if in its "judgment" the Senate did not decide otherwise. Even with that limitation, Monroe's motion was defeated by a vote of seven yeas to nineteen nays.[29] The voting patterns suggest that the issue of maintaining the closed-door policy was not, as might have been expected, purely a matter of party politics. The votes for and against retaining the policy were a mix of both pro and anti-administration Senators. Pro-administration Senators Butler, Foster, and King joined with anti-administration Senators Guinn, Macclay, and Monroe in voting for the resolution, while pro-administration Senators Carroll, Dickinson, and Ellsworth joined with anti-administration Senators Basset, Wingate, and Henry in voting against it.[30]

The Senate did open its proceedings slightly in early 1792, at least to the president. That change in policy was triggered by *The National Gazette's* unauthorized publication of the names of the two emissaries who had been appointed by President Washington to negotiate a treaty with Spain concerning the opening of the Mississippi River to American navigation. In order to ensure the confidentiality of future communications from the president, the Senate adopted a resolution on

January 27 providing "that the President of the United States shall be furnished an authenticated transcript of the executive sessions of the Senate, from time to time," but further providing "that no executive business, in [the] future, [shall] be published by the Secretary of the Senate." The president would be allowed to know what the Senate was doing in closed session, but no one else. Although the president was not bound by the Senate's rules of secrecy, there is no recorded case in which the executive proceedings of the Senate were publicly disclosed by the president. The Senate's "injunction of secrecy" remained in effect for the next 137 years, until June 18, 1929, when the Senate finally voted that all of its proceedings—both legislative and executive—were to be transacted in public."[31]

Whether because of Virginia's prodding or whether they were simply acting on their own initiative, a growing number of state legislatures by 1792 had begun to call for open Senate sessions. Some states saw open sessions as an indispensable part of the Constitution's call for popular sovereignty. How, after all, could the Senate reconcile the notion of popular sovereignty with its refusal to open its proceedings to public inspection? Other states had more practical concerns. Several states, most notable Virginia and North Carolina, were finding it increasingly difficult to "instruct" their Senators when nearly all of the Senate's work was being carried on behind closed doors, and when the only account of their Senators' conduct was largely limited to what was reported in the Senate journal.

Despite the growing call for the Senate to open its doors, those who supported a continuation of the closed-door policy were not without their own opposing arguments. Chief among them was that open sessions in the House of Representatives often led to oratory excesses, with House members playing to the partisan emotions of gallery onlookers. That was very often the case. In addition, House debates were frequently disrupted by visitors clapping, striking their canes on the floor, or shouting "Bravo" when a point was made with which they agreed.[32] The Senate, on the other hand, was a small group of relatively like-minded men. The Senate's closed-door policy was thought by many of its members to promote civil and rational discourse, free of boisterous distractions in the gallery. By contrast, the Senate was a model of decorum. Opening their chamber's doors to the public, many Senators feared, would cause the Senate to become too much like the House, which some Senators believed resembled more of a carnival than a deliberative legislative body.

Defenders of the closed-door policy also took issue with the claim that open sessions would lead to a broader dissemination of news about the Senate and its work. Here they pointed out, again with some factual basis, that press accounts of the House's activities were notoriously inaccurate. Because the House had no official shorthand reporters of its own, the public was dependent upon a handful of reporters—occasionally only a single reporter was present—who were employed by newspapers and assigned to cover House proceedings. The notes they took of the House's proceedings were often incomplete, inaccurate, and at times even slanted according to the reporter's own political bias. Some speeches that were made on the House floor were left out altogether.[33] The defenders of the Senate's policy saw no reason to introduce these same errors into the record of their chamber. In addition, because any Senate gallery that might be built would be occupied primarily by Philadelphians (where Congress was then meeting), the closed-door advocates were also able to claim, again not unreasonably, that there was a real danger that members of the Senate would be unduly influenced by local prejudices. "What may appear improper to Pennsylvanians," James Iredell of North Carolina warned, "may in fact be highly pleasing in North Carolina."[34]

Continued, but still unsuccessful attempts were made to open the Senate's doors, the next occurring on March 26, 1792 (made by Virginia Senators James Monroe and Richard Lee), and then again three weeks later on April 18 (by Georgia Senators William Few and James Gunn). Following the defeat of the first resolution, the scope of the second resolution was pared back, requiring only that members of the House of Representatives be allowed to attend debates, and even then only when the Senate was sitting in legislative session. While not providing general access to its legislative sessions, the resolution did permit each member of the Senate to "admit a number not exceeding two persons." In order to eliminate the risk of overcrowding, the resolution also included a provision deferring its effective date "until the Senate Chamber is sufficiently enlarged." Even as limited, though, the proposal went down to defeat.[35]

On January 3, 1793, the proponents of an open-door policy adopted a different strategy. Rather than merely calling for the opening of the

Senate's doors, they offered a more comprehensive resolution that undertook to rebut each of the several claims that had been made by those in favor of keeping the Senate's doors closed. This "speaking" resolution first declared that Senators are "individually responsible for their conduct to their constituents, who are entitled to such information as will enable them to form a justified estimate thereof." Here the resolution pointed out that "the Journals are too voluminous and expensive to circulate generally," and that even if that were not the case, "the information they contain as to the principles, motives, and designs of the individual members is inadequate." In many instances, there were deliberate attempts to conceal the existence of dissent by refusing to permit the entry of dissenting views in the journal. Unless a one-fifth vote could be mustered, even the yeas and nays might not be recorded. The information reported in the journal, the resolution's supporters went on to argue, "as defective as it is, becomes more inadequate and delusive as occasion for it increases, since the Senate make their own Journals." In other words, the journal's account of Senate deliberations on important matters was often less complete than it was on more routine matters. Finally, the resolution argued that "by withholding this information, the influence of their constituents over one branch of the legislature [the Senate] is in a great measure annihilated, and the best security which experience has devised against abuse of power and maladministration abandoned."[36] Without the restraining influence of public opinion, the Senate was more likely to act in ways that were contrary to the public good. This reduced influence worked in both directions, of course. Withholding information from the public also made it difficult for the Senate to build public support for its own legislative programs. Despite the strength and completeness of the proponents' arguments, the resolution went down to defeat by a vote of ten yeas to eighteen nays.[37] For some Senators, the open-doors movement was part of a general attack on the very style and substance of their political philosophy. Their instinctive response was simply to close ranks. Defending the Senate's closed-door policy became a matter of principle.

The pressure for a change in Senate policy continued to mount, however, and, in early 1794, the opportunity for change presented itself again. The occasion was the debate over whether Albert Gallatin, a Swiss-American who had been elected to the Senate by the Pennsylvania legislature in 1793, met the Constitutional requirement (in Article I) that a Senator "be a citizen for nine years." The Senate's jurisdiction over the question was based on Article I, Section 5 of the Constitution which provides that each chamber of Congress "shall be the Judge of the Elections, Returns and Qualifications of its own Members."

When the Third Congress opened on December 2, 1793, Gallatin (an anti–Federalist) took the oath of office. On that same day, several of Gallatin's political opponents (all Federalists) lodged a formal protest with the Senate alleging that Gallatin had not been a citizen for the required nine years. The committee to which the petition was referred for initial fact-finding found that Gallatin did not meet the residency requirement. Gallatin vigorously challenged the committee's report by pointing that he had lived in the United States for thirteen years and more important that he had served honorably in the Continental Army. "Every man," Gallatin argued, "who took an active part in the American Revolution was a citizen according to the great laws of reason and of nature, and when afterwards positive laws were made, they were retrospective in regard to persons under this [Gallatin's] predicament.... The new Constitution ... requires certain qualifications for members of Congress ... but it does not deprive citizens of their rights who were citizens before this Constitution was ratified."[38] The report and Gallatin's rebuttal were sent to a second committee, which confirmed the first committee's finding that Gallatin had not been a citizen for the required period. The matter was sent to the full Senate for final disposition.

The Senate was meeting in Philadelphia at the time and many of the Senators were keenly aware of the awkward position they were in— questioning, and perhaps even reversing, the decision of the Pennsylvania legislature which was then meeting in the building next door. Hoping to avoid the charge of "Star Chamber" that would surely follow a secret vote to unseat Gallatin, a majority of the Senate agreed, on February 11, 1794, "[t]hat the doors of the Senate be opened and continue open during the discussion of the contested election of Mr. Albert Gallatin."[39] Gallatin was ultimately removed from office on February 28 by a narrow party-line vote of fourteen to twelve.

The Senate's decision to open its doors during the Gallatin investigation succeeded in insulating it from the charge that is was sitting as a Star Chamber. The decision was of limited practical benefit to the public, though, since the Senate had no gallery at the time. There was no place for the public to watch the Gallatin deliberations. Members of the press were not even allowed on the Senate floor. They were required to cover the trial from the hallway. Nonetheless, the decision in the Gallatin case marked the first major break in the Senate's closed-door policy.

Several days later, on February 20, 1794, the Senate agreed at last to open its doors to the public, adopting a version of a motion that had been made earlier by North Carolina's Alexander Martin.[40] Those favoring an open-door policy had been turned back repeatedly over the past five years. Beginning with Martin's motion, however, circumstances began to change quickly. Several of the Federalist Senators from the northeast switched sides, joining with those other Senators who had long favored an open-door policy. Although *The National Gazette* was no longer being published by then, Freneau's broadsides had stoked the debate. More and more, political power in the United States was being seen as deriving its legitimacy from publicity and openness, not on the closed culture of aristocratic England. Against this change in public sentiment toward greater openness, the pro-secrecy forces were only able to secure amendments to Martin's motion that, first, delayed the change in policy until the next session; and second, that provided that the new open-door policy would only apply to legislative sessions. Martin's motion, as amended, was approved on December 9, 1795, by an overwhelming vote of nineteen to eight. Beginning with the next session of Congress, the Senate's galleries (which had yet to be built) were to be open to the public while the Senate was sitting in its legislative capacity, unless the majority of the Senate specifically ordered otherwise. Executive sessions, however, would remain closed.

Despite its margin of victory, the change in the Senate's policy was not achieved without cost. The debate on Martin's motion had been acrimonious, leaving political scars that would not quickly heal. After witnessing some of his closest colleagues being berated by several of the more radical open-door advocates, John Adams wrote to his wife that "[w]hat the effect of this measure ... will be, I know not; but it cannot produce greater evils than the contest about it, which was made an engine to render unpopular some of the ablest and most independent members."[41]

The Senate's expectation that its legislative sessions would be open to the public beginning with the next session was not to be realized. The construction of the visitor's gallery took nearly two years, primarily because of the delay in securing the necessary construction funds. As a result, Senate sessions throughout the entire second session of the Third Congress (November 3, 1794, through March 3, 1795) remained closed to the public. It was not until the beginning of the Fourth Congress (on December 7, 1795) that the Senate's legislative sessions were finally opened to the public. Two days later, on December 9, 1795, the Senate adopted an administrative resolution directing that "the gallery of the Senate chamber be permitted to be open every morning, subject to the restrictions therein mentioned, a suitable gallery having been erected and provided in the Senate chamber in the late recess of Congress for that purpose."[42] The Senate's executive sessions, however, would remain closed to the public for another 134 years, until 1929.

The public's response to the Senate's new open-door policy was not as effusive as its advocates had expected. As Senator Robert C. Byrd from West Virginia later wrote in his history of the U.S. Senate, "[n]o hordes rushed through to view the Senate at work. The sight of two dozen urbane gentlemen courteously discussing the issue of the day could hardly compete with the boisterous elegance downstairs in the House."[43] Nevertheless, the decision to open the Senate's doors was an important one—one whose significance would only grow over time. And although it did not suddenly bring the Senate into the public's good graces, it did eliminate a nagging irritant that had long alienated the public from the Senate.

Closed Sessions in Modern Times

Sessions of the House of Representatives were generally open to the public throughout its first twenty years under the new Constitution. During the War of 1812, though, the House resumed holding many of its sessions in secret. Although a fully functioning executive branch was in place by then—including a President, Secretary of War, and Secretary of State—both houses of Congress still retained an important role to play in matters of national defense and foreign policy. Deliberations on those matters, including confidential, war-related communications from the president, were all conducted in closed session.

Following the end of the War of 1812,[44] the House of Representatives resumed its practice of meeting in open session, closing its doors to the public only twice between the end of the war and 1830. Both sessions were held in order to receive confidential communications from the president: the first on December 27, 1825 (concerning relations with Indian tribes); and the second on May 27, 1830 (concerning trade relations with Great Britain). Since 1830, the House has met in secret session on only four occasions: January 20, 1979 (the Panama Canal Act of 1979); February 25, 1980 (Cuban and other Communist-block involvement in Nicaragua); July 19, 1983 (American support for paramilitary operations in Nicaragua); and March 13, 2008 (the Foreign Intelligence Surveillance Act).[45] Since 1929, when the Senate finally opened the doors to both its legislative and executive sessions, the Senate has meet in closed session on fifty-seven occasions, far more than the House of Representatives. The great majority of closed sessions were held to consider matters of national defense or foreign intelligence. Six of the more recent secret sessions, though, were held during the 1999 impeachment trial of President William J. Clinton: two involving procedural matters, and the other four during the Senate's final impeachment deliberations.[46]

The House and Senate nowadays almost always meet in open session. The standing rules of both chambers nonetheless make provision for their doors to be closed to the public: Rule XVII in the House and Rules XXI, XXIV, and XXXI in the Senate. Motions to close the doors in either chamber, including the procedures that are followed once the doors are closed, are ordinarily agreed to by that chamber's leadership in advance of the motion being made on the floor. When the House or Senate, or any of their committees or subcommittees, go into secret session, its chamber and galleries are cleared of everyone except members and officers or other employees who are specified in the chamber's rules (the House Secretary and Sergeant at Arms, for example) or those employees whose presence has been determined by the presiding officer as being essential to the matter under discussion. Once the chamber is cleared, its doors are closed. Staff members in the Senate are sworn to secrecy, while staff members in the House are required to sign a pledge of nondisclosure. Violations of the secrecy requirement are punishable under the disciplinary rules of each house. Members of both houses are subject to a variety of punishments, including loss of seniority, fine, reprimand, censure, or even expulsion. Officers and employees are subject to a range of disciplinary actions, up to and including dismissal.[47] The Senate did modify its rules slightly during the Clinton impeachment proceedings, though. Prior to going into the first of four closed-door deliberations the Senate agreed to a unanimous consent order allowing each of the Senators at the end of the trial "to place in the *Congressional Record* a statement of his or her views on the impeachment, [including] if a Senator so chose, a statement he or she had delivered during closed deliberations."[48] Each of the 100 Senators exercised the option under the consent order to include a statement in the *Congressional Record.*

Nearly all closed sessions are held in each house's own chamber. On two occasions, however, the Senate met secretly in the old Senate chamber. The old chamber was chosen because its lack of modern-day electronic equipment made it less susceptible to electronic eavesdropping.[49] One of those closed sessions was held on March 28, 1988, to discuss the Intermediate-Range Nuclear Force Missiles Treaty with the Soviet Union. The other was held on February 25, 1992, when, following the Tiananmen Square riots in 1989, the Senate met in secret to debate whether to extend China's "most favored nation" status.

The infrequency of closed sessions in the House and Senate these days is attributable in large measure to the fact that most of Congress' day-to-day work is now done by the various committees and subcommittees that have been established over the years. Future President Woodrow Wilson wrote in his doctoral dissertation, "Congressional Government," that when Congress is in session, it is on public display, but that the institution's real work is done in committee. "I know not how better to describe our form of government in a single phrase," Wilson wrote, "than by calling it a government by the chairmen of the Standing Committees of Congress."[50] Although neither the Constitution nor federal law requires a committee system, Congressional committees have served as the primary vehicle through which Congress has managed much of its work since the days of the First Congress. In addition to their role in drafting legislation, committees have also become the primary means by which Congress oversees executive agencies and participates in setting national policy. Given the growth in the role and importance of Congressional committees, it is in those committees that an injunction of secrecy is most often imposed.

The House currently has twenty-one standing committees, the Senate twenty. Most of the standing committees have multiple subcommittees. Committee and subcommittee meetings are ordinarily open to the public, unless the subject of the meeting is required by statute or chamber rule to be considered in closed session. The meetings that are open to the public also may be broadcast by radio and television under the rules that the particular committee has established. Some committees, such as the Committee on Agriculture, rarely meet in closed session. Those committees having jurisdiction over foreign intelligence, military appropriations, homeland security, counter-terrorism, and other classified subjects, meet in closed session far more often. Executive branch briefings of committees working in those classified areas are typically conducted in private.

Treaties and Impeachment Proceedings

In addition to those regular legislative and oversight matters that are taken up in closed session because of their sensitive nature, the Constitution imposes two additional, non-legislative duties on Congress that may also be carried out in closed session: Article II, Section 2, Clause 2, concerning treaties; and Article I, Section 3 Clause 6, concerning the impeachment of federal officials. The Constitution does not require the House or Senate to meet in closed session in either case, but neither does it require the sessions to be open to the public. Those decisions are made in accordance with each chamber's own rules.

The historic assumption was that the Senate would meet in closed session when a treaty is submitted to it for its "advice and consent" unless and "until the Senate shall, by their resolution, take off the injunction of secrecy." In the early years of the Senate, prior to its decision in December 1795 to open its doors to its legislative sessions, all of the Senate's treaty deliberations were conducted in closed executive session. Even after the Senate's decision in 1929 to admit the public to its executive sessions, the practice of debating treaties in secret session continued. Treaties were a part of the country's foreign affairs and advising the president on those matters was thought to be one of the Senate's most important executive functions. Although the terms of the treaty were eventually disclosed to the public, the negotiations leading up to the treaty were not.

The practice of considering treaties in closed session was first formalized in December 1800 when President Adams forwarded to the Senate the instructions he had given to America's envoys to the French Republic in connection with their negotiation of the Treaty of Montefontaine.[51] It was common practice for the president when submitting a treaty to the Senate also to submit the correspondence between him and the treaty's negotiators. Adams delivered the relevant correspondence, but added the request that "they may be considered in strict confidence." In response to Adams's request, the Senate adopted a new standing rule on December 22, 1800, directing "[t]hat all confidential communications made by the President of the United States shall be, by the members thereof, kept inviolably secret, and that all treaties which may hereafter be laid before the Senate, shall also be kept secret, until the Senate shall, by their resolution, take off the injunction of secrecy." The Senate's consideration of treaties was thereafter conducted behind closed session for the next eighty-eight years. Several attempts were made in the years following to have a pending treaty considered in open session, usually by the opponents of the treaty, but in all cases the motion was defeated.

A temporary break in the Senate's closed-door policy did occur when Democratic President Grover Cleveland submitted a treaty to the Senate that had been concluded with Great Britain in mid–February 1888. The Canadian Fisheries Treaty was intended by Cleveland to ease tensions with Great Britain over the two countries' respective fishing rights off the northeastern coast of North America. The motion to consider the treaty in open session was not made out of a principled conviction, but in an effort by the treaty's opponents to gain the upper hand politically. The new treaty with Great Britain generated intense anti–British opposition among Americans of Irish descent, and, in an effort to fuel that dissent even further, the Republican-controlled Senate amended the Senate's rules to allow the treaty to be debated in open session. The presidential election November 1888 was rapidly approaching and the Republican majority engineered the rule change in an effort to enhance its chances of capturing New York State's crucial thirty-six electoral votes and thus the presidency. The Senate debated the treaty throughout the summer, but as had been their intent all along, the

Republicans succeeded on August 21 in having the Senate reject the treaty. The vote was along party lines. Two weeks before the election, the Republicans also leaked a secret letter from the British ambassador disclosing that the government of Great Britain quietly supported the reelection of President Cleveland. The publication of that correspondence consolidated Irish-American support for the Republicans and played a large role in putting their nominee, former Senator Benjamin Harrison, in the White House. Following the election, the Senate returned to its former practice of holding closed sessions on treaties. That practice continued until 1929. Despite the closed sessions, however, news about the Senate's executive deliberations routinely leaked out to the press, enabling newspapers to publish full accounts of what had transpired. Members of the press reportedly joked that if the Senate wanted fuller coverage, it should conduct all of its business in secret.

The Senate's Rule XXIX still provides that "[a]ll confidential communications made by the President of the United States to the Senate shall be by the Senators and the officers of the Senate kept secret; and all treaties which may be laid before the Senate, and all remarks, votes, and proceedings thereon shall also be kept secret, until the Senate shall, by their resolution, take off the injunction of secrecy." Only infrequently, however, does the Senate decide to meet in secret session, and then most always because of classified information that may underlie the treaty or that may otherwise be relevant to the Senate's consideration of the treaty. The Committee on Foreign Relations, the Committee to which treaties are customarily referred for initial consideration, is also governed by Rule XXIX. In the great majority of cases, though, the injunction of secrecy is lifted by the full Senate simultaneously with its referral of the treaty to the Committee.[52]

Impeachment proceedings are a mix of both open and closed sessions. During the Constitutional Convention Benjamin Franklin warned his fellow delegates that presidents at times might "render [themselves] obnoxious." Rather than assassinating them, as had been the time-honored tradition, Franklin urged that there should be a regularized procedure for removing those officials. "What was the practice before this," Franklin asked, "in cases where the chief Magistrate rendered himself obnoxious? Why recourse was had to assassination in which he was not only deprived of his life but of the opportunity for vindicating his character? It would be the best way therefore to provide in the

Constitution for the regular punishment of the Executive when his misconduct should deserve it, and for his honorable acquittal when he should be unjustly accused."[53] The Constitution adopted by the delegates thus provides in Article II, Section 4 that "[t]he President, Vice President and all civil Officers of the United States, shall be removed from Office on Impeachment for, and Conviction of, Treason, Bribery, or other High crimes and Misdemeanors." Article I, Section 4, Clause 5 of the Constitution delegates to the House "the sole Power of Impeachment." Article I, Section 3, Clause 6 assigns the Senate the "sole Power to try all impeachments." Among all the powers granted to Congress by the Constitution, the power of impeachment is likely the greatest. If a federal official, including a president, is convicted, there is no appeal.

Impeachment proceedings may be initiated by the House against the President, Vice President, or other civil officer whom the President cannot remove, such as a federal judge, or an official whom the President does not wish to remove, such as a cabinet secretary.[54] In the modern era, the House Judiciary Committee has exercised jurisdiction over impeachments. After investigating the charges, the Committee votes on whether to pursue Articles of Impeachment against the accused official. If Articles of Impeachment are reported out of the Committee and then adopted by the full House (by simple majority vote), the impeachment charges are referred to the Senate for trial. Impeachment in the House is thus much like an indictment in today's criminal justice system.

The House has initiated impeachment proceedings sixty-two times. Articles of Impeachment have been issued on nineteen occasions. Of the nineteen that have resulted in trials in the Senate, there have been seven acquittals, eight convictions, three dismissals, and one resignation. Fifteen of the nineteen impeachments involved judges, including Supreme Court Justice Samuel Chase who was acquitted. Andrew Johnson (on February 24, 1868) and William J. Clinton (on December 19, 1998) are the only two presidents who have been impeached. Both were acquitted by the Senate, although in Johnson's case by only a single vote. President Richard Nixon resigned from office on August 9, 1974, before the impeachment proceeding against him in the House were concluded.

Impeachment proceedings in the Senate are a mix of both open and closed sessions. The Senate's governing rule provides that "[a]t all times while the Senate is sitting upon the trial of an impeachment the doors of the Senate shall be kept open." The Senate Secretary records and reports the trial phase of the impeachment proceedings "in the same manner as the legislative proceedings of the Senate." Once the trial phase is over, the Senate may, by a vote or upon motion without objection "direct the doors to be closed while deliberating its decisions." In nearly all cases, the doors are closed during the Senate's deliberations. The final vote on whether to remove the government official from office is taken in open session. The Senate's rules essentially parallel the practice followed in today's civil and criminal trials: the trial itself is generally held in open court, while the judge or judges' decision is considered and reached in the privacy of the judge's chambers.

Although the Senate's decisions to meet in secret have been free of controversy for the most part, the trial of President Clinton was an exception. Following the Senate's decision to deliberate in secret, Cable News Network filed a formal application with the Senate asking that it be "permitted to attend and view the debates, deliberations, and proceedings."[55] In a public statement accompanying its filing, CNN argued that "[e]xcept for a declaration of war, no proceeding of the Senate has such historic importance as ... the removal from office of an American president. Conducting these debates behind closed doors denies the people throughout the world the opportunity to judge the fairness of the proceedings and excludes firsthand information from being made available to the millions of American voters who have a vital stake in the trial's outcome."[56] CNN's application failed to gather the two/thirds vote necessary to suspend the Senate's rule and open the proceedings to public view.

6

Secrecy and the
Public Record

*In such a government as ours, where members are so removed
from the eye of their constituents, an easy and prompt circulation of public proceedings is peculiarly essential.*—James Madison, December 6, 1792

John Adams wrote in his *Dissertation on the Canon and Feudal
Law* that "the preservation of knowledge among the lower ranks is of
more importance to the public than all the property of all the rich men
in the country." "[N]one of the means of information," Adams went on
to write, "are more sacred, or have been cherished with more tender-
ness and care by the settlers of America, than the press."[1] Thomas Jefferson expressed the same view in 1787, writing that "[t]he basis of our
government being the opinion of the people, the very first object should
be to keep that right; were it left to me to decide whether we should
have a government without newspapers or newspapers without a government, I should not hesitate a moment to prefer the latter."[2]

Francis Lieber, who in 1853 chronicled America's growth through
its first half-century, singled out in particular the major role that newspapers played in pulling back even further the veil of secrecy between
Congress and the American people. "A modern free city-state can be
imagined without a public press," Lieber wrote, "a modern free country
cannot." As important as opening Congress' doors to public view was,
"without the ability of reporters to publish the transactions of public
bodies, the admission of the public would hardly amount to any publicity at all."[3] Openness without publicity is in many respects the func-
tional equivalent of acting in secret. Despite the Constitution's guarantee

of a free press, though, not all of America's political leaders were convinced of the wisdom of allowing the press to report on the debates of Congress. Many shared the attitude still prevailing in England's House of Commons that news reporters were nothing more than "pernicious interlopers and eavesdroppers."[4] In a letter written to his wife two years after the decision had been made to admit the press to House proceedings, John Adams expressed his concern that the correctness of that decision was not so clear-cut: "[t]his measure, by making the Debates public, will establish the national Government, or break the Confederation. I can conceive of no medium between these extremes."[5]

The introduction of press reporters into the House of Representatives occurred more or less simultaneously with the opening of the House's doors to the public. Reporters were eventually admitted to Senate sessions when the Senate gallery was constructed in 1795, but it was not until January 6, 1802, that the Senate finally voted to allow stenographers and other note takers to be admitted to the Senate floor and assigned to "such place as the [Senate] President shall allot."[6]

The first reporters functioned essentially as stenographers. Although the reporters were initially given seats on the House floor, an issue soon arose over whether to allow them to continue to sit on the House floor or to require them to take their notes from the visitor's gallery. Those House members who favored retaining floor privileges for the reporters argued that forcing them to take their notes while sitting some distance away in the gallery would inevitably lead to errors in their reporting. One reporter, apparently being unable to hear clearly from the gallery what was being said on the floor, was reported to have mistakenly converted a regulation of "harbors" into a regulation of "barbers."

Although a majority of House members were "anxious to have the shorthand reporters resume their seats in the House," a formal vote to that end was not taken for fear it would confer upon the reporters and their publications "a degree of legislative authority." Many members believed that the reporters' errors should be seen as theirs alone. Moreover, withholding any official imprimatur of the House made it easier for members to claim later on that they had been misquoted. The matter was finally settled by granting discretionary power to the Speaker "to admit such persons as he thought proper." The reporters would regain their seats on the floor, but without the official blessing of the House as a whole.

Even when the debates on the House floor were transcribed correctly, the news accounts that appeared in the newspaper were often partisan, emphasizing some points while downplaying, if not omitting, others. Partisanship on the part of the press was not viewed then in quite the same light as it is today. When John Adams and others spoke of the importance of the press, they were not speaking of the press in 21st century terms. Adams instead saw the press as not merely a chronicler of current events, but as a useful tool in the people's ongoing struggle against government tyranny. Rather than being an impartial reporter of the news, the role of the press, in Adams' view, was to serve as a partisan agent in the debate between the Federalists and the anti–Federalists: first during the ratification debates over the new Constitution, and later on as part of the growth of political parties.

The *Gazette of the United States,* founded in mid–April 1789, was the newspaper most supportive of the administration of George Washington and the other politicians who supported the emerging Federalist movement. At the other end of the political spectrum was the *National Gazette,* a rival newspaper founded at the urging of anti–Federalists Thomas Jefferson and James Madison. The *Gazette* was intended by the two to serve as a vehicle for spreading anti–Federalist political views. Indeed, so partisan was the *Gazette* in its reporting that Jefferson often wrote articles for the *Gazette* criticizing the Washington administration even though, as Secretary of State, he was a central part of it. The Philadelphia *Aurora,* another radical newspaper, also routinely denounced the Federalists, launching especially vitriolic attacks against the Washington and Adams administrations.

Not all newspapers, however, were as partisan in their reporting of the news. Newspapers such as the *New York Daily Gazette,* the *Philadelphia Gazette,* and the *National Intelligencer* attempted to report on Congressional proceedings in a more straightforward way, at least to the extent they regarded those proceedings as being newsworthy.[7] Newspaper editors pointedly asserted their right to omit material they found "eternally repetitious" or of little interest to their readers. The amount of available column space together with the limitations in existing shorthand methods also served to restrict the amount of reliable information that actually made its way to the public. Press coverage of Congressional proceedings was further hindered by the inability of the press to cover the Senate's executive sessions. Deliberations there remained a secret.

The First Steps Toward Greater Openness

The House's decision to open its doors to the public was unquestionably historic. Even so, the new policy was of practical benefit mostly to the forty thousand or so who lived in and around Philadelphia; and even then only to those who were lucky or politically connected enough to be able to secure a visitor's pass to the gallery. As for the other four million Americans, aside from those few who might occasionally travel to Philadelphia on government or other business, the flow of information from the members of the House to the people who elected them was sporadic at best. Two important steps were taken early in the second Congress to improve the flow of information to the public. Both measures were contained in the Post Office Act of 1792: the first concerning the Congressional franking privilege; and the second concerning the subsidized distribution of newspapers through the national mail system. Both were based on Congress' Constitutional power "to establish Post Offices and Post Roads." Although neither measure was front-page news at the time, both did much to bring the workings of the national government even more into the open.

Franking

The franking privilege allows members of Congress to send and receive mail under their signature without postage. Franking (from French, "to exempt from charge") and has its roots in 17th century Great Britain when, in 1660, the British House of Commons established the franking privilege for its members. The privilege in America was initially authorized in 1775 by the First Continental Congress and then reauthorized in 1782 by the Congress of the Confederation. The 1782 legislation provided that "the letters, packets, and dispatches to and from members of Congress, while actually attending Congress, shall pass and be carried free of charge."[8] By enabling members of Congress to convey information to their constituents about the work of government and the policy matters pending before Congress, those supporting the franking privilege saw it as playing a vital role in pulling back even further the curtain that, as a practical matter, still surrounded part of Congress' work. Franking was much less important in the Senate. Because Senators were elected by their respective state legislature, not by the people, they typically had less interest in keeping in touch with the public back home. Indeed, because the privilege also applied to mail that was sent to them, some Senators even saw the franking privilege as something of a nuisance. The debate for and against the continuation of the franking privilege thus took place mostly in the House.

Franked mail today plays only a small role in publicizing the work of Congress. Most Americans rarely receive mail from their Congressional representatives, and when they do it often goes unread. In the early days of the republic, though, franked mail was one of the primary sources of information about Congress and its work. Indeed, Representative James Alcorn from Mississippi later noted the historical significance of franking, declaring on the House floor that "through that means [franking] information was communicated everywhere to the people all over the country. The intelligence of the people was enlightened and promoted by reason of this franking privilege. The dissemination of knowledge was carried out to the uttermost confines of the land trough this franking privilege."[9] James Madison argued during the earlier 1782 debates that franking was the "principal channel" through which the citizenry secured its "general knowledge" of public affairs.[10]

Support for the franking privilege was not universal. A few members of the House, led by William Branch Giles of Virginia opposed the continuation of the privilege. Giles regarded franking as not only costly and discriminatory (an "unfair preferential benefit," he claimed), but also wholly "unnecessary, where public presses are established, the freedom of debate unrestrained, and the debates published in the newspapers." It is more than sufficient," Giles argued, that "every man [be] at liberty to express his sentiments in the papers, and that the public [be] free to read them."[11] The First Amendment was more than enough.

Those members of the House who supported the franking privilege responded to Giles' claims by arguing that the privilege was not granted to members of Congress as a personal benefit, "but as a benefit to their constituents, who, by means of it, derive information [about their government] from those who are best qualified to give it." Moreover, the supporters contended, "[t]he members also receive useful information through the same channel." The franking privilege was ultimately retained, but upon the express condition that it be used only for official correspondence.

Perhaps not surprisingly the franking privilege was often the subject of abuse. One House member boasted that if the envelopes were arranged properly, he could sign as many as three hundred in an hour. Some members even hired ghost-writers to sign their signature for them. Rumors were common that some members routinely franked their laundry home, or gave their signatures to family and friends for their personal use. One rumor even had it that an early nineteenth-century Senator attached a frank to his horse's bridle and sent the animal back to his home in Pittsburgh. Regardless of the truth of these rumors, members of Congress did routinely flood the mails with government documents, speeches, and packages of seeds. Some of the mailings were useful; many others were mostly aimed at bolstering their chances of reelection.

In light of these abuses, the Senate later voted on January 31, 1873, to abolish the Congressional franking privilege altogether, rejecting a House-passed bill that would have provided special stamps for the free mailing of printed Senate and House documents. Within two years, though, Congress began to carve out exceptions to the ban, authorizing free mailing of the Congressional Record, seeds, and agricultural reports. Finally, in 1891, observing that its members were the only government officials who were required to pay postage, Congress restored full franking privileges. The franking privilege is still used today by members of Congress, although with the advent of an increasingly broad array of modern-day print and electronic communications media, the value of franking as a communications tool has been greatly diminished.

Promoting the Growth of Newspapers

There was universal agreement within Congress that the widespread dissemination of information about the activities of government was essential to the preservation of national unity. Newspapers were seen as helping to bind America's far-flung population into a single nation. Dr. Benjamin Rush, one of the signers of the Declaration of Independence wrote to Dr. Richard Price, a minister and Welsh moral philosopher, commenting on the crippling effects on governing that the absence of newspapers can have: "[n]othing can be done by our public bodies till they carry the people along with them, and as the means of propagating intelligence and knowledge in our country are as yet but scanty, all their movements are marked with appearances of delay and procrastination."[12]

There was also the belief that in order to succeed as a democratic government, there must be an informed electorate, which, in turn, depends upon there being an ongoing exchange of news, ideas, and opinions. One of the key communication functions in the American form of government is thus that of providing the people with the information they need to participate in the process of creating and maintaining their own government. James Madison wrote in *The Federalist* that the people are the most powerful tool for controlling government, and to exercise that power the people must be informed. "If men were angels," Madison wrote, "no government would be necessary. If angels were to govern men, neither external nor internal controls on government would be necessary. In framing a government which is to be administered by men over men ... dependence on the people is, no doubt, the primary control on government."[13] Newspapers were seen as playing a vital, if not indispensable role in creating that informed electorate, particularly outside the country's urban population centers. To Benjamin Rush, it was "absolutely necessary" that the government circulate "knowledge of every kind ... through every part of the United States."[14] One New Hampshire newspaper wrote in early 1787 that "[o]ne great cause of discontent of the back country is their total want of regular intelligence. This gives designing men an opportunity of forging the greatest falsehoods, there being no publick newspapers to stare them in the face, and contradict what they assert."[15] Newspapers were thus seen by many as an important counterforce to secrecy. With the growth in investigative journalism, it would become even more so.

In his famous work *Democracy in America*, Alexis de Tocqueville wrote that in a democracy those who wish to shape public policy must "persuade every man whose help [he] require[s] that his private interest obliges him voluntarily to unite" with others of like mind. Only newspapers, de Tocqueville observed, are in a position to do that "habitually and conveniently [because] only newspapers can carry the same thought into a thousand minds at the same time." Newspapers cause "political life to circulate through all parts of that vast territory, detect[ing] the secret springs of political designs" and "summon[ing] the leaders of all parties to the bar of public opinion."[16]

Although there was no shortage of demand for newspapers in the late 1700s, printing and then distributing them was a difficult and expensive undertaking. Circulations were small. Rarely did a newspaper have more than a thousand subscribers. In an attempt to promote the growth and geographic expansion of American newspapers, Congress included in the Post Office Act of 1792 a provision that set a lower and preferential postage rate for newspapers. The legislation also authorized each newspaper to send, postage free, one copy of each of its editions to every other newspaper in the country. A publisher could then select articles of interest to his readers and reprint them in his own newspaper.

In making the case for the postage subsidy, Massachusetts Representative Elbridge Gerry—a leading proponent of low, uniform postage rates for newspapers—argued that "whenever information is freely circulating, there slavery cannot exist. However firmly liberty may be established in any country," Gerry continued, "it cannot long subsist if the channels of information be stopped."[17] James Madison, another advocate of low postage rates for newspapers (he thought that postage rates amounted to an improper tax) later wrote that "[i]n such a [government] as ours, where members are so removed from the eye of their constituents, an easy and prompt circulation of public proceedings is peculiarly essential."[18]

The Post Office Act of 1792 contained both the franking privilege and the authorization of lower postage rates for newspapers. The Act was passed by Congress on December 28, 1791, and signed into law by President Washington on February 20, 1792. Although Washington signed the legislation, he urged Congress a year later to repeal the section of the Act that continued to impose even the Act's modest postage on newspapers, terming it a "tax on the transportation of public prints."[19] In effect, Washington was proposing that the government circulate newspapers through the mail at no cost.

When Thomas Jefferson was sworn in as President in 1801 there were roughly two hundred newspapers in circulation throughout the United States. By the time Abraham Lincoln was elected president in 1860 there were nearly 3,000. This remarkable expansion of the press was attributable to a number of factors, including a growth in population, increased political participation by the working class, higher rates of literacy, and the advances in printing technology that allowed newspapers to be printed faster and more efficiently. An important part of the growth in newspapers and the number of people they reached, though, particularly during the first half of the 19th century, was the subsidized postal rates that Congress put into effect in 1792.

Permanent Record of Congressional Proceedings

The newspapers' primary role during the first half of the 19th century was, as it largely is today, to report on the news of the day. For many years, the only permanent record of Congressional proceedings was limited to what was contained in the House and Senate journals. Those wishing to learn what Congress had done in the past had those journals as their only ready resource. There was no other record to which the public could easily turn. In 1834, however, two commercial publishers, Joseph Gales and William Seaton, brothers-in-law who jointly owned *The National Intelligence*, began collecting and then selectively publishing existing accounts of past Congressional debates and legislative action. Gales and Seaton relied on the best records then available, primarily newspapers, including their own *Intelligencer*. The *Intelligencer* began publishing notes on the debates in Congress soon after Gales and Seaton purchased the paper from its founder, Samuel Harrison Smith, in 1810.

The summaries that Gales and Seaton prepared were included in a publication entitled the *Annals of Congress*.[20] The two publishers took great pride in the accuracy of their summaries, claiming at one point, for example, that "[t]his debate [concerning the Jay Treaty in 1796], as given here, possesses a character for authenticity and correctness which does not belong to the newspaper reports of the day, it having undergone the revision of the speakers themselves."[21] During their newspaper publishing days, Gales and Seaton enjoyed favored status in Congress, most likely because of their willingness to allow members to edit their own remarks before they were printed in the *Intelligencer*. The special status they enjoyed allowed Gales to sit next to the Senate president. Seaton covered the House from his place at the Speaker's side.

The *Annals* are organized by Congressional session into forty-two volumes covering the first eighteen Congresses—1789 through 1824. The Annals were not published contemporaneously, however, but were compiled and printed over the course of twenty-two years—from 1834 to 1856. Although the floor debates were summarized rather than presented verbatim, the *Annals'* record of those floor debates is substantially more complete than is contained in either the House or Senate journal. The *Annals* are consequently recognized as being the most authoritative source of Congressional activity during the period they cover. Funds appropriated by Congress in 1849 helped make possible the publication of the *Annals.*

In 1824, some ten years before Gales and Seaton began work on the *Annals*, the two publishers started a second publication, the *Register of Debates in Congress.* The *Register* was "intended to supply a deficiency in our Political Annals ... by present[ing] in a portable but durable form ... the History of the Legislation of the Government of the United States." The *Register* covered the years 1824 through 1837 and was published annually at the end of each Congressional session, thereby marking the first attempt to publish, more or less contemporaneously, an accurate account of the "leading debates and incidents" of Congress. The floor debates, though, were not reported verbatim in all cases. Many of the accounts were written in the third person. The House and Senate had begun allowing selected reporters on the floor by then, but because stenography was still in its early stages of development, the debates were typically recorded in longhand. In addition, speeches that were deemed to be lacking in general interest were often not reported at all. As had been the practice with the *Intelligencer*, members of Congress were also permitted to revise their remarks before the *Register* was published. Even with their shortcomings, though, Gales and Seaton confidently assured the *Register's* readers that "their substantial accuracy may be entirely relied upon."[22]

The third in the series of important historical records was the *Congressional Globe*, a newspaper-type publication that provided daily coverage of Congressional proceedings from 1833 to 1873 (the 23rd Congress through the 42nd Congress). Bound cumulative volumes of the *Globe* were published at the end of each session. The *Globe* was published by a new printing partnership formed in Washington, D.C., by Francis Blair and John Cook Rives. Much like the *Register*, the *Globe* did not initially provide its readers with a verbatim account of Congressional proceedings, but only "sketches of the debates and proceedings."

Although the *Globe* and the *Register* each had its supporters, the *Globe* was generally thought to be more partisan than the *Register*, frequently causing many members of Congress to claim that they were misquoted, misrepresented, or not even covered at all. The *Globe* was actively supported by President Andrew Jackson. Jackson saw the *Globe* as being more sympathetic to his administration. Many of Jackson's political adversaries distrusted the *Globe's* version of events in the House and Senate, branding Blair and Rives "habitual falsifiers of debate." The two partners encountered such resentment that they reportedly carried concealed weapons in order to protect themselves from angry members of Congress.[23] By the middle of the nineteenth century, however, improvements in shorthand, along with a willingness by Congress to pay the salaries of the reporters and for copies of their reports, enabled the *Globe* to provide a more accurate account of Congressional debates. With that greater accuracy, complaints against the *Globe* and its publishers subsided.

In 1846, the Senate authorized its members to subscribe to the political newspaper of their choice. By virtue of its popularity and the place it occupied in American politics, the *Globe* became the semiofficial publication of the Senate. The Senate contracted with newspapers two years later to furnish their coverage of Senate proceedings to the *Globe*. In 1850, the House entered into the same arrangement with the *Globe*. In light of the expectation that the *Globe* would act as a nonpartisan publication, the *Globe* began to make use of reporters who were trained in the latest stenographic techniques, thereby enabling the *Globe* to begin printing debates as first-person narratives rather than as third-person summations. Bound cumulative volumes of the *Globe* were published at the end of each session. Beginning with the 32nd Congress (1851), following the introduction of the phonetic shorthand method developed by Isaac Pitman, the *Globe* began reporting near-verbatim accounts of Congressional debates.

Despite the relative success of the *Globe*, the enormous number of floor debates that took place during the Civil War led Congress to consider adopting a more efficient and cost-effective system for recording its proceedings. Thus, when the *Globe's* contract expired on March 3, 1873, the 43rd Congress chose not to renew it, electing instead to establish a new publication, the *Congressional Record*, to be published by the Government Printing Office and staffed by Official Reporters of

Debates. Although reporters had been paid at government expense since 1855, it was not until the *Congressional Record* that Congress began hiring its own reporters directly.

The *Congressional Record* is now universally accepted as the most accurate and effective means of both recording and distributing information about Congress' activities. While early newspaper reporters insisted upon their right to omit material they did not believe "deserved particular notice," the *Congressional Record* has become what those editors resisted becoming—thoroughly comprehensive. The *Record* contains House and Senate floor proceedings in substantially verbatim form. As then-Senate Majority Leader Lyndon Johnson said in 1956, "Locked in its pages are the debates, the resolutions, the bills, the memorials, the petitions, and the legislative actions that are the reason for the existence of the Senate [and the House]." The work that Congress and its committees do in open session is now fully available for inspection by all.[24]

Although as a matter of practice most documents that Congress generates are publicly available, Congress and its committees may nonetheless designate certain documents, reports, and transcripts confidential or classified. In *Goland* v. *Central Intelligence Agency*, 607 F. 2d 339, 346 (D.C. Cir. 1978), the plaintiff sought "all of the reports of the Committees of the House and Senate [from] any hearings which may have been held ... on the authority, organization and administration of the CIA." The Court turned down the request, holding that "Congress has undoubted authority to keep its records secret, authority rooted in the Constitution, longstanding practice, and current congressional rules." There is no established procedure for gaining access to these documents. The declassification and release of them rests within the sole discretion of Congress.

Radio and Television Come to Congress

The public's ability to monitor the inner workings of Congress has progressed over the past two hundred years from a limited, often heavily edited account in the House and Senate journals, to the selected excerpts from the floor debate that were reconstructed by such private undertakings as the *Annals of Congress* and its successors, to the substantially verbatim accounts of floor debates in today's *Congressional Record*, to the live and unedited radio and television coverage of House and Senate floor sessions that is available today to nearly all Americans. The largest segment of the American public in history now has the opportunity to watch Congress at work firsthand. Except in those cases when the House or Senate is meeting in closed session, the veil of secrecy that once surrounded Congress has been torn away. Yet as was the case with the decisions to open the doors of Congress to the public and then to allow print reporters on the House and Senate floor, the decision to permit live coverage of Congressional proceedings, first with radio and then later with television, was neither quick in coming nor free of controversy.

The first effort to link the American people electronically with Congress occurred on February 22, 1922, when Michigan Representative Vincent M. Brennan introduced a bill authorizing live radio coverage of House proceedings. The purpose of Brennan's bill was straightforward: to "enable members of Congress as well as the country at large 'to listen in' on the doings of the floor of the House."[25] Brennan's bill gathered little support. Although the House was unwilling to put itself on live display, however, it was willing to allow its chamber to be used occasionally for the broadcast of other noteworthy events. President Warren G. Harding's Annual Address to a joint session of Congress was broadcast live from the House floor on December 19, 1922, as was President Calvin Coolidge's Annual Address the following year. The first radio broadcast of a presidential inauguration took place on March 4, 1925, when President Coolidge took the oath of office at the East Front of the Capitol. More than twenty-two million households tuned in to the broadcast.

Despite the large audiences that these radio broadcasts drew, Congress remained unwilling to allow live radio coverage of its own proceedings. On November 7, 1933, Congress denied the applications of several radio newsmen from CBS who sought admission to the press gallery. Much of the opposition to their applications came from forces outside Congress. Print journalists from around the country sent hundreds of telegrams to the Senate Rules Committee expressing their opposition to sharing their gallery with radio reporters. Many newspapers claimed that radio reporters could not be depended upon to report the news accurately and fairly. One publisher argued that radio "operates under a Federal License and its utterances can be directly controlled," whereas "the press cannot be controlled and therefore operates as a stabilizer of government," concluding that "there is no place in the press galleries for both." Another publisher wrote that allowing radio reporters into the press galleries would represent an "official recognition of radio broadcasting as a medium of disseminating news," which, because radio is licensed by the FCC, would amount to "an official sanction of the censorship of news" by government.[26] Other newspaper reporters opposed granting the broadcasters' applications on the more practical ground that the press galleries were too cramped to accommodate additional media members. The applications of the CBS newsmen were denied. Radio reporters were consigned to writing their stories for later broadcast from any public place they could find, reportedly even in Capitol broom closets.

In 1937, a reporter for William Randolph Hearst's *Washington Herald*, Fulton Lewis, Jr., gave up his newspaper job and began reporting political news on Washington radio station WOL. Lewis was a flamboyant commentator, popularly known as the "voice with a snarl." Lewis soon left WOL and began broadcasting his news reports on the Mutual Radio network. Mutual was owned and operated as a cooperative, with its own original programming, transmission and promotion expense, and advertising revenues. Lewis prided himself on doing his own reporting and when he stopped writing for newspapers, the press reporters who were unofficially in charge of the press gallery revoked his pass. The reporters took the rather self-serving position that if a radio station wanted someone to report on the news from Washington, they should hire someone from their ranks, "a working newspaperman," who could then appear on the radio every now and then and report the news. Lewis was outraged by the decision and began lobbying his friends in Congress to create a separate gallery for radio reporters. Although the newspaper reporters dismissed Lewis' lobbying effort as a publicity stunt, they had not counted on the eagerness of many members of Congress to have their proceedings covered by radio. Thus, on July 4, 1939, Congress reversed its policy and began admitting radio reporters to a new radio gallery that had been constructed separate and apart from the newspaper and other print media galleries.

Five years later, on September 15, 1955, Representative John Coffee from Washington introduced a bill authorizing live radio broadcasts of all House proceedings. Coffee's bill was introduced shortly after a similar bill had been introduced in the Senate by Florida's Clause Pepper. The two men argued that in light of the "mounting interest throughout the country," the time had finally come for Congress to allow its deliberations to be broadcast live. Other Congressmen, though, feared that permitting their deliberations to be broadcast would alter the culture of Congress for the worse. Coffee disputed that claim, responding that "the people are entitled to know what is going on in Congress, without editorial deletion or expurgation at the hands of radio or other commentators. Why should not the people judge for themselves?" Although the Joint Committee on the Organization of Congress held extensive hearings on the Coffee-Pepper initiative, their bill failed to attract enough votes to pass either house of Congress. The following year, though, a daily radio broadcast, "Congress Today" began airing. "Congress Today" was a fifteen-minute newscast devoted to the daily "doings of Congress and the cause and effect of current legislation."[27] Live, regular radio broadcasts of Congressional proceedings, however, were still many years away. Television coverage of Congress would be equally slow in coming.

The Federal Communications granted the nation's first television station license to W3XK in 1928. The station was located in Washington, D.C. On April 30, 1939, David Sarnoff, president of RCA, arranged for President Franklin Roosevelt to deliver the opening speech at the World's Fair from the RCA Pavilion in New York City. Roosevelt's speech was broadcast on station W2XBS, a station that was owned by RCA and operated by RCA's broadcasting affiliate, the National Broadcasting Company. Because there were very few television sets in operation then—probably no more than one hundred or so—NBC scattered several dozen additional sets throughout the city.

On January 3, 1947—nearly forty years after the FCC granted the first television license to W3XK—television cameras were allowed into the House chamber, but like radio before it, only on special occasions. The occasion for the maiden telecast was the opening of the 80th Congress. President Harry Truman's State of the Union address in 1947 was the first of the annual addresses to be televised. It would be another three decades, though, before the American television viewer would again be able to watch Congress at work.

Because so much of the work of Congress is done in committee, those committee hearings that were of particular national importance were also televised on occasion, including three that drew huge nationwide audiences: Senator Estes Kefauver's investigation into organized crime, Senator's Joseph McCarthy's investigation of Army security, and the Ervin-Baker committee's investigation of the Watergate break-in and subsequent cover-up. The three together served to whet the public's appetite for more live coverage of Congressional proceedings.

Although Kefauver's committee was not the first Congressional committee to have its proceedings televised, it was by far the most widely viewed. In March 1951, an estimated thirty million Americans tuned in to watch the live proceedings. "Never before had the attention of the nation been riveted so completely on a single matter," reported *Life* magazine. "The Senate investigation into interstate crime was almost the sole subject of national conversation."[28] "Television and radio make these events more vivid and alive to the general public than newspapers," explained one New York viewer. "I do not think any of you can possibly realize how much good it has done to have these hearings televised. It has made millions of us aware of conditions that we would never have fully realized even if we had read the newspaper accounts."[29]

The McCarthy hearings dominated national television three years later, from April through June 1954. Senator Joseph R. McCarthy, who earlier became infamous for his aggressive interrogation of suspected Communists, turned his committee's attention to the allegation that Communists had infiltrated the country's Armed forces. The Army responded by charging McCarthy with using improper influence to secure preferential treatment for a former staff member, David Schine, who had just been drafted. The McCarthy hearings were broadcast nationally on the ABC and DuMont networks, and in part by NBC. The hearings lasted thirty-six days. An estimated 80 million people watched at least part of the hearings. The cameras in the hearing room put McCarthy's aggressive methods and manner on full display, seriously weakening his popular support, and ultimately leading to his censure by the Senate on December 2, 1954.

Twenty years later, in 1973, the Senate Select Committee on Presidential Campaign Activities conducted what were to become known as the Watergate hearings. The committee was co-chaired by Senators Sam Ervin from North Carolina and Howard Baker from Tennessee. The committee's charge was to investigate whether "illegal, improper or unethical activities" had been committed in connection with President Richard Nixon's 1972 campaign for reelection—"What did the President know and when did he know it" was the question. Public television aired all 250 hours of the hearings, gavel-to-gavel. After the first week of testimony, however, the three commercial networks resumed their normal programming and rotated daily coverage of the hearings. The hearings nonetheless drew large nationwide audiences. An estimated eighty-five percent of Americans watched some portion of the Watergate hearings.

The growing demand for live television coverage of Congressional floor proceedings took a major step forward in 1973 with the formation of the Joint (House and Senate) Committee on Congressional Operations. The Committee's assignment was to examine the means by which Congress could better communicate with the American people. The Committee's subsequent recommendation that cameras be allowed in the House and Senate chambers met with different reactions in the two houses. As had been the case nearly 200 years earlier, the House was generally receptive to the idea of greater openness; the United States Senate was not.

In the House, Speaker Thomas (Tip) O'Neil from Massachusetts ordered that a House television system be installed on a trial basis. The trial began in March 1977. In order to avoid disrupting the normal flow of House business, remotely controlled cameras were placed at safe, out-of-the-way locations in the House chamber. The trial proceeded without incident. Full implementation of House television coverage could not be permanently implemented, however, until the House Rules Committee resolved the critical issue of who would be in charge of the television cameras: the House itself or the television networks who would remain independent of House authority. In June 1978, the Rules Committee decided that the House would be better served by retaining control of the cameras itself. The measure was approved by a vote of 235 to 150. Nine months later, on March 19, 197, the House's television system was in place and fully operational. The American public would be allowed to watch the House in action, but given the House's control of the cameras, only on the House's terms.

Once the House of Representatives began allowing gavel-to-gavel television coverage of its floor proceedings, pressure began to intensify on the Senate to follow suit. Shortly after he became Senate Majority

Leader in January 1981, Tennessee's Howard Baker introduced legislation authorizing live coverage of Senate floor proceedings. Baker argued to his colleagues that admitting television cameras to their chamber would restore "vigorous and well-informed debate" in the Senate. Senate debate, Baker said, "is stilted, truncated, ritualized, canned and read into the record with the conviction of a talking computer" and Senators "file into the chamber only to ratify in public what we have decided in private. Television could help change that," he said. "Any honest senator will concede that when the television lights are on in our committee hearing rooms, attendance is high and political competition is keen."

Despite the success in the House with television coverage, a number of influential senators remained firmly opposed to the idea for their chamber. Rhode Island's Claiborne Pell feared that "the presence of television will lead to more, longer, and less relevant speeches, to more posturing by Senators and to even less useful debate and efficient legislating than we have today." While conceding that television in the House seemed to be operating well enough, Pell cautioned his colleagues that "the unique character of the Senate and its very different rules and methods of floor operation make such a venture in the Senate much less likely to be positive." Russell Long from Louisiana also argued against the proposal, claiming that senators would posture in front of the cameras and that television would attract senators to the chamber floor when they should be doing the important work in committee meetings. Others feared that some senators, in an effort to compete with their House colleagues, would enlist the services of elocution coaches and even makeup experts. William Proxmire from Wisconsin, another opponent of televised proceedings, argued that television would make it harder for Senators to reach compromises in private because "senators will find that the positions they took in their opening statements have been engraved in film." "Television thrives on the dramatic," Proxmire said, and "any additional incentives to confrontation can only mean more argument—and probably worse legislation." The arguments of Pell, Long, and Proxmire were remarkably the same as had been made nearly two centuries earlier by those who opposed the opening of the Senate's doors to the public. In the end, Baker's proposal to allow gavel-to-gavel television and radio coverage of the Senate failed.

By early 1986, Majority Leader Bob Dole from Kansas and Democratic

Leader Robert C. Byrd of West Virginia began to worry that the absence of television coverage was turning the Senate into the nation's forgotten legislative body. House members were becoming far more visible to their constituents than were senators. History was again repeating itself. The upper house was in danger of becoming the forgotten house. The two leaders eventually engineered a vote in which the Senate agreed to a three-month trial period, with live national coverage to begin on June 2, 1986. Only a few weeks later, the Senate voted to make television coverage permanent. Not since the Senate voted in 1795 to end its policy of conducting its legislative sessions behind closed doors had the Senate taken such an important step toward openness in government. As one broadcast journalist is reported to have said, "they can still run, but now they have no place to hide."

C-SPAN

C-SPAN (Cable-Satellite Public Affairs Network) is a private, not-for-profit company that was created by the cable television industry on November 14, 1978. Its mission statement is "to make government more open to the American public." C-SPAN is available in 100 million homes in America, as well as millions more around the world through the Internet. C-SPAN provides twenty-four hour access to a variety of public affairs programming, including sessions of Congress, presidential addresses, and daily White House and State Department briefings. A survey conducted by Hart Research in 2013 showed that forty-seven million adults (twenty-four percent of adults with access to cable television) watch C-SPAN weekly.[30] C-SPAN's live television coverage of the House of Representatives began on March 19, 1979, the first day the House allowed television coverage of its floor debates. C-SPAN's coverage of the House that day consisted of a one-minute speech by then–Congressman Al Gore. The broadcast reached just the three million homes that had television cable or satellite hookups. C-SPAN was not carried on over-the-air networks then, nor is it today.

C-SPAN relies on live feeds from government-controlled cameras. Each chamber exercises tight control over the broadcast of its floor proceedings. The cameras are owned by Congress and operated remotely by Congressional staff members who are located in sublevel studios under each chamber. Although the feeds are not edited, the coverage provides the viewers only a limited view of what is actually taking place on the floor. The cameras are usually focused on the rostrum or on the member who is speaking. Senators typically speak from their desk; members of the House speak from one of two lecterns in the House well. Members who are talking with each other, reading the newspaper, or perhaps even napping are not shown. Only when voting is in progress do the cameras show the full chamber. Vote tallies by political party, but not by individual members, are superimposed on the screen.

C-SPAN has sought permission to add some of its own robotically operated cameras in order "to capture members' reactions during debate or to show other developments that occur away from the fixed lecterns where lawmakers speak, like a rank-and-file House member being worked over by party leaders to switch his or her vote." Party affiliation appears to have played no role in the decision to deny C-SPAN greater access to House floor proceedings. Permission to add its own cameras has been denied by former Republican Speakers Newt Gingrich and Dennis Hastert, and by Democratic Speaker Nancy Pelosi. The most recent denial came from Speaker John Boehner in 2011. "I believe the American people, and the dignity and decorum of the United States House of Representatives," Boehner said, "are best served by the current system of televised proceedings provided by the House Recording Studio." Precisely how "the American people ... are best served" by limiting C-SPAN's coverage of House proceedings was not explained. C-SPAN replied to Boehner's decision that "[w]e're disappointed to learn that despite 32 years of experience with televising its sessions and in an age of ubiquitous cameras in political life, the House of Representatives has chosen not to allow C-SPAN's cameras into its chamber to cover its sessions. We continue to feel that the public is best served by seeing a more complete picture of the legislative process than what's delivered by Congressionally—controlled cameras and will continue to work with Speaker Boehner and other leaders in the House in hope of one day gaining access on behalf of the media."[31] Although it would be inaccurate to suggest that Congress is continuing to act in secret, it fair to note that its insistence on controlling C-SPAN's cameras does deny the American viewing public a complete picture of what is taking place on the chamber floor.

7

Black Budgets
and the People's Money

Gentlemen, I want you to give me a billion dollars. I do not want you to ask me what it is going to be used for. It is a military secret, but I hope you will give me the money.—General George C. Marshall, 1942

The day-to-day work of the Continental Congresses was done out of the view of the public. In the majority of cases, though, the members of Congress were privy to Congress' work. But with the creation of secret funds—today's "black budgets"—neither the people nor in many cases even their representatives in Congress are fully aware of what the executive branch is doing. Indeed, in many cases members of Congress know little if any of the details of the black budget projects they are voting to fund.

A "black budget" is a budget that has been requested by the executive branch for the funding of a classified or covert operation. The spending amounts contained in the budget are shielded from public view and oftentimes from members of Congress. In many cases, the very existence of the project is not even publicly acknowledged. Top-secret documents leaked by former Booze Allen staffer Edward Snowden reveal that the federal government spent more than $52 billion in 2013 on clandestine spy programs alone. Yet despite the attention that black budgets have attracted in recent years, black budgets are anything but new.

The first black budget was established by Congress during the first term of President Gorge Washington. In his State of the Union Address on January 8, 1790, Washington asked Congress to establish "a competent fund designated for defraying the expenses incident to the conduct of foreign affairs." Part of the fund was to be used for traditional diplomatic activities. It was no secret, though, that a major part of the appropriation would be devoted to funding covert intelligence activities overseas.

The use of secret agents during the Revolutionary War had proved to be a valuable part of the country's war effort. General Washington reportedly spent ten percent of his military budget on intelligence gathering. "There is nothing more necessary than good intelligence to frustrate a designing enemy," Washington once wrote, "and nothing that requires greater pain to get."[1] Although the war was at an end, President Washington believed that maintaining an intelligence gathering capability was necessary not only to the conduct of America's foreign policy, but also to the preservation of America's territorial integrity. Great Britain was still intent on keeping her former colonies disorganized. The British continued to maintain her western posts in violation of the peace treaty, claiming that treaty violations on the part of the Americans justified its decision to retain those posts. Spain was active along America's southwest border attempting to persuade American settlers west of the Alleghany Mountains to switch their allegiance. The United States was also facing challenges from other European nations who were jockeying for territory in the still largely uncharted expanse of the New World. The foreign intelligence capabilities that were created during the War, however, such as John Jay's Committee for Detecting and Defeating Conspiracies in New York, were disbanded at the end of the War. Jay himself moved on to become Chief Justice of the United States Supreme Court. The secret fund that President Washington sought in 1790 was intended to help fill at least a part of that void.

The President and the members of Congress were both deliberately circumspect in discussing the purpose of the secret fund, generally avoiding any direct references to its use in funding clandestine activities. Indeed, those activities were rarely alluded to during the debates on Washington's request. In noting the various roles of foreign ministers, Representative William Smith from South Carolina hinted at the purpose of the fund on one occasion, observing that "many officers may be established in the diplomatic line without being concerned with making treaties. A minister may reside in France twenty years without being employed in the formation of any treaty whatever."[2] Congressman Thomas Scott from Pennsylvania, who also supported Washington's budget request, came the closest to exposing the secret nature of the fund. Scott predicted that when the Legislature is not sitting, "[occasions] will present themselves, when money for secret services may be required."[3] The real issue before the House was thus not the necessity of the fund—that was generally acknowledged—but rather the propriety of granting what amounted to a blank check to the president for the funding of secret diplomatic missions.

Alexander White from Virginia spoke for those in the House who supported Washington's request. White argued that it was not only "necessary to send ambassadors extraordinary" to foreign nations,"[4] but also that a special fund should be established so that the president would be able to dispatch foreign emissaries if an emergency arose at a time when Congress was not in session—Congress then met roughly six months a year. Money should be available to be withdrawn from the fund by the president in his sole discretion. Moreover, White argued, in order to protect the identity of the country's foreign agents and their missions, the details of how those funds were spent should be held in confidence by the president alone. The system of check and balances that the framers had very carefully put in place would have to be subordinated to the greater need for foreign intelligence.

William Smith from South Carolina also supported Washington's budget request. Smith downplayed the concern that granting the president such broad discretion in the use of a secret fund would undermine the House's oversight responsibilities or otherwise negate the system of checks and balances. To Smith, the notion of checks and balances was not a relevant consideration. Smith reasoned that it was not the province of the House to determine "when and where" foreign agents should be posted, adding that the role of the House was only "to provide for the payment of their salaries ... and this, if properly considered, was a competent check."[5] Furnishing the details of those agents' activities was unnecessary.

Other members of the House were not as willing to grant the president the authority to spend the public's money secretly and free of Congressional oversight. Representative Richard Bland Lee from Virginia conceded the need for the contingency fund, but argued that "the President ought not be empowered to draw money [from the fund] without [the Senate's] advice and consent."[6] James Jackson, a Congressman from Georgia also opposed the president's request, warning that "if we adopt the bill now, on some future occasion we shall have to go further; and the principle that one [the president] is more responsible than many [Congress] will lead to an arbitrary government."[7] Smith did not question the Senate's constitutional role in the appointment of foreign ministers, but countered that "if it [the secret fund] is not enjoined by the Constitution, it will be wrong to make such an arrangement [requiring the Senate's consent], because it will diminish the responsibility of the Executive officer."[8] James Madison also spoke in support of the president's request, pointing out that the president is responsible for appointing foreign service officers. Madison argued that the president can more efficiently carry out that role when acting "alone" than if he were "connected with a large body." Congressman Lee's amendment requiring the "advice and consent" of the Senate when appointing foreign agents, while gathering some support, was ultimately voted down. The House also voted to make the fund an annual appropriation.

The House officially notified the Senate of its passage of the bill on April 30, 1790. Because the Senate was still meeting in closed session at that point, little is known about the Senate's deliberations. The main point of contention appears not to have been the purpose of the secret fund. Indeed, allowing the president to operate in secret in some areas of foreign diplomacy enjoyed majority support in the Senate as well. The only issue in controversy appears to have been the size of the appropriation. The House bill provided for an initial funding of $40,000. The Senate amended the bill to provide for a funding of only $30,000. During the conference negotiations between the two chambers, the Senate acceded to the House's original funding of $40,000. Even then, not all of the Senators were pleased with the outcome. Senator William Maclay of Pennsylvania, an avowed isolationist, wrote in his private journal, "I consider the money as worse than thrown away. I know not a single thing that we have for a minister to do in a single court in Europe. Indeed, the less we have to do with them the better. I voted against every part of it."[9]

The legislation establishing the Contingency Fund for the Conduct of Foreign Intercourse took effect on July 1, 1790. The fund itself was not hidden from public view: it was openly accounted for in the Department of State's budget. Money could be withdrawn from the fund by the president on his signature alone. And although Congress did require the president to "certify" annually the amounts he spent, Congress also authorized the president, in his judgment, to conceal the purposes and recipients of the funds. The new law thus essentially granted the president an exemption from one of Congress's most important constitutional powers: the oversight of public expenditures. Neither Congress nor the public would know how the money was being spent or why. The initial funding provided by Congress would quickly prove to be inadequate. Less than two years later the fund ran short, forcing Secretary of State Thomas Jefferson to write to Treasury Secretary Alexander Hamilton that "I must ask the favor of a like draught on our bankers in Amsterdam for 40,000 dollars more."[10] By the third year of Washington's presidency, the secret fund had grown to $1 million, representing nearly twelve percent of the total federal budget.

The Contingency Fund would be drawn upon to fund an array of secret operations by many of the early 19th century presidents. America's second president, John Adams, had served as a foreign overseas agent of the Continental Congress and consequently brought with him to his presidency a first-hand understanding of the importance of intelligence gathering. Adams made use of the secret fund to "pay persons to serve the United States in foreign parts." America's third president, Thomas Jefferson is usually portrayed as an advocate of openness and accountability in government. Indeed, Jefferson was among the staunchest critics of the Constitutional Convention's decision to meet in secret. Yet it was Jefferson who became the "founding father" of covert activities under the Constitution, making use of the secret fund to a greater degree than any of the other early American presidents.

Jefferson's frequent use of the secret fund was rooted in his belief that it was the president's prerogative, when he thought circumstances warranted it, to conceal certain actions of government not only from the public, but from Congress as well. Jefferson's use of secrecy was especially pronounced in matters of foreign policy where he often dispatched private citizens to deliver diplomatic messages to foreign officials. Despite the official nature of their missions, Jefferson's private emissaries operated not only free of Congressional oversight, but often without the knowledge of the Secretary of State. Jefferson defended his use of the secret fund in a letter to James Monroe: "I can make private friendships instrumental to the public good by inspiring a confidence which is denied to public and official communications."[11]

Jefferson made use of these secret methods of communication for reasons of efficiency as well. After having dispatched a private envoy to Russia on one occasion, Jefferson explained his reasons for having done so in a letter to his Secretary of the Treasury, Albert Gallatin. Jefferson told Gallatin that waiting for formal approval from the Senate created too great a risk of the diplomatic opportunity being lost. Moving ahead with the diplomatic initiative was thus imperative. Jefferson also explained to Gallatin that involving the Senate in the matter created the additional risk of the communication's contents being disclosed publicly. Like Benjamin Franklin before, Jefferson had little faith in the ability of Congress to keep secrets. "We think secrecy also important," Jefferson wrote, "& that the mission should be as little known as possible, 'til it is in Petersburgh, which could not be, if known to the Senate."[12] In 1801 Thomas Jefferson withdrew money from the secret fund to finance the United States' first covert attempt to overthrow the government of a foreign nation, on this occasion the government in Tripoli, one of the Barbary Pirate states in North Africa. The overthrow failed.

Throughout his presidency, Jefferson generally kept the Senate in the dark in matters of foreign affairs. "The Senate is not supposed by the Constitution," Jefferson explained, "to be acquainted with the concerns of the Executive Department ... nor can they, therefore, be qualified to judge the necessity which calls for a mission to any particular place ... which special and secret circumstances may call for. All this is left to the President."[13] Although Jefferson's practice of withholding information from the Senate in matters of foreign affairs was sometimes questioned by one Senator or another, his position usually prevailed. The Contingency Fund was re-authorized by Congress in 1810 during his second term.

James Madison, the architect of the Constitution and the nation's fourth president, served as Jefferson's Secretary of State and was well aware of, and often was a part of, Jefferson's use of secrecy in foreign relations. In 1805, while serving as Jefferson's Secretary of State, Madison reportedly withdrew money from the secret fund to procure the services of a prostitute to enliven the visit of a foreign envoy from Tunisia.[14] As president, Madison was typically more deferential to Congress than Jefferson had been. Even so, he also made use of the secret fund from time to time. Between 1810 and 1812, Madison drew on the fund to finance clandestine operations—inciting "spontaneous" uprisings—that were aimed at helping the United States annex certain regions of Florida that were controlled by Spain. Although Madison's takeover plan failed, the United States did acquire Florida a few years later, in 1819, during the administration of President James Monroe. During the War of 1812, President Madison paid the pirate Jean Laffite and his men to scout, spy, and sometimes even fight for General Andrew Jackson.

From time to time during the early years of the secret fund, some members of Congress attempted to obtain a detailed accounting of the expenditures from the fund. A few even attempted to establish a measure of oversight of the activities that were financed out of the fund. None of those efforts succeeded. In 1846, however, during the administration of President James K. Polk, a major furor arose over the alleged misuse of the secret fund by Daniel Webster while serving as Secretary of State in the earlier administrations of Presidents William Henry Harrison (March 4 through April 4, 1841) and John Tyler (1841 through 1845).

The Treaty of Paris brought an end to the Revolutionary War, but not to all of the territorial disputes between the United States and Great Britain. The parties attempted in the Paris Peace Treaty of 1783 to prevent future "disputes which might arise [with Great Britain] on the subject of the boundaries of the United States" by setting out those boundaries as nearly as practicable. Despite their efforts, several of the boundary lines remained poorly defined, including the one between the State of Maine and the Canadian province of New Brunswick. Secretary Webster was determined to ease tensions with Britain and was therefore willing to entertain a compromise on the border issue. Public opinion among Maine's citizens, however, was vehemently opposed to any compromise that would result in the loss of American soil to the British. Webster undertook to manipulate public opinion in Maine through a well-orchestrated campaign that was financed with money from the secret Contingency Fund. Webster's clandestine operations included lobbying state legislators in Maine and planting articles in local newspapers that tended to support the British position. Webster's campaign even included the introduction of a map, very likely a forgery, that supposedly had belonged to Benjamin Franklin and that appeared to lend credence to Britain's boundary claim.

There were some in Congress who were troubled as a matter of principle by the use of secrecy generally, even in the conduct of foreign policy. Even more troubling were the recurring rumors that public funds had been secretly used by Webster to influence domestic public opinion. Using the fund to influence matters overseas was one thing; using it to influence matters at home was something else. When word leaked out about Webster's secret operations in Maine, the House of Representatives passed a resolution on April 19, 1846, calling upon President Polk "to cause to be furnished to the House an account of all payments made ... from the fund appropriated by law, through the agency of the State Department, for the contingent expenses of foreign intercourse ... concerning the northeastern boundary dispute with Great Britain." The resolution was offered by Charles J. Ingersoll, a Congressman from Pennsylvania and a staunch political opponent of Daniel Webster.

Although Ingersoll's resolution passed by an overwhelming vote, there were also members of the House who were adamant in their opposition to it. James I. McKay from North Carolina was concerned that requiring the president to supply the requested documents would eviscerate the very purpose of the statute that created the secret fund. "It has always been the policy of the Government to place at the disposition of the President ... a secret service fund." If the documents called for in the resolution are turned over to Congress," McKay argued, "the very object of the law authorizing these [secret] expenditures will be completely defeated and will stand as a precedent to justify a similar proceeding in all future cases."[15] Ingersoll responded that he "should be the last man to interfere with the ordinary application of the secret service money," but that this was an "extraordinary case" involving allegations of Webster's "great abuse of the fund by expend[ing] through vile agents part of that fund in corrupting the press ... for the purpose of accomplishing the treaty of the Northeastern boundary."[16] Ingersoll was drawing drawn a bright line between foreign and domestic affairs when it came to the use of the secret fund.

President Polk turned down the House's request for the financial accounting. In a Special Message issued on April 20, 1846, Polk emphasized that he himself had never made use of the secret fund and that it "would be an extreme case which would ever induce me to exercise this authority." Still, under the law authorizing the secret contingency fund, Polk pointed out, the president need only account specifically for those expenditures that "may in his judgment be made public, and by making a certificate of the amount of such [other] expenditures as he may think it advisable not to specify." Polk was making the point that there are "[t]wo distinct classes of expenditure that are authorized by this law—the one of a public and the other of a private and confidential character. The President in office at the time of the expenditure is made by the law the sole judge of whether it shall be public or private."

President Polk acknowledged that he was "fully aware of the strong and correct public feeling which exists throughout the country against secrecy of any kind in the administration of the Government, and especially in reference to public expenditures." There are exceptions, however. "The experience of every nation on earth has demonstrated that emergencies may arise in which it becomes necessary for ... the public good to make expenditures, the very subject of which would be defeated by publicity. In no nation is the application of such funds to be made public.... Useful projects ... might altogether be defeated ... if our purposes were to be known by the exhibition of the original papers and vouchers to the accounting offices of the Treasury."[17] "Foreign negotiations," Polk went on to explain, "are wisely and properly confined to the knowledge of the Executive during their pendency. Our laws require the accounts of every particular expenditure to be rendered and publicly settled. The single exception which exists is not that the amounts embraced under President's certificates shall be withheld from the public, but merely that the items of which these are composed shall not be divulged. To this extent, and no further, is secrecy observed." Polk was also quick to point out the "whole matter was terminated before I came into office."

The House's request in the Webster case also gave rise to the related question of "whether a subsequent President, either voluntarily or at the request of one branch of Congress, can without a violation of the spirit of the law revise the acts of his predecessor and expose to public view that which he had determined should not be made public. If not a matter of strict duty," Polk said, "it would certainly be a safe general rule that this should not be done. Indeed, it may well happen, and probably would happen, that the President for the time being would not be in possession of the information upon which his predecessor acted, and could not, therefore, have the means of judging whether he had exercised his discretion wisely or not."[18] No further official demands were made of Polk by Congress for a full accounting of presidential expenditures from the secret fund. President Polk's defiant stance regarding Congressional oversight effectively staved off for more than a century any further attempts by Congress to assert real oversight over executive branch covert operations. It was not until the end of World War II and the enactment of the National Security Act of 1947 that the Congress began to oversee executive branch intelligence and other covert activities.

The National Security Act of 1947 was enacted during the administration of President Harry S Truman. The purpose of the Act was to "integrate the policies and procedures for the departments, agencies, and functions of Government relating to national security." Among the Act's key provisions was one creating the Central Intelligence Agency, the nation's first permanent national intelligence-gathering entity. Both the House and Senate assigned oversight responsibility to their respective Armed Services Committee and Appropriations Defense Subcommittee. In actual practice, though, information about the CIA's and other intelligence agencies' activities was generally limited to the chairmen and ranking minority members of those committees and their subcommittees. Staff involvement was usually restricted to one or two senior staff members whose principal job was to make sure that the funding needs of the intelligence agencies were included in the annual Defense Department budget. Oversight, such as it was, was typically worked out by the Director of Central Intelligence and a few senior members of the Congress. The involvement of Congress as a whole was essentially nonexistent.

Although attempts were occasionally made during the 1950s and 1960s to exercise a more robust oversight by establishing select intelligence committees, none of the proposals were seriously considered. Most members of Congress tended to agree with the view expressed by Senator Leverett Saltonstall from Massachusetts who stated on the Senate floor in 1956 that this "is not a question of reluctance on the part of CIA officials to speak to us. Instead, it is a question of our reluctance, if you will, to seek information and knowledge on subjects which I personally, as a member of Congress and as a citizen, would rather not have."

The hands-off view of oversight expressed by Senator Saltonstall continued to be the accepted mode of Congressional oversight for more than a quarter of a century following the creation of the CIA. Many Congressional historians refer to the period as an "era of trust" or a period of "benign neglect." Even before then, though, Congress' hands-off approach to oversight was the norm. Perhaps no better example exits than the Manhattan Project during World War II.

Manhattan Project

James Madison explained to his fellow delegates during the Virginia ratification convention in June 1788 that the Constitution gave Congress control of the public purse strings. As a part of that control, however, Congress was granted "a necessary measure of discretion in deciding which expenditures may be withheld from public view." Congress exercised that discretion on a number of occasions over the years by excluding from both its official journal and the Constitutionally required "account of the public expenditures" those matters that it determined should be held in confidence. The funds that were needed for intelligence gathering activities and, during times of war, for secret military and other war-related operations were routinely hidden from public view.

Although shielding sensitive governmental activities from public view through the use of black budgets had been a common practice in government for nearly 150 years, World War II's Manhattan Project was unprecedented in its size, scope, and the number of people who were involved in both the project itself and in maintaining the ring of secrecy surrounding it. So secretive was the project that although Congress would be called upon to authorize nearly $2 billion in project funding (more than $20 billion in today's dollars), knowledge of the Manhattan Project was limited to only a handful of key governmental officials. The general public knew nothing about it.

The Manhattan Project was undertaken in 1939 initially as a basic research project aimed at determining the theoretically feasibility of constructing an atomic bomb. Following America's entry into World War II, the Manhattan Project was advanced to development status, eventually leading to the building of the world's first nuclear weapons: Little Boy, which was dropped on Hiroshima on August 6, 1945, and Fat Man, which was exploded over Nagasaki three days later.

The job of securing the necessary personnel and resources for the project was first assigned to the Office of Scientific Research and Development, the federal office in which most of the wartime research and development projects were administered. But given the number of facilities that had to be built, the overall management of the project was transferred to the Army Corps of Engineers under the command of Colonel Leslie Groves. The project's headquarters were located in Manhattan, New York, in the newly created Manhattan Engineer District, colloquially known as the Manhattan Project. By the end of the war, Groves (by then a Brigadier General) and his staff had spent approximately $1.89 billion on the construction of research, design, and production facilities at more than two dozen top secret locations.

The necessity of maintaining absolute secrecy around the Manhattan Project was paramount from the outset. Neither the Germans nor the Japanese could be allowed to learn of the project. And although the Soviet Union was officially an ally of the United States and Great Britain, President Roosevelt and England's Prime Minister, Winston Churchill, decided early on to keep the Soviet Union's leader, Joseph Stalin, in the dark as well. The Soviet Union was a repressive dictatorship that was regarded by both Roosevelt and Churchill as a potential future enemy.

The United States was successful in blocking Germany's attempts to infiltrate the Manhattan Project. Although Germany was able to deploy several spy rings in America, none of its spies ever penetrated the project's ring of secrecy. Rumors of the Manhattan Project reached Japan as well, but, like Germany, Japan was never able to discover the project's secrets. The Soviet Union was a different matter, however. Soviet spies were more successful in penetrating the Manhattan Project, principally because of their ability to play on the ideological sympathies of those Americans who were enamored of communist ideals. Indeed, the Soviet spy ring reportedly learned of the project before the FBI did. The Soviet's success at espionage ultimately proved instrumental in enabling it to develop its own atomic bomb only four years later.

Preventing America's war enemies from learning of the Manhattan Project meant that the project also had to be kept a secret from everyone else not actually a part of it. Even within the federal government in Washington, D.C., the necessity for strict secrecy required that the normal, even constitutional protocols for executive and legislative oversight had to be tempered, if not altogether ignored. Indeed, only a handful of government officials were even aware of the Manhattan Project's existence. In the White House, President Franklin Roosevelt, Secretary of War Henry Stimson, and General George C. Marshall (Army Chief of Staff) had access to the work of the Manhattan Project. There was also a small cadre of other executive branch officials who were directly involved in the project who were also privy to the project's secrets. But beyond these few key officials, the Manhattan Project remained cloaked in secrecy. In fact, Roosevelt's vice president, Harry Truman, did not learn of the project until he became president in April 1945, following President Roosevelt's death.

An article that *Life* magazine published in 1945 estimated that "probably no more than a few dozen men in the entire country knew the full meaning of the Manhattan Project, and perhaps only a thousand others [out of the approximately 100,000 who worked directly on the project] were even aware that they working on an atomic bomb."[19] The entire project was so vast and highly compartmentalized that no one below the highest clearance level was able to see more than a tiny fraction of the project's many facets. To Groves, "the compartmentalizing of knowledge ... was the very heart of secrecy ... each man should know everything he needs to know to do his job and nothing else." Thousands of men and women involved in the project, *Life* reported, "worked like moles in the dark."

Information about the Manhattan Project was generally withheld from Congress. In the House of Representatives, House Speaker Sam Rayburn of Texas, Majority Leader John W. McCormack of Massachusetts, and Minority Leader Joseph W. Martin also of Massachusetts, were regularly briefed on the project. In the Senate, Majority Leader Alben W. Barkley of Kentucky, Minority Leader Wallace H. White of Maine, and Senators Elmer Thomas of Oklahoma and Styles Bridges of New Hampshire, Chairman and Ranking Member, respectively, of the Military Appropriations Subcommittee, were also kept abreast of developments in the project. The Congressional briefings were given by Secretary of War Stimson, General Marshall, and Dr. Bush. The other 524 members of Congress were kept in the dark, as were the American people.

In 1962, General Groves, who was then retired, recounted one of the earliest of the Congressional briefings on the Manhattan Project. The Representatives who were in attendance, Rayburn, McCormack, and Martin agreed at the end of the briefing not only to finance the Manhattan Project to the extent necessary, but also to keep the project secret from other House members. According to Groves, "[t]he Congressmen indicated their approval without reservation. They said that, while the amount of money needed was large, they were in full agreement that the expenditures were justified, and they would do everything possible to have the necessary funds included in the upcoming Appropriations Bill. It would not be necessary, they said, to make any further explanations to the Appropriations Committee."[20] In 1947, Senator Millard Tydings described one committee meeting at which the "no questions" approach to funding the Manhattan Project was on full display. "General Marshall," Tydings said, "came before the Appropriations Committee one day and said in effect this: 'Gentlemen, I want you to give me a billion dollars. I do not want you to ask me what it is going to be used for. It is a military secret, but I hope you will give me the money.' The Committee responded by asking whether a billion dollars would be enough.'"[21]

Throughout the life of the Manhattan Project, the few Congressmen and Senators to whom knowledge of the project was entrusted were able to arrange quietly for its funding. For the most part, project funding was buried in the U.S. Army budget. Ferreting out the details was all but impossible. From time to time, though, a few members of Congress did have their suspicions about mysterious line items they would run across in the Army's budget. The stature of Sam Rayburn and Alben Barkley was so great among their Congressional colleagues, however, that the two were usually able to steer the Appropriations Committee and Subcommittee chairmen to "look the other way" and refrain from asking troublesome questions. On those few occasions when the two were unsuccessful, prying questions were met with a less than diplomatic response. "We make bubble gum," was the response given to then–Senator Harry Truman at a Congressional hearing concerning the unusually high expense levels at the "Richland Project," one of the towns that had been acquired to make way for the Hanford plutonium production facility.

Secrecy in government was certainly nothing new. The secrecy surrounding the Manhattan Project, however, was unprecedented, not only because of the strict limitations it placed on what government officials were allowed to disclose to the public—that had always been the case in highly confidential matters—but also because maintaining the required level of secrecy depended so heavily on the active support of the literally tens of thousands of ordinary Americans who worked on the project. Indeed, the project's cloak of secrecy often encompassed entire cities. The towns of Oak Ridge, Tennessee, and Hanford, Washington, were built by the federal government. Several thousand residents had to be relocated to make room for the new "towns." Military security personnel guarded the grounds surrounding the facilities. Communications within and between different research teams at the same facility were actively monitored. Official communications to other project centers were coded and encrypted. Personnel who were cleared to work on the Manhattan Project were "to read and sign either the Espionage Act or a special secrecy agreement," acknowledging their understanding of their secrecy obligations which, if breached, would constitute a basis for their dismissal.[22]

The scientists, engineers, and workers who were assigned to the various project facilities were under strict orders of secrecy not only when they were on the job, but also when they went home at the end of the workday. They were forbidden to discuss any aspect of their work with family or friends. The personal activities of the workers' families who lived in the new towns were also placed under severe restrictions. Private telephones and radios were prohibited in many locations. Personal mail was usually permitted, but was closely censored. Because the actual location of Los Alamos was itself a secret, residents who lived there were instructed to use the fictitious mailing address of "Box 1663, Santa Fe, New Mexico." Town residents were even encouraged to use made-up names when travelling outside the facility. Children were told not to use their full names in school. A large billboard near the exit gate at Oak Ridge summed up the secrecy code in clear and unmistakable terms: "What you see here, What you do here, What you hear here, When you leave here, Let it stay here."

In late 1942, President Roosevelt wrote to Vannevar Bush expressing his hope that, although the Manhattan Project's "work has been conducted in the utmost secrecy and without public recognition of any kind ... [s]ome day the full story of its accomplishments can be told."[23] Over the years it was.

Current Black Budgets

Although the term "black budget" is of fairly recent origin, the purpose of today's black budgets is the same as it was for the first black budget requested by President George Washington more than 225 years ago. Black budget programs continue to refer to those programs (including military, intelligence gathering, and homeland security operations) for which the government does not disclose funding levels or the program's operational detail. Although the funding for black budget activities is included in the federal budget, the existence of a program itself is classified and therefore not specifically disclosed, except to a handful of Congressional members who are directly involved in the oversight of the program. In some cases, the funding is simply folded into the funding for another, unclassified program. In other cases, the funding may be set out as a separate line item, but under a fictitious name with its costs deleted and its purposes disguised.

The arguments for and against the disclosure of intelligence spending levels have essentially centered on two competing considerations: the value of open political discourse that is promoted by a full accounting of government spending versus the danger of revealing useful information to actual or potential adversaries. The tension between these two considerations was directly addressed by the Senate Select Committee on Intelligence during hearings in April 1977. The Committee's hearings focused squarely on the question "Whether Disclosure of Funds Authorized for Intelligence Activities Is in the Public Interest."[24] The witnesses who appeared before the Committee were of mixed opinion. Those who argued for a greater disclosure of intelligence spending, such as Wisconsin's Senator William Proxmire, maintained that "people not only have a right to know, but [they] are going to have a much more efficient government when they do. We only make improvements when we get criticized and you can only criticize when you know what you're talking about, when you have some information." Even CIA Director Stansfield Turner agreed that "disclosure would help the public put into perspective the intelligence activities of their country," thereby enabling the public to make "rough judgments" about the relative spending priorities of their government. Those opposing the disclosure of even aggregate spending levels countered that without the details of that spending—which no one was calling for—the public would be in no better position than it already was to make an informed judgment about governmental spending on intelligence spending. Intelligence gathering should thus be seen as a special activity that does not lend itself to the oversight procedures that ordinarily apply in an open society. The Committee ultimately came down on the side of greater disclosure (but by only a single vote), concluding that "on a practical basis" greater disclosure will allow the people to know more than they do, thus allowing them to "weigh spending for intelligence against expenditures for health, education, or a particular weapon system." Despite the Committee's findings, legislation requiring the disclosure of intelligence spending, even in the aggregate, was not enacted. The black budget remained black.

The near total blackout surrounding covert intelligence operations came under attack again with the fall of the Soviet Union in December 1991. The advocates of greater openness argued that with the dissolution of the Soviet Union and the hoped-for end of the Cold War there was no longer a valid reason to keep secret the aggregate amounts that are spent by the United States on intelligence gathering activities. There were few foreign countries remaining, they claimed, that were able to make any effective use of information about total intelligence spending. Non-state terrorist organizations were even less able to exploit intelligence spending data. It was time for intelligence spending to be brought into the open.

During Congress' consideration of the 1992 Intelligence Authorization Act, the Senate Select Committee on Intelligence reported out a bill mandating the disclosure of certain intelligence and intelligence-related budget amounts. The amounts were only to be reported at an aggregated level, however. The Senate Armed Services Committee, which also took up the bill, was of a different view. That Committee pointed out that disclosing intelligence spending, even at an aggregated level, represented a major departure from the past practices of both Congress and the executive branch and that public disclosure could therefore have "profound implications for the conduct of ... intelligence activities and the formulation of intelligence policy which have not been considered in detail." The companion bill in the House of Representatives contained no provision calling for the public disclosure of intelligence spending. The House Committee instead recommended that the consideration of the budget reporting requirements be postponed until the following fiscal year (1993) in order to allow for a more detailed review. Congress ultimately adopted compromise language expressing the "sense of Congress" that "the aggregate amount requested and authorized for, and spent on, intelligence and intelligence-related activities should be disclosed to the public in an appropriate manner." The mandatory disclosure language in the Senate version may also have been dropped, at least in part, because of the strong opposition to it by the administration of President George H.W. Bush. Bush had been Director of the CIA and had testified earlier, in 1977, against public disclosure. Even in his signing statement for the 1992 Act, President Bush reiterated his opposition to disclosing intelligence spending, stating that "because secrecy is indispensable if intelligence activities are to succeed, the funding levels authorized by the Act are classified and should remain so."[25]

The issue of secrecy was not at an end, however. In the final report released on July 22, 2004, by the *National Commission on Terrorists Attacks Upon the United States* (more commonly known as the 9/11 Commission), the Commission recommended that "the overall amounts" spent by the country's national intelligence agencies no longer be kept secret. "The top-line figure itself," the Commission found, "provides little insight into U.S. intelligence sources and methods." And although the "intelligence communities should not be subject to [full detailed] disclosure ... when even aggregates amounts remain hidden, it is hard to judge priorities and foster accountability."[26]

Although the government has annually released the overall amount of intelligence spending since 2007, the government does not disclose how it spends the money or how its performance stacks up against the goals that were set by the president and Congress. In an article published on August 29, 2013, *The Washington Post* reported that the federal government appropriated $52.6 billion for black budget operations in fiscal year 2013. The information was taken from a 178-page top-secret document that was released by Edward Snowden, a former intelligence contractor who was employed by the consulting firm of Booz Allen Hamilton. The budget summary disclosed by Snowden details many of the objectives, successes, and failures of the sixteen spy agencies that make up the federal intelligence community. The *Post* described the secret budget as mapping "a bureaucratic and operation landscape that has been never been the subject of public scrutiny." The *Post* also opined that the budget includes many activities and projects that might not be funded if they were brought to light and debated publicly and in Congress. In another article written the following year by *The Daily Beast*, it was disclosed that the federal government planned to spend $58.7 billion on classified programs during fiscal year 2015.

Limited publicly available data suggest that intelligence spending, measured in constant dollars, has roughly doubled since the September 11, 2001, terrorist attacks. The tremendous growth that has taken place in black spy budgets was explained by the Director of National Intelligence in an open letter to the *Post* written shortly after the Snowden leak. Director James R. Clapper wrote that "[t]he United States has made a considerable investment since the terror attacks of 9/11, a time which includes wars in Iraq and Afghanistan, the proliferation of weapons of mass destruction technology, and asymmetric threats in such areas as cyber-warfare." Director Clapper also explained that "our budgets which are less than one percent of GDP are classified as they could provide insight for foreign intelligence services to discern our top national priorities, capabilities and sources and methods that allow us to obtain information to counter threats."[27]

The Intelligence Authorization Act of 2010 requires the Director of National Intelligence to disclose to the public the aggregate amount of funds appropriated each fiscal year by Congress for the National Intelligence Program. That program houses the intelligence gathering activities of sixteen federal agencies, including the Central Intelligence Agency and the National Security Agency. More than ninety percent of intelligence spending is contained in the Department of Defense budget. The 2010 law also authorizes the president to waive or postpone the required disclosure by submitting to the Senate and House Intelligence Committees: (1) a statement, in unclassified form, that the disclosure would damage national security; and (2) a statement detailing the reasons for the waiver or postponement, which may be submitted in classified form." The press release issued by the Director in connection with the annual disclosure report to the public is accompanied by a disclaimer: "Any and all subsidiary information concerning the NIP budge ... will not be disclosed. Beyond the disclosure of the NIP topline figure, there will be no other disclosures of currently classified NIP budget information, because such disclosures could harm national security." The country's black budget operations remain largely black.

8

Executive Secrecy
and Publicity

The president is the one person about whom a definite national opinion is formed and, therefore, the one person who can form opinion by his own direct influence and act upon the whole country at once.—Woodrow Wilson, March 24, 1908

The framers saw Congress as bearing the primary responsibility for keeping the public informed about the work of the government. It is, after all, the place where the nation's laws originate. Congress initially discharged that responsibility through the publication of its journals and later on by opening up its sessions to the public. The president, on the other hand, was seen by the framers as being a more distant, even regal figure. His relationship with the people would be more indirect: the people would play no direct role in his election, nor would they exercise any real influence over his conduct while in office. Much about the presidency would remain hidden from public view. However well informed individual members of Congress may be, though, their perspective is necessarily a limited one, both geographically and in matters of national policy. It is the president alone who has the sufficient national perspective to address those matters that affect the nation as a whole. Moreover, without the president's involvement, if not active assistance, Congress would be unable to carry out many of its Constitutional duties. The framers thus included in the Constitution an explicit statement of the president's duty to keep Congress informed, and through Congress the American people, about the state of their country.

The idea of requiring the president to keep the people informed

about the general state of affairs in the country appears to have originated in the constitutional plan that South Carolina's Charles Pinckney
submitted on May 29, 1787. Pinckney's plan provided that the president
"shall from time to time give information to the Legislature of the state
of the Union." Other than the requirement that the president provide
that information, though, Pinckney's plan offered no guidance concerning when or how often that information should be provided, nor
was there any enumeration of the subjects that the president should
address. Those matters were to left to the president's discretion. Based
upon the president's assessment of the state of the union, Pinckney's
plan also directed the president to recommend to Congress for its consideration "the measures he may think necessary." The Committee of
Detail incorporated a comparable provision into its draft of August 6,
1787. These two provisions—the State of the Union Clause and the so-
called Recommendation Clause—are the only two places in the Constitution where the president is required to speak directly to the people
and their elected representatives in Congress.

State of the Union Address

The State of the Union address is required by Article II, Section
3, Clause 1 of the Constitution. It is universally regarded as being the
most important presidential speech of the year. Although a president
may request to address Congress in joint session on other occasions,
such as President Roosevelt's December 8, 1941, "Address to Congress
Requesting a Declaration of War with Japan," the State of the Union is
the one time each year when the president is able not only to report
on the state of the country, but also to present his legislative priorities
for the coming year. Although presidents now communicate with Congress and the public on a regular basis through speeches, press con-
ferences, and interviews the State of the Union address provides the
president with a unique opportunity to speak to the entire nation in
single address. Standing before the American public to deliver the
annual address, the president is able to integrate into a single speech
his perspective on the country as seen from his several Constitutional
positions—as chief of state, chief executive, chief diplomat, commander-
in-chief of the military, and, in modern times, as chief legislator. The

State of the Union address is therefore an vitally important part of the people's right to know—the right to know what their president is thinking and why.

The State of the Union address has evolved significantly over the years. The format, delivery, and length of the speech have changed. The advent of radio and television has also greatly influenced the delivery, style, and political importance of the annual address. The address generates considerable discussion and analysis among newspaper and broadcast journalists, and, in recent times, bloggers and the Twitterverse. But even with these changes, the original purpose of the State of Union remains largely unchanged—to share with the American people the president's assessment of the state of their country.

President George Washington delivered the first President's Annual Message to Congress before a joint session of Congress on January 8, 1790. The address was delivered in the Senate chamber of Federal Hall in New York City, the provisional seat of government.[1] Washington's address was brief, consisting of only seven handwritten pages (1,089 words; President Clinton's 1995 address was the longest spoken address, coming in at 9,190 words). Washington emphasized at the beginning of his address "the rising credit and respectability of our Country—the general and increasing good will towards the Government of the Union—and the concord, peace and plenty, with which we are blessed." Washington went on to outline the challenges then facing the new country ("the many interesting objects, which will engage your attention," he said), including the need to fund and support his administration's efforts to promote the interests of the United States in foreign affairs and the organizing of a standing army in order to ensure the continuation of the "peace and plenty with which we are blessed." On the domestic front, Washington encouraged Congress to establish a national currency, a uniform rule of naturalization, a Post Office and Post Roads, a system of public education, and a plan for establishing public credit and repaying the public debt. Compared with modern day practice, Washington's address was remarkably free of politics. Washington's message struck just the right balance between strong executive leadership and a proper respect for the role of Congress, and therefore earned favorable responses from members of both the House and the Senate. The press's coverage of the address was positive as well, with many newspapers printing Washington's address in its entirety.

When Thomas Jefferson became president in 1801, he decided against delivering the annual address to Congress in person. Jefferson thought it was too "kingly" in appearance, too closely resembling the "Speech from the Throne" that the British monarch delivered to Parliament each year. Jefferson submitted a written address instead. The explanation given by Jefferson in a letter to the Senate president for not delivering the address in person was that "[i]n doing this I have had principal regard to the convenience of the Legislature, to the economy of their time, to their relief from the embarrassment of immediate answers on subjects not yet fully before them, and to the benefits thence relating to the public affairs."[2] Some historians also speculate that because Jefferson was not a good public speaker—his Inaugural Address had been barely audible and was unfavorably received[3]—he may not have wanted to deliver the Annual Address orally.[4]

The practice of delivering a written message to Congress continued for more than a hundred years. It was not until 1913 that President Woodrow Wilson broke with tradition and addressed a joint session of Congress in person. Wilson believed that the presidency was more than a remote branch of government and that visible and personal leadership was needed by both the people and the Congress—the kind of leadership that could only be demonstrated by addressing the people directly. Wilson's poor health prevented him from delivering his address in person in 1919 and 1920. Warren Harding's two annual messages (1921 and 1922) were delivered in person. When then–vice president Calvin Coolidge succeeded President Harding in office, following the death of Harding in August 1923, Coolidge's annual message (in December 1923) was broadcast live on radio. Although Franklin Roosevelt is generally regarded as being the president who made the most effective use of radio (Franklin delivered thirty "fireside chats" between 1933 and 1944), it was Calvin Coolidge who first made use of radio to speak to the entire nation. The broadcast was a national event. Indeed, on December 5, the day before Coolidge's radio address, the *New York Times* wrote that "[t]he voice of President Coolidge addressing Congress tomorrow will be carried over a greater portion of the United States and will be heard by more people than the voice of any man in history."[5] Coolidge's remaining State of the Union addresses (1924 through 1928), and all four of Herbert Hoover's annual addresses (1929 through 1932), were submitted in writing.[6]

In 1934, Franklin D. Roosevelt resumed the practice of delivering the State of the Union address in person. It was Roosevelt's message that year that was first described as the "State of the Union," although it was not until the presidency of Harry S Truman that the term came into common usage. Although the general practice since Roosevelt has been to deliver the State of the Union address in person, there have been exceptions. Presidents Truman (in 1946 and 1953), Eisenhower (in 1961), and Carter (in 1981) all returned to the former practice of delivering their annual message in writing. In 1972, President Nixon presented both an oral address and a written message. In 1973 and 1974, President Nixon delivered a series of six written messages to Congress, each bearing the title "State of the Union." President Carter also delivered both written and oral addresses to Congress in 1978, 1979, and 1980. Roosevelt's last address (1945) and Eisenhower's fourth address (1956), although delivered in writing to Congress, were also summarized in radio broadcasts to the American people. Harry Truman's State of the Union address in 1942 was the first to be televised.

The Recommendation Clause

Despite the Article I provision that "All legislative Powers herein granted shall be vested in a Congress of the United States," the Constitution assigns the president, as James Madison described it in *The Federalist* No. 47, an important "partial agency" in the legislative process. That agency directs the president to "recommend to their [Congress'] consideration such measures as he shall judge necessary and expedient." This so-called Recommendation Clause reflects the fact that the president's position as chief executive affords him a breadth of perspective on the overall state of the union that members of Congress rarely have. It also recognizes that the president alone is the one public official who is duty-bound to represent all of the people.

At the Constitutional Convention, the Recommendation Clause originally used the word "Matters," but was changed by the framers to "Measures" in order to make clear the expectation that the president was to recommend specific legislation, and not just general ideas. On the motion of Gouverneur Morris, the Convention also changed the word "may" to "shall," as Morris explained, "in order to make it the duty of the President to recommend, & thence prevent umbrage or cavil at his doing it."[7] The word change shielded the president from any charge that he was meddling in the affairs of Congress. Beyond these changes, there was little discussion of the provision. As important as the Recommendation Clause has become, Alexander Hamilton listed it (in *The Federalist* No. 77) among several minor presidential powers, noting that "no objection has been made to this class of authorities; nor could they possibly admit of any."[8]

While the Recommendation Clause technically imposes an affirmative duty on the president, its execution rests entirely with the president. The framers included no provision in the clause requiring the president to document the reasons for his proposals or otherwise provide such information to Congress as it might require in its consideration of those proposals. Moreover, Congress possesses no Constitutional power to compel the president to recommend legislation since he alone is the "judge" of what is "necessary and expedient."

Other than in times of emergency or war, America's early presidents played a limited role in the legislative process. A president's role was mainly to carry out the laws that Congress enacted. President Washington sent only three proposals to Congress. President Jefferson was more active in attempting to influence the work of Congress, but generally preferred to work behind the scenes rather than through the formal submission of specific legislative proposals. As the national government became more involved in the economy, however, beginning during the latter half of the 19th century, presidents became increasingly active in attempting to influence Congressional action. The turning point of the modern presidency's involvement in the legislative process is generally thought to have occurred during President Franklin D. Roosevelt's legendary "Hundred Days." After calling the 73rd Congress into special session on March 9, 1933, shortly after his inauguration, Roosevelt sent to Congress over the next 100 days nearly a dozen pieces of proposed legislation, many drafted in the White House, that were aimed at helping the American people cope with the severe economic consequences of the Great Depression. Many of Roosevelt's proposals were enacted by the Democratic-controlled Congress without formal hearings or, in many cases, without serious legislative scrutiny.

Although the president is constitutionally required to speak on only two occasions, the Constitution has been supplemented over the years by federal laws that require the president to submit a variety of fiscal and budgetary reports to Congress. Chief among them is the president's annual budget and annual economic message. The budget message required by the Budget and Accounting Act of 1921 lays out the president's taxing and spending proposals for the upcoming fiscal year. Under the former system, each government agency appeared independently before Congress to appeal for funds. This landmark legislation established the general framework for today's federal budget. In the view of many political science scholars "[t]he modern presidency, judged in terms of institutional responsibilities, began on June 10, 1921, the day that President Warren G. Harding signed the Budget and Accounting Act."[9] The Employment Act of 1946, signed into law by President Harry S Truman on February 20, 1946, assigns overall responsibility for economic stability to the executive branch and, as a part of the responsibility, calls for the president to provide his assessment of the national economy and the details of the his economic projections for the coming fiscal year. The Budget Act and the Employment Act are not the only two statutes, though, that require the federal government to disclose information to the people. Indeed, by statute, Congress also requires virtually all federal executive departments and independent agencies, as well as the president and certain parts of the legislative and judicial branches, to prepare and submit several thousand reports each year covering a broad range of domestic and foreign policy topics. The great majority of the reports are available for review by the people. Most of the reports are listed in a Library of Congress publication entitled "Popular Names of U.S. Documents."

9

Executive Privilege: The President's Power to Withhold Information

*All nations have found it necessary, for the advantageous con-
duct of their affairs, that some of these proceedings ... should
remain known to their executive functionary only. He ... must
be the sole judge of which of them the public interests will permit
publication.*—Thomas Jefferson, June 17, 1807

The system of governance that the delegates to the Constitutional
Convention adopted generally separates the executive and legislative
functions of government. The framers did not go so far in that separation, however, as to enable one branch to act entirely free of the other.
Checks and balances were provided throughout the Constitution. For
every power that is vested by the Constitution in one branch of government there is typically a counterbalancing power vested in another.
The president thus is designated the commander-in-chief of the military, but the power to declare war, as well as the power to appropriate
the funds that are necessary to conduct a war, are reserved to Congress.
The president is empowered to enter into treaties, but those treaties
cannot take effect without the approval of the Senate. Congress is given
broad power to enact laws, but it is the president's responsibility to
enforce them. The president's power "to grant Reprieves and Pardons
for Offenses against the United States," as provided for in Article II,
Section 2, Clause 1 of the Constitution, is the only power which the
president may exercise without the involvement of Congress or the
possibility of reversal by the courts.

A system of governance that provides for a sharing of power

between the executive and legislative branches necessarily requires that information also be shared. Without the sharing of information neither branch would be able in many cases to carry out its Constitutional duties. Yet as important and obvious as the need to share information is, the Constitution does little to require it. It has little to say about government communications in general or about secrecy in particular. Indeed, other than the State of the Union and Recommendation Clauses, the president is under no explicit duty to supply information to Congress or to comply with a request by Congress for information or documents that are in the executive's possession. The framers may well have thought it too difficult to anticipate the many possible situations in which Congress might call for information from the president, or to set out the procedures that should be followed in the event the president refuses. Thus, rather than attempting to specify the myriad situations in which information should be shared, the framers chose instead to rely on the practical, often political, incentives that each branch has under the Constitution to release or withhold information. It was the framers' evident hope, if not expectation, that those incentives, or if need be the sheer force of necessity, would be sufficient to lead to procedures being put in place for resolving any disputes that might disrupt the necessary flow of information between the president and Congress. The president's right of executive privilege versus Congress' power to call for information has been one of the most contentious of the roadblocks to that free flow of information.

Among the most important of Congress' "checks" on the executive branch is Congress' power to investigate and oversee the actions of the executive. The Constitution does not expressly authorize Congress to investigate the executive branch, however, nor does it expressly grant Congress the right of access to the records or other information that is in executive's possession. Yet without those powers, Congress would be unable to monitor what the executive is doing, or to determine how existing programs are being administered, or to assess whether executive branch officials are executing the laws consistent with Congressional intent. The president would be free in many cases to operate in secrecy. The power to demand information from the executive is thus an implied one. As the United States Supreme Court observed nearly one hundred years ago, "a legislative body cannot legislate wisely or effectively in the absence of information respecting the conditions which the legislation is intended to affect or change; and where the legislative body does not itself possess the requisite information—which not infrequently is the case—recourse must be had to those who possess it." And because "experience has taught that mere requests for such information often are unavailing," the Court explained, "some means of compulsion are essential to obtain what is needed."[1] The power to investigate, and with it the power to demand information from the executive branch, is thus an integral part of the Constitution's system of checks and balances. It is also an indispensable tool in ensuring openness in government.

Congress' power to require information from the executive implies a corresponding duty on the part of the executive to provide the requested information. That duty, however, is not absolute one. The president may assert executive privilege when, in his judgment, disclosing the requested information would disrupt the executive branch's functions or decision-making processes. Like Congress' power to investigate, the president's power of executive privilege is not explicitly provided for in the Constitution. It is an implied power rooted in the Constitution's separation of powers and in the primacy of the president when discharging his Constitutional duties.

The president's authority to withhold documents or other information from disclosure historically has fallen into two categories: the state secrets privilege, covering military, diplomatic, and national security secrets; and the communications privilege, covering communications between the president and his advisors. The privilege essentially enables the president to act in secret. Indeed, one of the primary considerations that led the framers to settle on a single executive, rather than a multiple executive as some of the delegates had preferred, was the greater ability of a single executive to operate with "secrecy, vigor & dispatch." Although the privilege has been asserted numerous times over the years, it was not until the presidency of President Dwight Eisenhower that the term "executive privilege" became a part of the political lexicon.

The scope of the president's right of executive privilege and Congress' power to call for information have both evolved over the years. But like so many other aspects of modern day governance, the foundation of the executive privilege was laid early on during the administration of President George Washington. Three of those early cases are of particular importance—St. Clair's Defeat, the Morris Affair, and the Jay Treaty. A fourth case, involving President Richard Nixon's refusal to turn over certain documents in a judicial proceeding, marked the outer limits of executive privilege: limits beyond which not even a president may go.

St. Clair's Defeat

The claim of executive privilege was first asserted by George Washington in 1792. The issue arose when Congress demanded information from Washington's Secretary of War, Henry Knox, concerning a major defeat that had been suffered in November the year before by the U.S. military forces at the Battle of the Wabash. The defeat was inflicted by a confederation of Miami and Shawnee Indians who disputed America's claim of sovereignty in the Northwest Territory. The American troops were under the command of General Arthur St. Clair, the Governor of the Territory and a Continental Army veteran. Nearly half of St. Clair's command of 1,400 was either killed or wounded.[2]

The nation and Congress were in a state of shock at the defeat. After debating briefly about whether an investigation should be undertaken by the House of Representatives or whether the president should be allowed to investigate the matter internally, the House decided on February 2 to appoint a special committee to inquire into the causes of St. Clair's defeat. The decision to launch the investigation was unprecedented, representing as South Carolina Representative William L. Smith pointed out, "the first instance of a proposition of this House to inquire into the conduct of officers who are immediately under the control of the Executive."[3] Implicit in the House's investigation was also the question of the extent to which, if any, the executive branch is under a duty to provide information to the legislative branch.

The House appointed the committee on March 27, 1792, and directed it "to inquire into the causes of the failure of the late expedition under Major General St. Clair." In order to facilitate the inquiry, the committee was expressly "empowered to call for such persons, papers, and records as may be necessary to assist their inquiries."[4] On March 30, the committee directed Secretary Knox to deliver to the committee all of the documents that were in his possession pertaining to St. Clair's defeat. Knox promptly wrote to Washington seeking his guidance.

Washington's usual practice in dealing with important policy questions, particularly those of first impression, was to call for written opinions from his department heads. Face-to-face meetings were rare. In this case, though, Washington convened his full Cabinet to discuss the House's request. Washington recognized the precedential effect that the decisions he made, as the first president, would have on future presidents. As Washington wrote some years earlier to James Madison, "[a]s the first of everything, in our situation will serve to establish a precedent, it is devoutly wished on my part that these precedents be fixed on true principles."[5]

Washington met with his cabinet on March 31, 1792. Thomas Jefferson, Secretary of State, Alexander Hamilton, Secretary of the Treasury, Henry Knox, Secretary of War, and Edmund Randolph, Attorney General were in attendance. Although minutes of the meeting were not kept, Jefferson recorded in his personal notes that "[t]he President said he had called us to consult, merely because it was the first example, and he wished that so far as it should become a precedent, it should be rightly conducted." Jefferson also recorded that Washington "neither acknowledged nor even doubted the propriety of what the House was doing." But just as Washington acknowledged Congress' right of inquiry, he also foresaw the possibility that "there might be papers of so secret a nature that they ought not to be given up."[6] The question in Washington's mind was whether he, as president, had the Constitutional authority to withhold information from Congress and the American people.

A second meeting was held on April 1 at which, according to Jefferson, President Washington and his cabinet agreed to four central points: "We had all considered, and were of one mind, that, first, that the House was an inquest and therefore might institute inquiries. Second, that it might call for papers generally. Third, that the Executive ought to communicate such papers as the public good would permit and ought to refuse those the disclosure of which would injure the public: consequently [all parties] were to exercise a discretion. Fourth, that neither the committee nor the House had a right to call on the Head of a Department, who and whose papers were under the President alone; but that the committee should instruct their chairman to move the House to address the President."[7]

Washington eventually decided to cooperate with the Congressional inquiry and, on April 4, ordered Secretary Knox to turn over all of the papers the House had requested. Washington's decision was based on his judgment that public disclosure of the papers would not harm the national interest. As Jefferson recorded, "[f]inally agreed to speak separately to members of the committee and bring them by persuasion into the right channel. It was agreed in this case, that there was not a paper which might not be properly produced."[8] Although the House was given the documents it requested, Washington had laid the groundwork for the presidential use of executive privilege. Only two years later, in 1794, President Washington would again be required to consider the use of executive privilege when confronted with another Congressional demand for executive branch documents.

The Morris Affair

Political debate in the United States concerning the legitimacy of the French Revolution was deepening already-existing political divisions in the 1790s, causing many of America's political leaders to align themselves along pro–French and pro–British lines. France and Great Britain were then engaged in the first post–French Revolutionary war. Former Secretary of State Thomas Jefferson led the pro–French Democratic-Republican Party that shared many of the republican ideals of the French Revolution. The Federalist Party, led by Secretary of the Treasury Alexander Hamilton, viewed the revolution in France with great skepticism and sought to preserve existing commercial ties with Great Britain.

On January 24, 1794, during Washington's second term, the Senate adopted a resolution, by a vote of thirteen to eleven, directing that the President "be requested to lay before the Senate the correspondences which have been had between the Minister of the United States at the Republic of France [Gouverneur Morris] and between said Minister and the office of the Secretary of State [Edmund Randolph]."[9] The concern among many in the Senate was that Morris's conservative, pro-monarchy views were lessening his effectiveness as a diplomatic representative to the Revolutionary regime in France. Morris was critical of the Revolution and was continuing to give advice to the King,

Louis XVI, even though by that time the King was essentially without power.

Secretary of State Randolph reviewed his files and reported to Washington that Morris's correspondence contained "little of what is exceptional." Even so, there were several passages in Morris's correspondence, Randolph founded, that might be "impolitic" to disclose. As he had done in 1792, Washington sought the advice of his cabinet— Secretary of War Knox, Secretary of the Treasury Hamilton, and Secretary of State Randolph. The meeting was held on January 28. Although there was some divergence of opinion among the three Secretaries over the outer limits of the president's power to withhold information from Congress, all three agreed that Washington was under no duty in this case to comply strictly with the letter of the Senate's resolution, particularly given its unqualified breadth.[10]

President Washington ultimately accepted the advice of his cabinet, and, on February 26, 1794, provided the Senate with copies of the requested documents, but with the sensitive parts redacted. Washington explained in his transmittal letter that "[a]fter an examination [of the Morris correspondence], I directed copies and translations to be made; except in those particulars which, in my judgment, for public consideration, ought not to be communicated."[11] The Senate accepted Washington's partial response without serious protest. Indeed, Secretary of State Randolph reported to Washington that his response to the Senate's request "appears to have given general satisfaction." Randolph also reported that Representative James Madison was overheard in conversation conceding that "the discretion of President was always to be the guide" in such matters."[12] In making that concession, Madison was essentially recognizing the growing consensus that the president has the right to withhold information from Congress "for public consideration." The president did not offer, however, nor did the Senate require, the articulation of definite standards for determining when information requested of the president might properly be withheld. Nor did the Senate articulate any limits on its own discretion in releasing such information to the public as might be confided to it. The Senate's request for the Morris correspondence was not to be the last of President Washington's confrontations with Congress. In March 1796, the House would request that it be given all of the documents concerning the controversial Jay Treaty.

The Jay Treaty

Although the war between the United States and Great Britain had been over for more than ten years, relations between the two countries continued to be strained. Two of the ongoing sources of friction were Great Britain's continued military presence in America's northwestern territory and its repeated efforts to interfere with American trade and shipping. In an attempt to improve those relations, the two countries agreed to seek a negotiated settlement of their disputes. The result of those negotiations, the Jay Treaty, was signed by the two parties in London on November 19, 1794, and approved by the United States Senate on June 24, 1795. John Jay, Chief Justice of the Supreme Court, served as America's chief negotiator.

The treaty received less than a favorable reception in the United States. Although the treaty was negotiated by his own administration, not even President Washington was entirely satisfied with it. "My concern respecting the treaty," Washington said, "is the same now that it was, namely, not favorable to it, but that better to ratify it than to suffer matters to remain as they are." The Senate ultimately approved the treaty, (on June 24, 1795), but by a vote of only twenty to ten, exactly the two-thirds majority required by the Constitution for Senate approval of a treaty.

Opponents of the Jay Treaty claimed that it ceded too much to the British. The treaty's opponents in the House attempted to derail it by claiming that although the Constitution assigned primary responsibility for treaty-making to the president and the Senate, the House also had "a discretionary power of carrying the Treaty into effect, or refusing their sanction." The Congress had the power to regulate commerce by laying and collecting taxes, the House's reasoning went, and if the president and Senate alone could enter into a binding treaty, then they could effectively legislate without the approval, or even involvement, of the people's representatives in the House.

Representative Edward Livingston of New York introduced a resolution in the House calling upon President Washington to "lay before this House a copy of the instructions to the Minister [John Jay] who negotiated with the King of Great Britain ... together with the correspondence and other documents relative to the said Treaty."[13] Livingston later learned that there were a few negotiations that "were probably unfinished [and that the disclosure of the papers relating to those negotiations] might embarrass the Executive." In light of those unfinished negotiations, Livingston amended his resolution by "excepting such of said papers as any existing negotiation may render improper to be disclosed."[14] James Madison, who during the Morris affair had seemed to recognize the president's right of executive privilege, questioned the constitutionality of the House's demand, and attempted to "throw the resolution into such form as not to bear even the appearance of encroaching on the Constitutional rights of the Executive." Madison's proposed amendment scaled back the demands of the resolution by "[e]xcept[ing] so much of the papers as, in his judgment, it may it not be consistent with the interests of the United States, at this time to disclose." Madison's amendment was defeated by a vote of thirty-seven to forty-seven.

Not everyone in the House who objected to the Jay Treaty agreed with Livingston's call for the treaty documents. Uriah Tracy from Connecticut argued that although "the House certainly had a right to call for any papers or statements from its officers created under the laws which it had participated in making, it had no role to play in approving a treaty." If the Constitution was examined," Tracy said, "it would be found that the treaty-making power was given to the President; and no ... right was given to any other ... but to the two-thirds of the Senate, and that by way of consent and advice."[15] On March 24, 1796, following more than two weeks of debate, the House adopted Livingston's resolution calling for the documents.

On March 30, 1796, Washington advised the House in a written message that "the duty of my office, under all the circumstances of this case, forbids a compliance with your request." Washington's decision to withhold the requested information was based on two grounds. First, that as a matter of Constitutional provision, "the power of making treaties is exclusively vested in the President, by and with the advice and consent of the Senate, provided two-thirds of the Senators present concur." "It is perfectly clear" Washington told the House, "that the assent of the House of Representatives is not necessary to the validity of a treaty." Second, Washington explained, "[t]he nature of foreign negotiations require caution ... and secrecy; and even when brought to a conclusion a full disclosure of all the measures, demands, or eventual concessions which may have been proposed ... would be extremely impolitic; for this might have a pernicious influence on future negotiations ... perhaps danger and mischief, in relation to other powers."[16]

Washington's decision to withhold the Jay Treaty documents from the House was not, as a technical matter, an exercise of executive privilege. The decision was based primarily on the absence of a Constitutional provision authorizing the House's involvement in treaty-making. Although Congress may demand information from the executive branch, it may only do so when the information is necessary to the discharge of a specific Constitutional duty. Absent that duty, the president is under no obligation to comply. In this case, as Washington pointed out, "all the papers affecting the negotiation with Great Britain were laid before the Senate when the treaty itself was communicated for their consideration and advice." Because the House had no role to play in the treaty, it had no right to call for those papers.

The House debated at some length over the response it should make to Washington's refusal to turn of the Jay Treaty documents. Ultimately the House took no substantive action, other than to adopt two nonbinding, largely face-saving resolutions. Both resolutions were offered on April 6 by North Carolina Representative Thomas Blount.[17] The first of Blount's resolutions acknowledged the right of the president, with the Senate's concurrence, to make treaties, but nonetheless argued that when a treaty has provisions whose execution depends on the House taking some action—in this case providing the funds necessary to carry out the treaty—it was the right of the House "to deliberate on the expediency or inexpediency of carrying such Treaty into effect, and to determine and act thereon, as, in their judgment, may be most conducive to the public good." Blount's second resolution declared that when the House requested information from the president "which may relate to any Constitutional functions of the House," such as appropriating funds, the House need not specify "the purpose for which such information may be wanted, or to which the same may be applied." Both of the resolutions passed in the House the next day, April 7. On April 14, six weeks after Washington had submitted the Jay Treaty to the Senate, the House took up another resolution recommending that the appropriations that were necessary to fund the treaty be approved. On May 3, after debating other alternative resolutions, the House passed a bill providing the necessary appropriations.[18] The bill was sent to the Senate on May 4. It became law on May 6, 1796.

United States v. Nixon

Presidential claims of a right to preserve the confidentiality of information and documents in the face of legislative demands have figured prominently, although intermittently, in executive-congressional relations since 1792. Few of the inter-branch disputes, though, have made their way to the courts for substantive resolution. The vast majority of disputes have been resolved through political negotiation and accommodation. Indeed, it was not until the Watergate-related litigation in the 1970s that the Supreme Court confirmed for the first time the existence of a presidential executive privilege as being a necessary derivative of the president's role under the Constitution. The case arose out of President Richard M. Nixon's refusal, based on a claim of executive privilege, to turn over to the Watergate Special Prosecutor certain tape recordings and documents pertaining to Nixon's conversations with close aides and advisors. The tapes allegedly contained evidence revealing President Nixon's personal involvement in a cover-up of illegal activities of political operatives connected with his re-election campaign. The Supreme Court issued its opinion on July 24, 1974.[19] Although the Court found a constitutional basis for a president's right of executive privilege—based on "the supremacy of each branch within its assigned area of constitutional duties" and in the separation of powers—the Court rejected Nixon claim that the privilege was absolute.

Nixon's claim that he need not provide the requested documents rested on two grounds. Nixon first argued that executive privilege is necessary to ensure the confidentiality of communications between a president and other high-ranking executive officials and those who advise them in the performance of their official duties. The Court acknowledged the importance of protecting those communications, noting that the principle underlying the privilege "is too plain to require further discussion. Human experience teaches that those who expect public dissemination of their remarks may well temper candor with a concern for appearances and for their own interests to the detriment of the decision-making process." The Court also made clear, however, that even though the claim of confidentiality of communications between a president and his advisers is entitled to "great deference" from the courts, it is not absolute: "when the privilege depends solely on the broad, undifferentiated claim of public interest in the confidentiality of such conversations, a confrontation with other values arise." Thus, although the need to protect military, diplomatic, or sensitive national security secrets fall within the scope of executive privilege, the Court found it "difficult to accept the argument that even the very important interest in confidentiality of Presidential communications is significantly diminished by production of such material for *in camera* inspection [before the judge alone] with all the protection that a district court will be obliged to provide." In other words, a judge's private inspection of the requested documents would not compromise the confidentiality of any document to which a claim of executive privilege legitimately applies.

The second ground asserted by the President Nixon rested on the doctrine of separation of powers. Here the president argued that the executive's independence is absolute when operating "within its own sphere." In this case, though, the Court found that Nixon was attempting to protect himself from possible criminal prosecution, rather than carrying out a Constitutional duty or otherwise promoting a public interest. "Thus, while the executive privilege is a legitimate presidential power, it is not an absolute one. Particularly in criminal proceedings, where evidence is needed to achieve a just result, the balancing test implied in the Constitution in this case weighed in favor of requiring the president to turn over the White House tapes."

In prior cases, executive privilege had been asserted by a president as a defense to Congress' demand for documents in his possession. The dispute had always been one between the executive and legislative branches. In the *Nixon* case, however, the dispute over executive privilege arose between the executive and judicial branches; and here the Court made clear that just as executive privilege may not be asserted in an effort to defeat a legitimate request for information by Congress when discharging its Constitutional duties, neither can it be used to block the judiciary from discharging its duties: "[t]he impediment that an absolute, unqualified privilege would place in the way of the primary constitutional duty of the Judicial Branch to do justice in criminal prosecutions," the Court wrote, "would plainly conflict with the function of the courts under Art. III." The judiciary is therefore as entitled to information from the executive branch as is the legislature. "While the Constitution diffuses power the better to secure liberty, it also contemplates that practice will integrate the dispersed powers into a workable government. It enjoins upon its branches separateness but interdependence, autonomy but reciprocity." The Court rejected Nixon's claim of executive privilege in an 8 to 0 decision.

As is the case with many other Constitutional powers, executive privilege is always subject to a balancing test. Presidents and their advisers undeniably need confidentiality in their discussions and in carrying out their Constitutional duties. Congress and the judiciary have their Constitutional duties as well, however, and often they must have access to executive branch information if they are to carry out their duties. When a dispute arises between the branches, a claim of executive privilege must thus be weighed against the other branch's need for the information it needs to carry out its own Constitutional role. Neither power is absolute.

There have been proposals in Congress over the years to develop a clear statutory definition of executive privilege. No legislation attempting to do that has been enacted. It is not likely that it ever will. Yet just as the framers intended, the three branches of government have been able so far to negotiate successfully the disputes that have arisen between them over a president's claim of executive privilege.

10

Federal Records and the People's Right to Know

Sunlight is said to be the best of disinfectants; sunlight the most efficient policeman.—Justice Louis D. Brandeis, March 1914

Public access to the records that are created by the executive branch of government is an essential part of the people's right to know, especially in light of the ever-increasing role that the executive branch plays in the lives of everyday Americans. Indeed, the federal government generates an estimated six million cubic feet of documents annually.[1] These documents capture first-hand the actions of the many departments and agencies within the executive branch. The records are therefore critical tools in understanding and monitoring the powers and operations of the executive branch: they are critical tools in reducing the level of secrecy in government.

The explosive growth of federal agencies and programs during the New Deal era led to a corresponding increase in the number of rules and regulations that were being issued by those agencies. More than a dozen major agencies were created during the 1930s as part of the New Deal, including the Federal Communications Commission, Securities Exchange Commission, National Labor Relations Board, Social Security Administration, and the Federal Deposit Insurance Corporation. Many in Congress and even the executive branch became concerned about the overall lack of standards governing the issuance of agency regulations and the absence of any uniformity among the agencies in how those regulations were administered once they were issued. In early 1939, Attorney General Frank Murphy, acting at the direction of President Roosevelt, appointed a blue-ribbon committee to develop a set of procedures for the administrative agencies. The committee's final report was submitted to the Senate on January 29, 1941.[2]

Although Murphy's committee focused on agency administration, another of its key goals was the elimination of the secrecy that surrounded so much of the work of those agencies. That secrecy bred a natural distrust of the entire administrative process. As Murphy's committee noted in its final report, "[w]here necessary information must be secured through oral discussion or inquiry, it is natural that parties should complain of 'a government of men.' Where public regulation is not adequately expressed in rules, complaints regarding 'unrestrained delegation of legislative authority' are aggravated. Where the process of decision is not clearly outlined, charges of 'star chamber proceedings' may be anticipated."[3] The committee thus recommended that legislation be enacted requiring the publication of agency policies and interpretations and the adoption of rules ensuring a broader disclosure of agency documents to the public. Final legislative action on the committee's recommendation was delayed, however, by the outbreak of World War II and the resulting demands that were placed on Congress' time and attention. Following the end of the war, Congress resumed its consideration of the Murphy committee's recommendations. Its response to those recommendations was the Administrative Procedure Act, introduced in the Senate on October 19, 1945, by Senator Patrick McCarran of Nevada and signed into law by President Harry S Truman on June 11, 1946.

The public information section of the new law, Section 3, was seen by Congress as being a matter of particular importance. Prior to the APA's enactment, the public had no legal right of access to executive branch records. As the Senate Judiciary Committee reported, "[t]he section [3] has been drawn upon the theory that administrative operations and procedures are public property which the general public, rather than a few specialists or lobbyists, is entitled to know or to have the ready means of knowing with definiteness and assurance."[4] The House Judiciary Committee reached the same conclusion, declaring that "all administrative operations should as a matter of policy be disclosed to the public except as secrecy may obviously be required."[5]

Despite Congress' intent that the workings of government be opened up to the people, the APA did relatively little to put that intent into actual practice. Much of the failure is attributable to the many

158

disclosure exceptions that were provided for in the law. Thus although the APA required federal agencies to publish detailed information about their function, organization, and administrative procedures, specifically excepted were materials pertaining to "any function of the United States requiring secrecy in the public interest." That "public interest" term, however, as the Senate later found when considering amendments to the APA, "has been subject to conflicting interpretations, often colored by personal prejudices and predilections ... serv[ing] in many cases to defeat the very purpose for which it was intended—the public's right to know the operations of its government."[6] And although "matters of official record" were also to be made available under the APA, only those "persons properly and directly concerned" with the particular agency proceeding were granted access to the official record. Even then, the record could be "held confidential for good cause found." Indeed, an agency's opinions and orders could also be withheld from the public upon a finding of "good cause," unless they were to be cited as precedent in future agency proceedings. The public, the press, and even some Congressional committees were often rebuffed when seeking information from executive branch agencies. In many respects, the new Administrative Procedure Act made the bureaucrats the final judge of their own compliance. The exceptions provided for in the Act tended to become the general rule. Despite the need for reform, genuine public disclosure would await Congress' passage of the Freedom of Information Act twenty years later.

Freedom of Information Act

A democracy requires accountability, and accountability requires transparency. As President Barack Obama said in 2009, "[i]n our democracy, the Freedom of Information Act, which encourages accountability through transparency, is the most prominent expression of a profound national commitment to ensuring an open Government. At the heart of that commitment is the idea that accountability is in the interest of the Government and the citizenry alike."[7]

The failure of the APA's Section 3 to provide efficient and predictable access to government records, often even to those directly affected by an agency's action, led Congress on June 20, 1966, to enact the Freedom of Information Act, signed into law on July 4 by President Lyndon B. Johnson. The road to the adoption of FOIA was not an easy one, however. Its enactment followed more than eleven years of investigation, legislative development, and deliberation in the House of Representatives and nearly five years in the Senate

The Freedom of Information Act replaced and greatly expanded the public information section of the Administrative Procedure Act. It was intended by Congress to remove the barriers to the public's access to federal agency records. Unlike the APA, FOIA was intended to be a disclosure statute, not a withholding statute. FOIA does not apply to the legislative or judicial branches, however, nor does it apply to state or local governments. Records that are generated by Congress are not included in FOIA because of Congress' determination that its own proceedings were already sufficiently subject to public inspection through press, radio, and television coverage and the publication of the *Congressional Record.* The judiciary was also exempted because of Congress' satisfaction with the general openness of the federal court system's files and courtrooms.

FOIA is often referred to as the embodiment of the "people's right to know" about the activities and operations of their government. The Act establishes the statutory presumption that the public has a legally enforceable right of access to information that is held by federal agencies and departments. Under the former public information section of the APA, those who requested information from a federal agency were generally required to demonstrate a need for the information they sought. Under FOIA, however, any person, whether individual or corporate, is entitled to review existing, identifiable, and unpublished agency records. No longer must a person first demonstrate a need for the requested record. Indeed, curiosity alone is sufficient.

The driving force behind the enactment of FOIA, as well as its principal author, was John E. Moss, a Democratic Congressman from Sacramento, California. Prompted by lobbying by newspaper editors and the growing demand generally for greater openness in government, Moss's Special Subcommittee on Government Operations conducted a series of hearings in 1955 that uncovered numerous instances of excessive secrecy within the executive branch. Moss drafted legislation aimed at reducing that level of secrecy. Moss was unable to gather much support for his bill from the Republican members of the House, however, largely because of the opposition from Republican President Dwight Eisenhower.

Following the elections of Presidents John F. Kennedy in 1960 and Lyndon B. Johnson in 1964, the Republicans in Congress, freed of pressure from the White House, became increasingly open to Moss' legislation, including in particular Donald H. Rumsfeld, a thirty-year-old Republican Congressman from Illinois. Rumsfeld was assigned to Moss's subcommittee and soon signed on to become a co-sponsor of Moss's FOIA bill. Rumsfeld was wholehearted in his support of the purpose of the legislation: "[t]he unanimous action after years of delay results from the growing size and complexity of the federal government, of its increased role in our lives, and from the increasing awareness of the threat involved in Government secrecy in vital records affecting their fate.... With the continuing tendency toward managed news and suppression of public information that the people are entitled to have, the issues have at last been brought home to the public...."[8]

With a Democratic president in office, Represented Moss assumed that his FOIA legislation would receive White House support. President Johnson, however, proved to be no more supportive of the public's right of access to government information than had been President Eisenhower. No detailed explanation was given by the White House for its opposition to Moss's legislation. It may simply have been the political reality that no president, regardless of party affiliation, ever wants the internal affairs—and mistakes—of his administration to be revealed to the press and the public. Regardless of the reason, White House support was not forthcoming. Rumsfeld in particular denounced what he saw as the Johnson administration's "continuing tendency toward managed news and suppression of public information that the people are entitled to have."[9] The relations between Moss and the White House were made even worse by Congressman Moss's insistence that "I will not agree to any language that grants statutory recognition to executive privilege."[10]

Twenty-seven federal agencies and departments testified during Moss's committee hearings. All of them opposed the bill. The Johnson administration's chief witness, Assistant Attorney General, Norbert A. Schliel, made clear his opposition to the idea of a national freedom of information law, telling the committee that "the problem is too vast, too protean to yield to any such solution." Even though officially acknowledging that a lack of transparency did exist, Schiel offered no alternatives to Moss's FOIA bill and even hinted that a presidential veto might be exercised if the bill was passed. Moss continued to forge ahead and, with the continuing efforts of Rumsfeld and others, gradually succeeded in building greater support among Republicans for his legislation. The addition of House Republicans, together with the public's growing interest in a more open government, finally led to FOIA's enactment on June 20, 1966. President Johnson signed FOIA into law while vacationing at his ranch in Texas, although he did so with little enthusiasm. While Johnson's usual practice was to hand out signing pens at public bill signings, Johnson refused to hold a formal signing ceremony for FOIA. Indeed, across the bottom of a memorandum he received concerning the bill's signing, Johnson wrote, "No ceremony, L."[11]

President Johnson remained adamant to the end in his opposition to the new law, reportedly telling his assistant, Billy Don "Bill" Moyers, that FOIA would "screw my administration." In his signing statement of July 4, 1966, Johnson was politically astute enough, though, to conceal his true feelings, declaring that "[a] democracy works best when the people have all the information that the security of the Nation permits," adding that "[n]o one should be able to pull curtains of secrecy around decisions which can be revealed without injury to the public interest." But Johnson also emphasized that "[a]t the same time, the welfare of the Nation or the rights of individuals may require that some documents not be made available." Likely in response to the absence of any provision in FOIA recognizing a president's power of executive privilege, Johnson also made clear his position that "this bill in no way impairs the President's power under our Constitution to provide for confidentiality when the national interest so requires."[12]

Although FOIA establishes the public's legal right to obtain executive agency documents, the implementation of FOIA has not been uniform across all presidential administrations. The shadow of the leader is still an important force. Some presidents have interpreted FOIA's requirements rather narrowly while others have given the Act's provisions a more liberal interpretation. While generally known as a limited-government advocate both before and during his presidency, President Ronald Reagan's attitude toward FOIA was generally a restrictive one, defending as a matter of policy decisions to withhold requested material that was arguably exempt under FOIA. Reagan's policy marked a change in the way FOIA had been implemented in the previous administrations of Presidents Ford and Carter. Prior to Reagan's administration, agencies generally tended to release as much information as possible, even if in some instances a case could be made that the requested information was exempt under FOIA. Reagan's policy continued in effect until President William Clinton adopted a more pro-disclosure policy in 1993. A policy more closely aligned with Reagan's policy was subsequently adopted by President George W. Bush when he assumed office. The Department of Justice under President Bush advised federal agencies to give "full and deliberate consideration of the institutional, commercial, and personal privacy interests when making disclosure determinations" and assured the agencies that the Department of Justice would defend their decisions in court "unless they lack[ed] a sound legal basis or present[ed] an unwarranted risk of adverse impact on the ability of other agencies to protect other important records."[13] The administration of President Barack Obama, by contrast, implemented a pro-disclosure policy, directing federal agencies "to adopt a presumption in favor of disclosure."[14]

As important as FOIA is in regularizing the federal administrative process, it is arguably the electoral process, and not just the administrative process, that is the true beneficiary of the Freedom of Information Act. Indeed, in a case decided six years later, in 1972, the Second Circuit Court of Appeals found that "the ultimate purpose [of FOIA] was to enable the public to have sufficient information in order to be able, through the electoral process, to make intelligent, informed choices with respect to the nature, scope, and procedure of federal government activities."[15] FOIA is an antidote to secrecy.

FOIA has been in place in the United States for fifty years. The Act's requirements apply to approximately one hundred federal agencies. Individuals, whether citizens or not, are able to compel the government to turn over federal records at little or no cost. Anyone who requests information—by filing a FOIA request with an agency—is generally entitled to receive it unless disclosure would harm national security, violate personal privacy, or reveal a business trade secret. FOIA also provides for judicial enforcement of its disclosure policy. United States District Courts are empowered to grant *de novo* review of denials of access to records and also to enjoin agencies from improper denials. The agencies in those cases bear the burden of demonstrating that their refusal to provide a requested document is "specifically" permitted by one of the statute's exemptions.

More than 700,000 FOIA requests were filed in 2014. Government data submitted by the Attorney General reveal that the government responded to nearly 650,000 requests that year, including requests that had been made in prior years. In roughly forty percent of the cases, the requested information was provided. In the remaining cases, the requested materials were either censored or withheld altogether.[16] Even so, the Freedom of Information Act represents the clearest statutory expression of the American people's right to know.

Presidential Records Act

Presidential records are those documentary materials that are created by the president and vice-president and their immediate staffs. Prior to the passage of the Presidential Records Act of 1978, the public's knowledge of the day-to-day activities of the president was mostly limited to what the president wished to disclose. Although presidents generate a great many documents while in office, those documents prior to the Act were under the total control of the president whose administration generated them, not only while the president was in office, but also after his term ended. A president's records were essentially his own personal property, and could be removed, disclosed, or destroyed by him at his discretion upon leaving office. The records and their contents were thus secret to the extent the president wished to keep them secret. The public had no legal right of access. The single exception to that rule involved the records of President Nixon. Because of the unique circumstances surrounding Nixon's resignation from office and a president's broad authority to dispose of his records as he saw fit, Congress enacted a special law governing his, and only his, presidential records—the Presidential Recordings and Materials Preservation Act of 1974.[17] That Act was introduced on September 18, 1974, by Senator Gaylord Nelson from Wisconsin. The legislation passed both houses of Congress on December 9 and was signed into law by President Gerald Ford on December 19, 1974. The immediate purpose of the Act was to prevent the destruction of Nixon's presidential papers. Under the Act, the

Administrator of the General Services Administration was directed to take "complete possession and control "of virtually all documents, including tape recordings produced within the White House during the previous [Nixon] Administration." The Administrator was also directed to develop regulations to govern the public's access to the Nixon tapes and other materials, taking into account the goal of providing the public with the "full truth" about the abuses of governmental power that took place during "Watergate."

The Presidential Records Act of 1978 was enacted in the aftermath of the post–Watergate controversy over President Nixon's records. The Act established the principle that presidential documents are public, not personal documents, and that they should be generally available for public inspection. Because of the Presidential Records Act, a president's records are now owned, possessed, and controlled by the people of the United States, not the president. Excluded, however, are the "personal records" of a president; that is, those records or documentary materials that are "of a purely private or nonpublic character which do not relate to or have an effect on the carrying out of the constitutional, statutory, or other official or ceremonial duties of the President." Personal records typically include diaries, journals, or other personal notes; materials relating to private political associations; or materials that relate exclusively to the president's election to office. The records of President Ronald Reagan were the first to be the subject to the Act.

Although the PRA allows the public access to presidential records, it does not come into play until after a president leaves office. While in office, a president continues to exercise virtually complete control over his presidential records. During his term, a president is generally permitted to destroy those records that no longer have administrative, historical, informational, or evidentiary value. For the first five years after a president leaves office his records are generally exempt from public access, including requests made under the Freedom of Information Act. For the next seven years, anyone can request access to a president's records through a FOIA, subject, however, to several exemptions, including national security information that is properly classified, confidential communications between a president and his advisors, and information which, if disclosed, would constitute an unwarranted invasion of personal privacy. After twelve years, the PRA's exemptions no longer apply, including the automatic twelve-year exemption for communications between a president and his advisors. The expiration of that exemption, however, does not mean that a president's confidential communications may no longer be protected from public disclosure. The PRA expressly provides that "nothing within this Act shall be construed to confirm, limit, or expand any constitutionally-based privilege which may be available to an incumbent or former President."[18] Even after twelve years, both former and current presidents may still review presidential records prior to their release in order to decide whether to assert executive privilege in connection with a president's confidential communications with his advisors.[19]

The enactment of the Presidential Records Act does not mean that presidential records before 1978 were not available for public inspection. The records of many former presidents, beginning with President Herbert Hoover (1929 to 1933), were donated to the federal government and are now generally available in presidential libraries. The Presidential Libraries Act of 1955[20] formalized that practice and authorized the National Archivist to accept donations of presidential records. These records are available to the public through a network of thirteen presidential libraries that are administered by the Office of Presidential Libraries, a part of the National Archives and Records Administration. Official fundraising for the Barack Obama Presidential Library and Museum, the fourteenth in the presidential library system, began in January 2014. It will be located in Chicago and is expected to open in 2020.

11

Security Classification

The public is entitled to know as much as possible about Government's activities. Classification should be used only to protect legitimate national security secrets and never to cover up mistakes or improper activities.—President Jimmy Carter, June 29, 1978

Even the most ardent supporters of the people's right to know do not quarrel with the proposition that there are types of information, such as the country's nuclear launch codes, that must be protected from public disclosure. By the same token, even those who come down the hardest on the side of greater protection of government documents make no claim that the lunch menu at the White House mess, for instance, should be given a restrictive security classification. The challenge over the years has been, and remains so today, deciding which information should be classified and which should not.

Throughout most of America's early history with secrecy, the national government was occupied primarily with protecting a relatively small amount of information pertaining to military and diplomatic matters. Formalized procedures for deciding what and how that information should be protected were essentially non-existent, however. During the Revolutionary War, General George Washington and other higher-ranking officers decided what information should be protected on a case-by-case basis and then attempted to protect it by simply writing "Secret" or "Confidential" on the communiqués or other documents containing the information. The terms were used in their ordinary meanings and were intended to advise the document's recipient that the information contained in it was private and that it should not to be disclosed. This unofficial system of protecting military information remained in place throughout the War of 1812 and the Civil War.

During the Civil War, the control of sensitive information appears to have been limited generally to the war zones that fell under the jurisdiction of the military. Even then, though, the rules were not consistent. Reporters were often allowed relatively easy access to military secrets, while at other times strict measures were taken to preserve their secrecy. In a few instances, newspapers were even seized or suppressed by Union military commanders.[1] In most cases, though, the public's access to news about the war was unrestricted. On one occasion, President Lincoln instructed a Union general on how to deal with sensitive information: "You will only arrest individuals and suppress assemblies or newspapers," Lincoln said, "when they may be working palpable injury to the military in your charge, and in no other case will you interfere with the expression of opinion in any form or allow it to be interfered with violently by others. In this you have a direction to exercise great caution, calmness, and forbearance."[2] Although President Lincoln himself occasionally authorized the censorship of some mail and the suppression of a few newspapers, most of the information about the progress of the Civil War, good and bad, was readily available to the public. Indeed, during his Second Inaugural Address, Lincoln pointed to the generally unrestricted flow of information to the people about the war: "The progress of our arms, upon which all else chiefly depends, is as well known to the public as to myself."[3]

The security classification practices that were followed during the Civil War remained essentially in place throughout the remainder of the nineteenth century and even through the end of World War I. With the beginning of World War II, however, the practice of classifying information underwent a significant expansion. It was also during World War II that the government began classifying other defense-related scientific and technical information as well. More formalized classification procedures were also put in place governing both the type of information that should be protected and the specific safeguarding procedures that were to be followed.

The public's access to national security information has ebbed and flowed since the end of World War II. At times, access has been influenced by the philosophical inclinations of individual presidential administrations, while at other times world events have influenced the extent to which the federal government protected sensitive information. In most cases, the flow of information to the public has been influenced by both. Regardless of those ebbs and flows, though, the overall growth in the government's document classification system has grown steadily: first because of the unprecedented increase in the size of the federal government during and after World War II; and second because of the increased secrecy demands of the Cold War. The ongoing threats of terrorism against the American homeland in recent years have taken the classification of information to new levels.

Although Congress occasionally enacted legislation in an attempt to define the scope and direction of America's security classification policy, it has been the executive branch, through the issuance of presidential executive orders, that has played the primary role in setting and implementing classification policy. The president's authority to issue executive orders is based upon three sources: statutory (by authorization of Congress), constitutional (in his role as commander-in-chief, for example), and inherent (in his role as chief executive). Presidential claims of inherent authority have been the most controversial of the three because they are less subject, if at all, to counter-balancing restraints. Statutory and constitutional sources of authority to withhold information from the public originate outside the executive branch and are therefore subject to greater external controls. Presidential executive orders involving the protection of national defense information have been based at one time or another on all three of these sources of authority.

Today's classification system traces its origins to Executive Order 8381, issued by Franklin Roosevelt on March 22, 1940. Prior to Roosevelt's Executive Order, sensitive defense-related information was classified secret by military personnel pursuant to a succession of Army and Navy general orders.[4] But with the events leading up to the beginning of World War I, Congress enacted legislation directing the president "in the interests of national defense" to designate "vital military and naval installations ... [that] require protection against general dissemination of information relative thereto."[5]

Roosevelt's executive order simply formalized in many respects the classification practices that had been in effect throughout the nineteenth century. The order set out broad definitions of the type of military information that should be classified and specified in descending order of importance the three security designations that were to be applied: Secret, Confidential, and Restricted. The order's classification requirements were broad in scope, applying not only to military facilities, but also, for the first time, to "any commercial establishment engaged in the development or manufacture of military equipment." Information about the Manhattan Project, for example, was classified under Executive Order 8381.

Following the end of World War II and the beginning of the Cold War, President Harry S Truman issued two executive orders that expanded and enhanced presidential control over the classification process. The first of Truman's Executive Orders, 10104, was issued on February 1, 1950. Although the order superseded Roosevelt's Executive Order 8381, it retained most of the substantive provisions of the former order. The principal change was to add a fourth security designation—Top Secret—thereby bringing America's security classifications into line with those of its NATO allies. Only eighteen months later, on September 24, 1951, President Truman issued a new Executive Order, 10290. This order implemented sweeping changes in America's security classification policy. First, rather than relying on Congressional legislation as the basis of his authority to issue the order, Truman instead relied only on "the authority vested in me by the Constitution and statutes, and as President of the United States." The president's authority to set official secrecy policy was thus based not solely on his Constitutional obligation to "take care that the laws [enacted by Congress] be faithfully executed," but also on his own inherent Constitutional standing as president of the country and Commander-in-Chief of its military. The addition of these two additional sources of authority enabled the president to act on his own initiative in certain areas without authorization of Congress. Although Congress has never explicitly authorized the use of executive orders in dealing with the classification of information, it has given its implicit approval of the practice on several occasions, including a provision of the Freedom of Information Act that exempts from disclosure documents that have been classified under an executive order.[6] In addition, the "national defense" standard that had been effect since the beginning of America's classification system was replaced by a broader and more flexible standard of "national security"—a standard that included not only national defense, as that term was historically understood, but potentially other considerations as well. Finally,

Truman's order was applicable not only to "all departments and agencies of the Executive Branch of the Government," but also to "those [civilian individuals and companies] who deal with the Federal Government."

The substantial discretion that Truman's Executive Order granted to the president and other officials in the executive branch to classify information drew wide criticism from both the press and the public. Many of the order's critics saw it as a form of censorship that was unwarranted at any time, but even less so during times of peace. Federal agencies having little to do with national security, such as the Battle Monuments Commission, the Commission on Fine Arts, and the Indian Claims Commission were authorized to classify information. Allowing the president to classify information on the basis of the new "national security" standard also drew especially sharp criticism. Since the earliest days of the Revolutionary War, the meaning and intention of "national defense" was commonly understood. The new "national security" standard had no historical definition, however, and was thus subject to widely differing interpretations. Coming in for criticism as well was the order's creation of a new designation "Restricted," to be applied to information concerning the manufacture or utilization of atomic weapons, or the production or use of fissionable material. Critics of the new designation thought it so vague as to encourage over-classification.

Shortly after the election of President Dwight Eisenhower in 1956, Secretary of Defense Charles Wilson directed that a study be made of the Defense Department's classification policies and procedures. The study was undertaken by the Committee on Classified Information, established in mid–August 1956 and headed by former Assistant Defense Secretary Charles Coolidge. The Coolidge Committee issued its final report three months later, on November 8, 1956. In its report, the Committee noted the fundamental principle that "[b]eing a democracy, the government cannot cloak its operations in secrecy. Adequate information as to its activities must be given to its citizens or the foundations of its democracy will be eaten away."[7] The Committee also pointed out, though, that "our democracy can be destroyed in another way, namely, by giving a potential enemy such information as will enable him to conquer us by war." The task before Coolidge's Committee was to strike a proper balance between the two competing objectives.

Coolidge's Committee submitted twenty-eight specific recommendations, ten of which dealt with the bureaucratic tendency toward over-classification. Classifying innocuous information, the Committee found, poses a serious a risk of creating a degree of disrespect for government classification that actually serves to increase the chances of genuinely sensitive information being leaked. "When much is classified that should not be classified at all," the report concluded, "respect for the system is diminished and the extra effort required to adhere faithfully to the security procedures seems unreasonable."[8]

Against the background of the widespread the criticisms that had been leveled at President Truman's Executive Order 10290, President Eisenhower also directed Attorney General Herbert Brownell "to make a study for the purpose of advising him [Eisenhower] how the flow of information could be increased without jeopardizing our national defense."[9] The specific assignment given to Brownell was to create a new policy that would balance the legitimate need to safeguard certain kinds of official information, in the name of national defense, with the equally legitimate need to avoid censoring the free flow of information from the government to the people.

The challenge of designing a new classification policy was made even more difficult by the onset of the Cold War and the Soviet Union's continuing efforts to steal American secrets. The classification of sensitive military information had been thought of historically as coming into play particularly during times of war. Battle strategies and plans were thus routinely protected from disclosure. But with the launch of the Cold War, protecting sensitive information about the country's national defense capabilities became an ongoing necessity.

The United States and the Soviet Union were both devoting significant resources to recruiting and training agents and spies and then deploying them around the world. The primary purpose of the two countries' espionage programs was to gather information and intelligence not only about the other side's military and technical capabilities, but also about their actions and intentions. Even in the absence of an actual military conflict, protecting that information took on a wartime importance.

On November 6, 1953, Brownell delivered an address to a meeting in Chicago of the Associated Press Managing Editors Association. Brownell criticized Truman's executive order for permitting government officials to withhold many types of information that could be disclosed to the public without endangering the national safety. "There was a tendency," Brownell said, "to follow the dangerous policy heretofore used by dictator government officials to use the term 'National Security' indiscriminately, and thereby throw a veil of secrecy over many items which historically have been open to the people." Brownell also faulted the order because it "authorized classification of too many kinds of documents, [which] tended to promote a careless attitude on the part of some Government employees who handle matters which should be kept secret."[10] Brownell was additionally concerned that Truman's order was "so broadly drawn and loosely administered as to make it possible for government to cover up their mistakes and even their wrongdoing under the guise of protecting national security."

On December 15, 1953, President Eisenhower issued Executive Order 10501. Eisenhower's new order pared back significantly the scope of Truman's executive order. The order withdrew classification authority from twenty-eight executive agencies, limited the authority in seventeen other agencies to the agency's head, and reinstituted the "national defense" standard for applying a secrecy classification. Eisenhower's order also did away with the "Restricted" classification and set forth clearer definitions of the remaining three classifications reflecting the degree of damage that disclosure would cause—Top Secret (exceptionally grave damage), Secret (serious damage), and Confidential (prejudicial to the defense interests of the nation). Eisenhower's order, though, although a positive reform in the judgment of many, did little to reduce the amount of material that was being classified. During a series of Congressional hearings held in the late 1950s several classification absurdities came to light. The Department of Labor, as one example, classified statistics on the amount peanut butter purchased by the Army on the ground that the information would enable an enemy to estimate the number of military personnel.[11]

The next five presidents—Presidents Kennedy, Johnson, Nixon, Ford, and Carter—issued executive orders that generally tracked the provisions of President Eisenhower's Executive Order 10501. In April 1982, however, President Ronald Reagan issued Executive Order 12356. Reagan's order expanded the executive branch's ability to protect national security information from unauthorized or premature disclosure by expanding the categories of classifiable material. Although the stated purpose of the order was to enhance national security "without increasing the quantity of classified information," the order reversed in important respect the trend toward reducing the number of classified federal documents. Reagan's executive order also required that all information falling within those categories must be classified, and directed those who classify information to resolve any classification doubt they might have in the favor of classification until the doubt could be resolved. The operating instruction for classifiers was "when in doubt, find out."

Another important change made by Reagan's order was the elimination of the so-called "balancing test." Under President Jimmy Carter's Executive Order 12065, officials who were charged with deciding whether to declassify and release information that had been classified were to "balance" the public interest in having the information disclosed with the damage to national security that could be expected to result from the information's disclosure.[12] President Regan's Department of Justice issued a written overview of the new order on January 1, 1982. In that overview, the Department acknowledged that the "balancing test" may be a "laudable principle," but defended its elimination on the ground that "including an explicit requirement in the executive order only invited others to substitute their judgment for that of executive branch officials possessed with the expertise and experience to exercise this responsibility. That invitation significantly complicated the task of protecting legitimately classified information in court and added no countervailing benefit."[13]

Shortly after President Obama took office in January 2009, he ordered that a review be undertaken of the nation's classification policy and procedures. On May 27, 2009, the President wrote that "my Administration is committed to operating with an unprecedented level of openness. While the Government must be able to prevent the public disclosure of information where such disclosure would compromise the privacy of American citizens, national security, or other legitimate interests, a democratic government accountable to the people must be as transparent as possible and must not withhold information for self-serving reasons or simply to avoid embarrassment."[14]

On December 29, 2009, President Obama issued Executive Order 13526,[15] which, while confirming the need to protect genuinely sensitive information, sought to eliminate the bias toward classification by providing that "if there is significant doubt about the need to classify information, it shall not be classified."[16] And if there is proper justification for classifying information, the order provided that "if there is significant doubt about the appropriate level of classification, it shall be classified at the lower level."[17]

Chapter Notes

Chapter 1

1. The Congress had been scheduled to convene on Thursday, September 1, 1774, but because too few delegates had arrived by then, the opening was held over until the following Monday, September 5.

2. New York Committee of Fifty-One to Boston Committee of Correspondence, May 23, 1774, The Avalon Project, Goldman Law Library, Yale University Law School. The City of New York had appointed a committee "consisting of fifty-one persons to correspondence with our sister colonies on this and every other matter of public moment."

3. John Adams, Diary, August 16, 1774, *Founders Online*, National Archives, www.founders.archives.gov/documents/Adams [Original source, L.H. Butterfield, ed., *The Papers, Diary, and Autobiography of John Adams*, vol. 2, 1771–1781 (Harvard University Press, 1961, pp. 99–100).

4. *Journals of the American Congress From 1774 to 1788*, vol. 1 (Sept. 5, 1774, to Dec. 31, 1776), p. 55.

5. Constitution of New York, art. XV (Apr. 20, 1777).

6. Constitution of Pennsylvania, Sect. 13 (Sept. 28, 1776).

7. Caesar Rodney to Thomas Rodney, September 12, 1774, Edmund Cody Burnett, ed. *Letters of Members of the Continental Congress*, vol. 1 (Washington, D.C., Carnegie Institution, 1921) pp. 29–30.

8. Thomas Cushing to Peyton Randolph, June 2, 1773, William Pitt Palmer et al. eds. *Calendar of Virginia State Papers and Other* Manuscripts, vol. 8 (Richmond, 1890), p. 19.

9. William Pitt (Jan. 29, 1775), *Celebrated Speeches of CHATAM, BURKE, AND ERSKINE*, Selected by Philadelphia Bar Association (E. C. & J. Biddle, Philadelphia, 1845) p. 32.

10. Isaac Kramnik, ed. *The Portable Edmund Burke*, "Speech on Conciliation with the Colonies" (March 25, 1775) (Penguin, New York, 1999).

11. A.J. Langguth, *Patriots* (Simon & Schuster, New York, 1988), p. 208. The Virginians had been arguing about what they would do if armed conflict broke out between the Bostonians and the British. Washington is reported to have said, "I will raise a thousand men, subsist them at my own expense and march myself at their head for the relief of Boston."

12. John Adolphus, *The History of England from the Accession to the Decease of King George the Third*, vol. II (A. E. Mallett, London, 1841), p. 118.

13. W.C. Ford, ed., *Journals of the Continental Congress 1774–1789* vol. I (Washington, D.C., GPO, 1904), p. 15.

14. *Ibid.*, 15 (*e.g.* instructions to Delaware delegates).

15. John E. Hall, ed. *The Port Folio* vol. xviii (Harrison Hall, Philadelphia, 1824), p. 411.

16. Joseph Federico and Matthew McHenry, *Galloway Township* (Arcadia Publishing, Philadelphia, 2011), pp. 7–8.

17. L.H. Butterfield, ed., *The Papers, Diary, and Autobiography of John Adams*, vol. 2

(Harvard University Press Cambridge, MA, 1961), p. 107. *See also* National Archives, Monday, Aug. 22, 1774, *Founders Online, founders.archives.gov/documents/Adams.*

18. William P. Massey, *A History of England During the Reign of George the Third,* vol. II (John W. Parker and Son, London, 1858) p. 202.

19. John Adams to Abigail Adams, September 18, 1774 [electronic edition]. *Adams Family Papers: An Electronic Archive.* Massachusetts Historical Society www.masshist.org/digitaladams.

20. *Ibid.,* John Adams to Abigail Adams, September 8, 1774.

21. John Adams to Elbridge Gerry, November 5, 1775, Edmund C. Burnett, ed., *Letters of Members of Continental Congress,* vol. I (Carnegie Institution, Washington, D.C., 1921), p. 249.

22. Silas Deane to Mrs. [Elizabeth] Deane, September 5–6, 1774. Conn. Hist. Soc. *Collections:* vol. II, p. 172; *See also* Edward C. Burnett, ed., *Letters of Members of the Continental Congress,* vol. I (Carnegie Institution, Washington, D.C., 1921), p. 11.

23. Samuel Adams to the Boston Committee of Correspondence, September 17, 1774, Harry Alonzo Cushing, ed., *The Writings of Samuel Adams,* vol. III (G.P. Putnam's Sons, New York, 1907), p. 154.

24. William P. Massey, *A History of England During the Reign of George The Third,* vol. II (John W. Parker and Son, London, 1858) p. 197.

25. Worthington Chauncey Ford, ed., *Some Papers Laid Before the Continental Congress, 1775* (Gov. Printing Office, Washington, D.C. 1905), p. 27.

26. Peyton returned from Virginia in September, 1775. Some delegates urged Peyton to step down. The issue was shortly resolved with Peyton's sudden death (from apoplexy) on October 22.

27. "A Century of lawmaking for a New Nation: U.S. Congressional Documents and Debates, 1774–1785," *Journals of the Continental Congress,* vol. 2, May 11, 1775 (Library of Congress, Washington D.C., 1904–1937) p. 22 (hereinafter *Journals of the Second Continental Congress*).

28. *Ibid.,* at 49.

29. *Journals of the Second Continental Congress,* vol. 5, at 435.

30. *Journals of the Continental Congress,* vol. 2, at 68–69. The letter was translated into French. A thousand copies were printed, sent to Canada, and "dispersed among the Inhabitants there." *Ibid.,* at 69.

31. *William and Mary College Quarterly Historical Magazine,* vol. 20 (Whittet & Shepperson, Richmond, VA, 1912), pp. 123–24.

32. *Journals of the Continental Congress,* vol. II, at 342–342.

33. *Journals of Continental Congress,* vol. 1, at 101–102.

34. *Journals of the Continental Congress,* vol. 2, at 208.

35. *Journals of the Continental Congress,* vol. 3, at 393.

36. *Ibid.,* at 427.

37. Lewis Harley, *The Life of Charles Thomson* (George W. Jacobs & Co., Philadelphia, 1900), p. 95.

38. Charles Francis Adams, *The Works of John Adams* (Charles C. Little and James Brown, Boston, 1856), p. 30.

39. John Adams autobiography, Part 1, *John Adams* (Feb. 17, 1776), sheet 31 of 53 [electronic edition]. *Adams Family Papers.* [electronic edition]. *Adams Family Papers: An Electronic Archive.* Massachusetts Historical Society www.masshist.org/digitaladams.

40. Moss Coit Tyler, ed., *Patrick* Henry (Houghton, Mifflin and Company, Boston, 1890), p. 97. *See also American Quarterly Review,* vol. 1, p. 30.

41. Lewis Harley, *The Life of Charles Thomson* (George W. Jacobs & Co., Philadelphia, 1900), p. 95.

42. *Journals of the Continental Congress,* vol. I, at 49–51.

43. "Galloway's Plan for the Union of Great Britain and the Colonies," www.ushistory. org; *See also* Julian B. Boyd, *Anglo-American Union: Joseph Galloway's Plan to Preserve the British Empire, 1774–1778* (Octagon Books, New York, 1970).

44. Edmund C. Burnett, ed., *Letters of Members of the Continental Congress,* vol. 1 (Carnegie Institution, Washington, D.C., 1921), p. 55.

45. William Franklin to the Earl of Dartmouth, Dec. 6, 1774. Chauncey Ford, ed., *Journals of the Continental Congress* (Gov. Printing Office, Washington, D.C.; 1904), p. 51 n. 1. Franklin had been given a copy of the plan by Galloway, a close personal friend, following the plan's rejection and expunging from the record, both actions that had outraged Galloway.

46. *Journals of the Continental Congress,* vol. 2, at 253.

47. "The Committee of Secret Correspondence: Instructions to William Bingham June 3, 1776," *Founders Online,* National Archives, www.fonders.archives.gov/ocuments/ Franklin [Original source: William B. Willcox, ed., *The Papers of Benjamin Franklin,* vol. 22 (Yale University Press, New Haven, 1982, pp. 43–447].

48. *Journals of the Continental Congress,* vol. 3, at 392.

49. *Journals of the Continental Congress,* vol. 4, at 345.

50. *Journals of Continental Congress,* vol. 26, at 331–332.

51. Peter Force, ed., "American Archives, Fifth Series," vol. II, at 818–819 (Statement of members Benjamin Franklin and Robert Morris; concurred in by Richard Henry Lee and William Hooper) (M. St. Claire Clark and Peter Force, Washington, D.C., 1851).

52. In 1778, Paine accused a member of Congress, Silas Deane, of trying to profit personally from the French aid. In substantiating his claim, Paine quoted from documents he had access to as the committee's secretary. Paine was fired the following year.

53. *Journals of the Continental Congress,* vol. 13, at 5.

54. John C. Rives, ed., "Abridgement of the Debates of Congress from 1789 to 1856," vol. vi (D. Appleton and Co., New York, 1858), pp. 493–494.

55. An earlier resolution adopted by Congress on March 27, 1818 called for the publication of the Secret Journals, but "except[ed] such parts of the foreign correspondence as the President may deem improper at this time to publish." The resolution of April 21, 1820 removed that exception.

Chapter 2

1. A draft of the Articles had been sketched out by Benjamin Franklin more than two years earlier. Franklin's draft was read in Congress on July 21, 1775, but was not acted upon. The colonies had not yet declared their independence from England. Franklin nonetheless hoped that the draft would serve to motivate the delegates to begin thinking about the present and future needs of America. He emphasized, though, that it was only a draft and that Congress could probably come up with a more perfect instrument.

2. "A Century of lawmaking for a New Nation: Congressional Documents and Debates, 1774–1875," *Letters of Delegates to Congress,* Thomas Rodney's Diary, March, 1781. (hereinafter *Letters of Delegates to Congress).*

3. Thomas Jefferson to Spencer Roane, September 6, 1819, Library of Congress, electronic format www.loc.gov/exhibits/Jefferson.

4. Articles of Confederation, Art. II.

5. Articles of Confederation, Art. IX, clause 7.

6. *Ibid.*

7. George Washington to the Rev. William Gordon, July 8, 1783, The University of Chicago Press, "The Founders' Constitution," vol. 1, ch. 7, doc. 6, www.press-pubs.uchicago.edu/founders/documents.

8. Thomas Jefferson to George Washington, March 15, 1784, The Avalon Project (Lillian Goldman Law Library, Yale Law School); *see also* Jared Sparks, ed. *Correspondence of the American Revolution,* vol. 4 (Little, Brown, and Company, Boston, 1853), pp. 62–63.

9. Jared Sparks, ed., "The North American Review," vol. xxv (Hilliard, Metcalf & Co., Cambridge, 1827). p. 254.

10. *The Federalist,* No. 22, "The Project Gutenberg EBook of the Federalist Papers."

11. *Massachusetts Sentinel,* April 11, 1787, in Merrill Jensen et al. eds., "The Documentary History of the Ratification of the Constitution" (State Historical Society of Wisconsin) at 13:79.

12. Charles C. Tansill, ed., *Documents Illustrative of the Formation of the Union of*

the American States (Government Printing Office, Washington, D.C., 1927): "Resolution of the General Assembly of Virginia Proposing a Joint Meeting of Commissioners from the States to Consider and Recommend a Federal Plan for Regulating Commerce" (January 21, 1786).

13. *Ibid.* (September 14, 1786).

14. Sydney Howard Gay, ed., *American Statesman: James Madison,* Vol. XII (Houghton, Mifflin and Company, New York, 1899), pp. 59–60.

15. "Report of the Annapolis Convention to the Legislatures of Virginia, Delaware, Pennsylvania, New Jersey, and New York," n. 12.

16. Galliard Hunt, ed., *The Writings of James Madison: 1803–1807,* James Madison to Noah Webster, October 12, 1804 (G.P. Putnam's Sons, New York, 1908), p. 163.

17. *Ibid.,* at 162.

18. Max Farrand, *The Fathers of the Constitution, a Chronicle of the Establishment of the Union* (Yale University Press, New Haven, 1921), p. 105.

19. George Washington to James Madison November 5, 1786, John P. Kaminski and Jill Adair McCaughan, eds., *A Great and Good Man: George Washington in the Eyes of His Contemporaries* (Rowan & Littlefield, Lanham, MD, 1989), p. 49.

20. George Washington to Henry Knox February 3, 1787, *Founders Online,* National Archives, www.founders.archives.gov/documents/Washington.

21. Joseph C. Clayton, "The American Lawyer," vol. 15 (Corporation Legal Manual Company, New York, 1907), p. 19.

22. Many of Shay's followers were Revolutionary War veterans who had received little in the way of pay or expense reimbursement for their military service. Merchants began to initiate legal proceedings (often foreclosures) against them in order to collect the debts they were owed. Merchants and banks also began refusing further credit or loans, while merchants began demanding payment in cash for any future goods or services. This demand for hard currency eventually placed the average borrower under unrealistic payment schedules, given the small amount of cash in circulation. Shay and his followers demanded that Massachusetts begin printing more money in order to alleviate that cash shortage.

23. Thomas Jefferson was of a different view. In a letter to James Madison about Shays' Rebellion, Jefferson said that "I hold that a little rebellion now and then is a good thing, and as necessary in the political world as storms in the physical." Thomas Jefferson to James Madison, June 30, 1787. *See* J.P. Gordy, *A History of Political Parties in the United States,* vol. 1 (Henry Holt and Company, New York, 1900), p. 134.

24. Stephen Higginson to Gen. Henry Knox, November 25, 1786, Michael J. Klarman, *The Framers' Coup: The Making of the United States Constitution* (Oxford University Press, New York, 2016), p. 96.

25. George Washington to Henry Knox, December 26, 1786, John C. Fitzpatrick, ed., *The Writings of George Washington,* vol. 29 (Government Printing Office, Washington, D.C., 1939), p. 121.

26. *Ibid.,* 126.

27. *Boston Independent Chronicle,* February 15, 1787.

28. *Charleston* (MA) *American Recorder,* March 16, 1787.

29. *Journals of the Continental Congress,* vol. 32, at 74.

30. *Ibid.*

Chapter 3

1. George Mason to George Mason, Jr., May 20,1787, Online Library of Liberty, XV, www.oll.libertyfund.org/titles/1787 (hereinafter Online Library of Liberty); source: Max Farrand, ed., *The Records of the Federal Convention of 1787,* vol. 3 (Yale University Press, New Haven, 1911).

2. James Madison to Thomas Jefferson, May 15, 1787, *Ibid.,* at IX.

3. George Washington to George Augustine Washington, May 17, 1787, ConSource. www.onsource.org/document/george-washington-to-george-augustine-washington;

source: James H. Hudson, ed., *Supplement to Max Farrand's The Records of The Federal Constitution of 1787* (Yale University Press, New Haven, 1987).

4. George Washington to Arthur Lee, May 20, 1787, Online Library of Liberty at XIV.

5. The Convention did not meet on: (1) Sundays; (2) between May 15 and May 24; (3) on July 3 and 4; and (4) between July 27 and August 25. John R. Vile, *The Constitutional Convention of 1787; A Comprehensive Encyclopedia of America's Founding* (ABC-CLIO, Santa Barbara, CA, 2005), pp. 33–34.

6. John Marshall, *The Life of George Washington, Commander in Chief of the American Forces*, vol. 2 (C.P. Wayne, 1805), p. 125.

7. Charles Warren, *The Making of the Constitution* (Little, Brown & Co., Boston, 1937), p. 132, fn. 1.

8. James Madison to James Monroe, June 10, 1787, Michael Klarman, *The Framers' Coup: The Making of the Constitution* (Oxford University Press, Oxford, 2016), n. 30.

9. Edmund Randolph to Beverly Randolph, May 27, 1787, William D. Palmer, ed., *Calendar of Virginia State Papers from January 1, 1785 to July 2, 1789*, vol. 4 (Legislature of Virginia, Richmond, 1884), pp. 290–291.

10. Max Farrand, ed., *The Records of the Federal Convention of 1787*, vol. 3 (Yale University Press, New Haven, 1911), pp. 557–559 [hereinafter *Farrand's Records*].

11. James McGregor Burns, *Transforming Leadership* (Grove Press, New York, 2003), p. 83.

12. John Adams to James Sullivan, May 26, 1776, Robert J. Taylor, ed., *Papers of John Adams* (Massachusetts Historical Society, 1979), pp. 209–213.

13. *Farrand's Records*, vol. 3., "Report Delivered by Luther Martin to Maryland State Legislature," App. A (December 28, 1787).

14. William Temple Franklin, *Memoirs of the Life and Writings of Benjamin Franklin* (London, 1818), p. 197.

15. *Pennsylvania Packet and Daily Advertiser*, May 14, 1787, cited in John P. Kamkinski and Jill Adair McCaughan, *A Great and Good Man: George Washington in the Eyes of His Contemporaries* (Madison Hope Publishers, Madison, WI, 1989), p. 83.

16. George Washington to Edmund Randolph, March 28, 1787, Jared Sparks, ed., *The Writings of George Washington* (Russell, Odiorne, and Metcalf, Boston, 1835), p. 244.

17. Max Farrand, *The Faming of the Constitution of the United States* (Yale University Press, New Haven, 1913), p. 66.

18. Daniel N. Hoffman, *Governmental Secrecy And The Founding Fathers: A Study in Constitutional Controls* (Greenwood Press, Westport, CT, 1981), p. 21.

19. *Farrand's Records*, vol. 1, p. 17.

20. In addition to providing a measure of privacy, the closed draperies also acted as a barrier against the swarming flies from a nearby livery.

21. Washington Irving, ed., *The Life of Georg Washington*, vol. 4 (Cosimo Classics, New York, 2005), pp. 105–106.

22. Jonathan Elliot, ed., *Debates on the Adoption of the Federal Constitution*, vol. 1 (Burt Franklin, New York, 1888), p. 143.

23. Joseph C. Morton, *Shapers of The Great Debate at The Constitutional Convention of 1787* (Greenwood Press, Westport, CT, 2006), p. 48, n. 1 [citing *Farrand's Records*, vol. 1, pp. 13,15].

24. Luther Martin's Speech Before the Maryland House of Representatives, January 27, 1788, Jonathan Elliot, ed., *Debates in the Several State Conventions on the Adoption of the Federal Constitution*, vol. 1 (J.B. Lippincott & Co., Washington, D.C., 1863), p. 345.

25. James H. Hutson, ed., *Supplement to Max Farrand's The Records of The Federal Convention of 1787* (Yale University Press, New Haven, 1987) p. 25 (hereinafter *Farrand Supplement*); George Washington Diary, May 28, 1787, George Washington Papers at Library of Congress, 1741–1799.

26. John P. Kaminski, *Secrecy and the Constitutional Convention*, p. 11, n. 11 (University of Wisconsin, Madison, 2005, p. 11, n. 11).

27. Alexander Hamilton (*Amicus*), *National Gazette*, September 11, 1792.

28. Gordon S. Wood, *The Creation of the American Republic 1776–1787* (University of North Carolina Press, Chapel Hill, 1969), pp. 142–143.

29. *Farrand Supplement*, p. 67.

30. *Ibid.*

31. James Madison to Thomas Jefferson, July 18, 1787, R. Worthington, ed., *Letters and Other Writings of James Madison*, vol. 1 (New York, 1884), p. 334.

32. George Mason to George Mason, Jr., June 1, 1787, *Farrand's Records*, vol. 3, pp. 32–33.

33. Alexander Martin to Gov. Richard Caswell, July 27, 1787, *Farrand's Records*, vol. 3, p. 64.

34. Jude M. Pfister, ed., *"Charting an American Republic: The Origins and Writing of the Federalist Papers* (McFarland & Company, Jefferson, NC, 2016), p. 127.

35. Edward Carrington to James Madison, June 13, 1787, Robert A. Rutland et al. eds., *The Papers of James Madison*, vol. 10 (University of Chicago Press, Chicago, 1977), pp. 52–53.

36. Edmund Pendleton to James Madison, August 12, 1787, David B. Mattern et al. eds., *The Papers of James Madison*, vol. 17 (University of Virginia Press, Charlottesville, VA, 1991), pp. 518–519.

37. Richard Henry Lee to Arthur Lee, July 14, 1778, Moncure Daniel Conway, *Omitted Chapters of History Disclosed in the Life and Papers of Edmund Randolph* (G.P. Putnam's Sons, New York, 1888), p. 86.

38. Madison notes include an introduction describing how he prepared them. "In pursuance of the task I had assumed I chose a seat in front of the presiding member, with the other members on my right & left hands. In this favorable position for hearing all that passed, I noted in terms legible & in abbreviations & marks intelligible to myself what was read from the chair or spoken by the members; and losing not a moment unnecessarily between adjournment and reassembling of the convention I was enabled to write out my daily notes ... in the extent and form presented in my own hand on my files." 1 *Farrand's Records*, vol. 1, p. xvi (quoting Madison's introduction).

39. The Rev. James Madison to James Madison, August 1, 1787, Robert A. Rutland et al. eds. (University of Chicago Press, Chicago, 1977), pp. 120–121.

40. Madison to Jefferson (Philadelphia, July 18, 1787), *Ibid.*, pp. 105–106.

41. Luther Martin's Speech Before the Maryland House of Representatives, January 27, 1788, Jonathan Elliot, ed., *Debates in the Several State Conventions on the Adoption of the Federal Constitution*, vol. 1 (J.B. Lippincott & Co., Washington, 1836), p. 345.

42. *A Plebeian,* "An Address to the People of the State of New York" (April 17, 1788). The twenty-six page pamphlet was reprinted in four installments in Philadelphia's *Independent Gazetteer* on May 23, 24, 27, and 28.

43. Thomas Jefferson to John Adams, August 30, 1787, *The Diplomatic Correspondence of the United States*, vol. 2 (Blaire & Rives, Washington, D.C., 1837), p. 83–84.

44. James Madison to Thomas Jefferson, June 6, 1787, Sidney M. Milkis and Michael Nelson, eds. *The American Presidency* (CQ Press, Los Angeles, 2016), ch. 1, n. 26.

45. James Madison to Thomas Jefferson, June 6, 1787, Robert A. Rutland et al. eds. (University of Chicago Press, Chicago, 1977), pp. 105–106.

46. *Farrand Supplement*, pp. 41–42.

47. Nicholas Gilman to Joseph Gilman, July 31, 1787, "Annual Report of the American Historical Association," vol. 1 (Government Printing Office, Washington, D.C., 1903), p. 91.

48. Nathaniel Gorham to Nathan Dane, June 3, 1787, www.consource.org/document/nathaniel-gorham-to-nathan-dane-1787-6-3.

49. William Blount to John Gray Blount, June 15, 1787, *Farrand Supplement*, p. 76.

50. *Pennsylvania Herald*, June 2, 1787.

51. *Pennsylvania Journal and Weekly Advertiser*, October 6, 1787.

52. John Church Hamilton, *Life of Alexander Hamilton*, vol. 3 (Houghton, Osgood and Co., Boston, 1879), p. 330.

53. *Pennsylvania Herald*, August 18, 1787.

54. Henry D. Gilpin, *The Papers of James Madison*, vol. 3 (Langley & O'Sullivan, Washington, D.C., 1840), p. 1294.

55. *Ibid.*

56. *Ibid.*, at 1547.

57. Louis Fisher, *Presidential Spending Power* (Princeton University Press, Princeton, 1975), p. 203.

58. Harry D. Gilpin, *The Papers of James Madison*, vol. 1 (J & H.G. Langley, Washington, D.C., 1841), p. 1580.

59. *Ibid.*, at 1851.

60. J. of Senate, 1st Sess., September 8, 1789, p. 74.

61. Act of Sept. 2, 1789, Ch. 12, sec. 4.

62. Act of Sept. 29, 1789, Ch. 23 sec. 1.

63. 2 *Annals. of Cong.*, December 30, 1791 (Gales and Seaton, Washington, D.C., 1849), p. 300.

64. *Ibid.*

65. The Committee of Style and Arrangement consisted of Alexander Hamilton, James Madison, William Samuel Johnson, Gouveneur Morris, and Rufus King.

66. "Papers of Dr. James McHenry on the Federal Constitution, September 15, 1787," The Avalon Project (Lillian Goldman Law Library, Yale Law School, New Haven). Text and notes reprinted from the "American Historical Review (Washington, D.C., 1905–1906), pp. 596–618.

67. George Washington, Diary, September 15, 1787. Donald Jackson and Dorothy Twohig, eds. "The Diaries of George Washington, July 1786–December 1789," vol. v (University of Virginia Press, Charlottesville, 1979).

68. As Franklin was waiting to sign the Constitution, he studied the carving on the back of George Washington's chair—a carving of half a sun. He stared at it for a minute and then said, "I have often looked at that picture behind the president without being able to tell whether it was a rising or setting sun. Now at length I have the happiness to know that it is indeed a rising, not a setting sun." The Avalon Project (Lillian Goldman Law Library, Yale Law School, New Haven); source: Madison's "Notes on the Debates in the Federal Convention, September 17, 1787.

69. Benjamin Franklin to Nathan Gorham, November 14, 1787. Franklin told Gorham that "I have hitherto refused to permit its Publication, but your judgment that it may do good weighs much more with me than my own Temples."

70. "America's Founding Fathers—Delegates to the Constitutional Convention". The U.S. National Archives and Records Administration (Washington, D.C.).

71. Two of New York's three delegates, John Lansing, Jr., and Robert Yates, left the Convention because of their opposition to the direction the proceedings were taking, leaving only Alexander Hamilton to represent the state, but without the required quorum for voting. Washington's diary entry for the day, Monday, September 17, read: "Met in Convention when the Constitution received the unanimous assent of 11 states and Colonel Hamilton from New York."

72. George Washington, Diary, September 17, 1787, *Founders Online*, National Archives, www.founders.archives.gov/documents/Washington.

73. *Journals of the Continental Congress*, vol. 33, at 548.

74. *See* U.S. Constitution, art. VIII (setting forth the ratification process).

75. Charles R. King, ed., *The Life and Correspondence of Rufus King*, vol. 1 (G.P. Putnam's Sons, New York, 1894), p. 232.

76. *Journals of the Continental Congress*, vol. 33, at 543.

77. *Founders' Constitution*, "Article 2, Section 2, Clauses 2 and 3," vol. 4, Doc. 22 (University of Chicago Press, Chicago, 1787).

78. *Ibid.*

79. Dr. James McHenry, Diary, September 17, 1787, The Avalon Project (Lillian Goldman Law Library, Yale Law School, New Haven).

80. *Ibid.*, Benjamin Franklin, September, 17, 1787.

81. John C. Hamilton, ed., *The Works of Alexander Hamilton*, vol. vii (Charles S, Francis & Company, New York, 1851), p. 32.

82. *Farrand* Supplement, p. 315.

83. "Centinel: No. XIV, *Independent Gazetteer*, Philadelphia, February 5, 1778.

84. Jonathan Elliot, ed., *Debates on the Adoption of the Federal Constitution*, vol. v (Washington, D.C., 1845), p. 558.

85. National Archives, "Records of the Continental Congress and Confederation Congress and the Constitutional Convention," Record Group 360 *et seq.* (Washington, D.C.).

86. John Quincy Adams to James Madison, October 22, 1818; John Church Hamilton, ed., *Life of Alexander Hamilton: A History of the Republic of the United States*, vol. 3 (Houghton, Osgood and Company, Boson, 1879), *note* to page 347.

87. *Ibid.*

88. James Madison to John Q. Adams, November 28, 1818, Online Library of Liberty, www.oll.libertyfund.org p. 301.

89. William Jackson to George Washington, September 17, 1787, W.W. Abbot, ed., "The Papers of George Washington: Confederation Series 329," vol. 5 (University of Virginia Press, Charlottesville, 1997).

90. Jared Sparks, "The North American Review, vol. 25 (Boston, 1827), p. 251.

91. Madison was not entirely consistent, however. In February, 1791, during a debate in the House of Representatives concerning the chartering of a national bank, Madison said "how [he] well recalled that the power to grant charters of incorporation had been proposed in the Great Convention and rejected." Former Convention delegate Elbridge Gerry of Massachusetts (who was also serving in the first Congress) criticized Madison for using his memory of those debates as authority for future political guidance. Madison agreed with Gerry that the better course would be not to divulge the proceedings of the Convention. *Annals of Cong.* vol. 2, February 2, 1791 (Gales and Seaton, Washington, D.C., 1834), p. 1945.

92. *Annals of Cong.* vol. 4, April 6, 1796 (Gales and Seaton, Washington, D.C., 1855), p. 1855.

93. "The North American Review," vol. xxv (Frederick T. Gray, Boston, October, 1827), p. 252.

94. George Washington, "Message to the House of Representatives Declining to Submit Diplomatic Instructions and Correspondence," March 30, 1796.

95. Jonathan Elliot, ed., *Debates on the Adoption of the Federal Constitution*, vol. 5, (Washington, D.C., 1845), p. 553; Joseph C. Morton, *Shapers of the Great Debate at the Constitutional Convention of 1787* (Greenwood Press, Westport, CT, 2006), p. 203.

Chapter 4

1. *A Plebeian*, "An Address to the People of the State of New York (April 17, 1788).

2. John K. Alexander, *The Selling of The Constitution: A History of News Coverage* (Madison House, Madison, WI, 1990), p. 392, n. 2.

3. Statement of William Davie, Debate in North Carolina Ratifying Convention (July 24, 1788); Jonathan Elliot, ed., *The Debates on the Several State Conventions on the Adoption of the Federal Constitution*, vol. iv (Washington, D.C., 1836), p. 23.

4. Jerry Holmes, ed., *Thomas Jefferson, A Chronology of His Thoughts* (Rowan & Littlefield, Lanham, MD, 2002), p. 258; Edwin Morris Betts and James Adam Bear, Jr., eds., *The Family Letters of Thomas Jefferson* (University of Virginia Press, Charlottesville, 1966), p. 415.

5. Herbert J. Storing, ed., *The Complete Anti-Federalist*, vol. 1 (University of Chicago Press, Chicago, 1981), 3.6.9, p. 70.

6. *Centinel*, No. II, *Freeman's Journal* (Philadelphia, October 20, 1787); John P. Kaminski, *Secrecy at the Constitutional Convention* (University of Wisconsin, Madison, 2005), p. 19 and n. 30.

7. Robert Allen Rutland, *The Ordeal of the Constitution: The Antifederalists and the Ratification Struggles of 177–1788* (University of Oklahoma Press, Norman, 1966), p. 38.

8. William H. Riker, *The Strategy of Rhetoric: Campaigning for the American Constitution* (Yale University Press, New Haven, 1996), pp. 26–28.

9. John P. Kaminski and Gaspare J. Saladino, *Commentaries on the Constitution, Public and Private*, vol. 1 (State Historical Society of Wisconsin, Madison, 1981), p. 243.

10. *Centinel* No. 4, *Independent Gazetteer* (Philadelphia, November 30, 1787).

11. *Centinel* No. II, *Freeman's Journal* (Philadelphia, October 24, 1787).

12. John P. Kaminski and Gaspare J. Saladino, *Commentaries on the Constitution, Public and Private,* vol. 1 (State Historical Society of Wisconsin, Madison, 1981), p. 215.

13. Kidd, Thomas J., *Patrick Henry: First Among Patriots* (Basic Books, New York, 2011). p. 183. The rat that Henry "smelt" was the notion of replacing the Articles of Confederation with a new constitution creating a strong national government.

14. Jonathan Elliot, ed., *The Debates in the Several State Conventions on the Adoption of the Federal Constitution,* vol. III (J.P. Lippincott & Co., Philadelphia, 1876), p. 170.

15. George Clinton, New York Ratifying Convention, July 11, 1788, "The Founders Constitution," vol. 1, Ch. 8, Document 39 (University of Chicago Press, Chicago, 1981).

16. Lynn Hudson Parsons, *John Quincy Adams* (Rowman & Littlefield Publishers, Lanham, MD, 1998). p. 37.

17. *Annals of Congress,* vol. 1 (Gales and Seaton, Washington, D.C., 1834), p. viii.

18. The *Federalist* No. 64, *Independent Journal,* March 5, 1788.

19. Jonathan Elliot, ed. *Debates, Resolutions, and Other Proceedings of the Convention of Virginia,* vol. II (Washington, D.C., 1828), p. 339.

20. Gen. George Washington to Col. Elias Dayton, July 26, 1777; ed. John C. Fitzpatrick, *The Writings of George Washington* vol. viii (Government Printing Office, 1933), p. 478–479.

21. Act of July 27, 1789, 1 Stat. 28, Sec. 1.

22. The *Federalist* No. 84, "Certain General and Miscellaneous Objections to the Constitution Considered and Answered," July 16, 1788 (Lillian Goldman Law Library, Yale Law School, New Haven, 2008).

23. Speech of Patrick Henry in Virginia Convention (June 5, 1788); The Founders' Constitution, vol. 1, ch. 14, document 39 (University of Chicago, Chicago, 1987).

24. John P. Kamanski, ed., *The Documentary History of the Ratification of the Constitution Digital Edition,* Speech of Patrick Henry in Virginia Convention (June 17, 1788) (University of Virginia Press, Charlottesville, 2009).

25. J. of Senate, 1st Sess., September 8, 1789 (Gales and Seaton, vol. 1, p. 74).

26. Jonathan Elliott, ed. *The Debates in the Several Conventions on the Adoption of the Federal Constitution,* vol. 1 (New York Ratifying Convention, July 26, 1778) (Washington, D.C.), p. 330.

27. James Madison to Edmond Randolph, August 21, 1789; Gaillard Hunt, ed., *The Writings of James* Madison, vol. 5 (G.P. Putnam's Sons, New York, 1904), pp. 417–418.

Chapter 5

1. Pennsylvania Constitution, Sec. 13 (Sept. 28, 1776).

2. New York Constitution, Art. XV (April 20, 1777).

3. Gordon Lloyd, ed., *James Madison's Notes of Debates in the Federal Convention of 1787* (Ashbrook University, Ashbrook, OH, 2014), p. 331.

4. Gaillard Hunt, ed., *Journals of the Continental Congress,* vol. xxiv (Government Printing Office, Washington, D.C., 1922), p. 313.

5. *Ibid.* at 313–15.

6. Paul Blumenthal, "The History of Transparency—Part I: Opening the Channels of Information to the People in the 18th Century" (Sunlight Foundation, Washington, D.C., March 23, 2010).

7. *Annals of Congress,* U.S. Senate, 3d Congress, 2d Session, January 27, 1795 (Gales and Seaton, Washington, D.C., 1855), p. 1146.

8. Roy Swanstrom, *A Dissertation on the First Fourteen Years Of The Upper Legislative Branch,* U.S. Senate Bicentennial Publication No. 4 (Washington, D.C., 1988), p. 241, n. 17.

9. *Annals of Congress,* House of Representatives, Eighth Congress, Second Session, November 7 and 8, 1804 (Gales and Seaton, Washington, D.C., 1852), p. 680.

10. Annals of Congress (Gales and Seaton, Washington, D.C., 1849), p. 348.

11. *Ibid.,* at 414.

12. On March 4, 1789, there were eleven states that had ratified the Constitution and

which were thus eligible to send a delegation to Congress. Only five states, however, were present on March 4. Given the absence of a quorum, the Senate adjourned from day-to-day until April 6, when Richard Henry Lee, from Virginia, arrived and took his seat, thereby establishing a six-state quorum. Letters had been sent to the absent Senators on March 11 and March 18, "requesting their immediate attending," and expressing the hope that "you will not suffer our, and the public expectations, to be disappointed." Senate Journal, First Session, pp. 5–6 (March 4, 1789) (Washington, D.C., 1820).

13. United States Senate, Senate Historical Office; source, Roy Swanstrom, *A Dissertation on the First Fourteen Years Of The Upper Legislative Branch*, U.S. Senate Bicentennial Publication No. 4 (Washington, D.C., 1988).

14. Executive Journal of Senate, vol. 1, p. 19 (August 21, 1789).

15. Rule 11 of the Rules of the First United States Senate; *Journal of William Mcclay*, Edgar S. Mcclay, ed. (D. Appleton and Co., New York, 1890), p. xiv.

16. *Ibid*. Rule 16.

17. An excellent discussion of the origin of the title "President" may be found in Randolph Keim, *Society in Washington* (Harrisburg Publishing Co., Washington, D.C., 1887), pp. 31–33.

18. Swift, Elaine, *The Making of an American Senate: Reconstitutive Change in Congress, 1787–1841* (University of Michigan Press, Ann Harbor, 1996), pp. 58–59.

19. *Annals of Congress*, Senate, First Congress, First Session, May 19, 1789 (Gales and Seaton, Washington, D.C., 1834), p. 39.

20. *Ibid.*

21. *Ibid.* at 44.

22. *Gazette of the United States*, March 17, 1792.

23. Robert C. Byrd. ed. Mary Sharon Hall, *The Senate 1789–1989: Addresses on the History of the United States Senate*, vol. 1 (Washington, D.C., Government Printing Office 1988). p. 27.

24. John C. Fitzpatrick, ed., *The Writings of George Washington*, vol. 30 (George Washington Bicentennial Commission, Washington, D.C., 1939), p. 363.

25. *National Gazette*, February 13, 1793.

26. *National Gazette*, August. 8, 1792, quoting the *National Asylum*.

27. Samuel E. Forman, "Political Activities of Philip Freneau," in "The Johns Hopkins University Studies in Historical and Political Science," vol. XX (Johns Hopkins Press, Baltimore, 1902), p. 528.

28. *Annals of Congress*, Senate, First Session, April 29, 1790 (Gales & Seaton, Washington D.C., 1820), p. 135.

29. *Ibid.* at 287.

30. *Ibid.*; for further commentary *see* Francis Lieber and Theodore Dwight Woolsey, *On Civil Liberty and Self-Government* (J.B. Lippincott and Co., London, 1888), pp. 139–140.

31. United States Senate, "The Senate in Session," Senate Historical Office Online; Mildred Amer, "Secret Sessions of Congress: A Brief Historical Overview," Congressional Research Service: Library of Congress (Washington, D.C., 2004), p. 2.

32. Reported, e.g., in *Gazette of the United States*, March 17, 1792; *also* Roy Swanstrom, United States Senate, Senate Historical Office; *A Dissertation on the First Fourteen Years Of The Upper Legislative Branch*, U.S. Senate Bicentennial Publication No. 4 (Washington D.C., 1988), p. 243, n. 25.

33. McPherson, pp. 10–20.

34. Justice James Iredell to John Hay, April 14, 1791, Griffith J. McRee, *Life and Correspondence of James Iredell*, vol. 2 (D. Appleton and Company, New York, 1857), p. 328.

35. Journal of the Senate, April 18, 1792, p. 429.

36. Journal of the Senate, January 3, 1793, p. 467.

37. *Ibid.*

38. "Compilation of Senate Election Cases From 1789 To 1913," pp. 162–63, Senate Doc. 1063 (Washington. D.C., Government Printing Office, 1913).

39. Journal of the Senate, February 11, 1794, p. 43.

40. The arguments that Senator Martin made summed up all of the arguments that

had been made over the past five years in support of an open door policy: "[t]he mode adopted by the Senate of publishing their journals, and Extracts from them, in newspapers, is not adequate for the purpose of circulating satisfactory information. When the principle and designs of individual members are withheld from the public, responsibility is destroyed, which, on the publicity of their deliberations, would be more influential over the other branch of the Legislature: abuse of power, and mal-administration in office more easily destroyed and corrected; jealousies rising in the public mind from secret legislation, prevented; and greater confidence placed by our fellow citizens in the National Government, by which their lives, liberties, and properties, are to be served and protected." Journal of the Senate, January 16, 1794, p. 22.

41. John Adams to Abigail Adams, February 23, 1794; "Adams Family Papers: An Electronic Archive," Massachusetts Historical Society.

42. Journal of the Senate, December 9, 1795, p. 197.

43. Robert C. Byrd, "The Senate 1789–1989, Addresses on the History of the United States Senate," vol. 1, ed. Mary Sharon Hall (Government Printing Office, 1988), p. 128.

44. The United States suffered several costly defeats during the War of 1812, including the capture and burning of the nation's capital, Washington, D.C., on August 24, 1814. American troops were successful in turning back British invasions in New York, Baltimore and New Orleans, however, thereby forcing Great Britain to the peace table. Hostilities ended with the signing of the Treaty of Ghent on December 24, 1814. The treaty was formally ratified by the Senate on February 16, 1815.

45. *See* Christopher M. Davis, "Secret Sessions of the House and Senate," Table 2 (Congressional Research Service, December 30, 2014).

46. *Ibid.* at Table 1.

47. *See* Christopher M. Davis, "Secret Sessions of the House and Senate: Authority, Confidentiality, and Frequency" (Congressional Research Service, December 30, 2014).

48. 145 *Cong. Rec.*, H1386–87 (daily ed. Feb. 9, 1999).

49. The old Senate chamber is located north of the Capitol rotunda on the second floor of the Capitol. It was home to the Senate from 1810 to 1859, and then to the Supreme Court from 1860 to 1935. The chamber was renovated during the Bicentennial in 1976 and now is preserved as a museum and an occasional meeting place for the Senate.

50. Wilson, Woodrow, *Congressional Government: A Study in American Politics* (Johns Hopkins University, Baltimore, 1885).

51. The Treaty of Mortefontaine brought to a close the hostilities between the United States and France in the Quasi-War which had been fought primarily in the Caribbean.

52. *See, e.g.,* Removal of Injunction of Secrecy—Treaty Document No. 108-2, Motion of Senator Orin Hatch (Cong. Rec., vol. 149, no. 25, S2227, Feb. 11, 2003).

53. Madison's Notes, July 20, 1787, The Avalon Project (Lillian Goldman Law Library, Yale Law School, New Haven, 2008); Alex Simpson, ed., "A Treatise on Federal Impeachments" (The Law Association of Philadelphia, 1916), p. 11.

54. *See* U.S. Const. Art. II, Sec. 4.

55. United States Senate, "Application Of Cable News Network For A Determination That The Closure Of The Proceedings Violates The First Amendment To The United States Constitution" (January 29, 1999).

56. CNN.com (January 29, 1999).

Chapter 6

1. George A. Peeks, Jr., ed., *The Political Writings of John Adams* (reprinted by Hackett Publishing Company, Indianapolis, IN, 2003), p. 13.

2. Thomas Jefferson to Edward Carrington, January 16, 1787, "The Founders Constitution," vol. 5, Amendment 1, University of Chicago, www.press-pubs.uchicago.edu/founders (1987).

3. Francis Lieber, Theodore Woolsey, ed., "On Civil Liberty and Self-Government" (J.B. Lippincott Company, London, 1888) p. 128.

4. Michael MacDonagh, *The Book of Parliament* (Isbister and Co., London, 1897),

p. 313. It was only by bribing a doorkeeper that a publisher could obtain a seat for his reporter in the "strangers" gallery. Even then a reporter had to take his notes by stealth. If he was observed from the floor taking notes he ran he risk of being expelled or brought by the sergeant-at-arms to the Bar and charged with violating the House of Commons rule against the publication of its proceedings. It was not until 1834 that a small gallery was set aside for reporters.

5. John Adams to Abigail Adams, April 19, 1789, "Adams Family Papers: An Electronic Archive," Massachusetts Historical Society.

6. Elizabeth G. McPherson, "Reporting the Debates of Congress," *Quarterly Journal of Speech*, vol. 28, Issue 2 (1942), pp. 141–142 [Taylor & Francis Online, 2009].

7. The *Pennsylvania Gazette* was the most prominent of America's newspapers, often referred to as the *New York Times* of the 18th century. The paper was partly owned and published by Benjamin Franklin from 1730 to 1748.

8. Journals of the Continental Congress, vol. 23, at 678 (October 18, 1782).

9. Cong. Rec. vol. II, 4676 (June 8, 1874) (statement of James L. Alcorn).

10. Richard R. John, *Spreading the News: The American Postal System from Franklin to Morse* (Harvard University Press, Cambridge, 1995), p. 32.

11. *Annals of Congress*, December 28, 1791 (Gales and Seaton, Washington, D.C., 1849), p. 290.

12. Dr. Benjamin Rush to Dr. Richard Price, April 22, 1786, "Proceedings of the Massachusetts Historical Society," vol. xvii (1903), p. 341.

13. "The Federalist Papers, The Federalist No. 51, February. 6, 1788 (Lillian Goldman Law Library, Yale Law School, New Haven, 2008).

14. Benjamin Rush, "Address to the People of the United States," *American Museum*, vol. I (January,1787), pp. 9–10.

15. *New Hampshire Spy*, February 16, 1787.

16. Alexis De Toqueville, *Democracy in America*, "Liberty of the Press in the United States," ch. XI (Saunders and Otley, London, 1935).

17. *Annals of Congress*, December 28, 1791 (Gales and Seaton, Washington, D.C., 1849), p. 289.

18. James Madison to Edmund Pendleton, December 6, 1792, National Archives, Founders Online at *www.founders.archives.gov/documents/Madison* Original source: Robert A. Rutland, ed., *The Papers of James Madison*, vol. 14 (University of Virginia Press, Charlottesville, 1983), pp. 420–421.

19. George Washington: "Fifth Annual Message," December 3, 1793. Online by Gerhard Peters and John T. Woolley, *The American Presidency Project*. http://www.presidency.ucsb.edu.

20. The *Annals* were first known as *The Debates and Proceedings in the Congress of the United States*.

21. *Annals of Congress*, March 7, 1796 (Gales and Seaton, Washington, D.C., 1855), p. 426.

22. *Register of Debates in Congress*, Preface, vol. 1 *Preface* (Gales and Seaton, Washington, D.C., 1825).

23. United States Senate, Senate Historical Office, *Reporters of Debate and the Congressional Record*, www.Senate.gov/artandhistory.

24. The daily edition of the *Congressional Record* is usually available the day after each day's session. The *Record* is distributed to more than 4,000 subscribers in legislative offices, government agencies, and depository libraries. It is also available online.

25. History, Art & Archives, U.S. House of Representatives, "Radio and Congress: Connecting the House to the Home."

26. Gweneth L. Jackaway, *Media at War: Radio Challenges to the Newspapers, 1929–1939* (Praeger Publishers, Westport, CN, 1995), pp. 129–130.

27. "The Billboard" March 30, 1946, p. 7.

28. United States Senate Historical Office, Notable Senate Investigations, "Special Committee on Organized Crime in Interstate Commerce" (Washington, D.C.).

29. *Ibid.*

30. Press release, "C-SPAN at 34," March 19, 2013.

31. "C-SPAN Denied Cameras in the House of Representatives, Again," *Washington Post* staff writer, Rachel Weiner; February 4, 2011.

Chapter 7

1. George Washington to Robert Hunter Morris (Gov. of Pa.), January 1, 1756, National Archives, Founders Online at www.founders.archives.gov/documents/Washington Original source: W.W. Abbot, ed., *The Papers of George Washington* Colonial Series, vol. 2 (University of Virginia Press, Charlottesville, 1983), pp. 249–250.

2. *Annals of Congress*, January 26, 1790 (Gales and Seaton, Washington, D.C., 1834), p. 1123.

3. *Ibid.*, at 1129 (Jan. 27, 1790).

4. *Ibid.*, at 1100 (Jan. 19, 1790.

5. *Ibid.*, at 1101.

6. *Ibid.*, at 1119 (Jan. 26, 1790).

7. *Ibid.*, at 1126 (Jan. 27, 1790).

8. *Ibid.*, 1119 (Jan. 26, 1790).

9. William Maclay, Edgar S. Maclay, ed., "Journal of William Maclay," Ch. X (D. Appleton and Co., New York, 1890), p 304 (digitized by Cornel University).

10. Thomas Jefferson to Alexander Hamilton, June 24, 1792, National Archives, Founders Online at www.founders.archives.gov/documents/Jefferson. Original source: Charleston T. Cullen, ed., *The Papers of Thomas Jefferson* vol. 23 (Princeton University Press, Princeton, 1990), pp. 62–63.

11. Thomas Jefferson to James Monroe, January 8, 1804, Thomas Jefferson, *The Works of Thomas Jefferson*, vol. X (Cosimo Classics, New York, 2010), p. 61.

12. Thomas Jefferson to Albert Gallatin, August 30, 1880, "Papers of Albert Gallatin," National Archives, Founders Online, "Papers of Albert Gallatin," www.founders.archives.gov/documents/Jefferson.

13. Thomas Jefferson to George Washington, April 24, 1790, National Archives, Founders Online at www.founders.archives.gov/documents/Washington. Original source: Dorothy Twohig et al. eds. *The Papers of George Washington*, Presidential Series, vol. 5 (University of Virginia Press, Charlottesville, 1996), pp. 342–346.

14. Stephen F. Knott (guest columnist) "America Was Founded on Secrets and Lies," *Pittsburgh Post-Gazette* (April 24, 2016).

15. *The Congressional Globe*, April 10, 1846 (Blair & Rives, Washington, D.C.), p. 637.

16. *Ibid.*

17. President James K. Polk, Special Message to the House of Representatives, April 20, 1846. Online by John Wolley and Gerhard Peters, *The American Presidency Project*, www.presidency.ucsb.edu.

18. *Ibid.*

19. "Mystery Town Cradled Bomb: 75,000 in Oak Ridge, Tenn." Worked Hard and Wondered About Their Secret Job," *Life* (Aug. 20, 1945), p. 111 (retrieved Feb. 12, 2016).

20. Gen. Leslie M. Groves, *It Can Now Be Told: The Story of the Manhattan Project* (Da Capo Press, New York, 1962), pp. 362–363.

21. "The CIA's Secret Funding and the Constitution," Yale Law Journal, 84 Yale L.J. 608 (January 1975), pp. 21–22; U.S. Senate, Committee on Armed Services, Hearings on the National Security Act, 80th Congress, 1st Session (Washington, D.C.: 1947), Part 2, p. 623.

22. Anthony Cave Brown and Charles B. McDonald, *The Secret History of the Atomic Bomb* (Penguin, New York, 1977), p. 210.

23. Franklin D. Roosevelt to Vannevar Bush, November 17, 1942; Online: Special Collections & Archives Research Center, Oregon State University, 2015.

24. Senate Select Committee on Intelligence, "Whether Disclosure of Authorized for Intelligence Activities Is in the Public Interest, 95th Cong., 1st Session, April 27–28, 1977 (Government Printing Office, Washington, D.C.), p. 4.

25. President George H. W. Bush, Statement on Signing the Intelligence Authorization Act, Fiscal Year 1992 (The White House, December 4, 1991).

26. National Commission on Terrorist Attacks Upon the United States, *The 9/11 Commission Report* (Government Printing Office, Washington, D.C., 2004), p. 416.

27. Statement of James R. Clapper, *The Washington Post*, August 29, 2013.

Chapter 8

1. George Washington, *State of the Union Address*, January 8, 1790 (Federal Hall, New York).

2. Thomas Jefferson: "Letter to the President of the Senate and to the Speaker of the House of Representatives Regarding the President's Annual Message," December 8, 1801. Online by Gerhard Peters and John T. Woolley, *The American Presidency Project* http://www.presidency.ucsb.edu.

3. Gerhard Casper, "Executive-Congressional Separation of Powers During the Presidency of Thomas Jefferson," Stanford Law Review, vol. 47, no. 3 (February 1995), p. 480.

4. *The Jefferson Monticello*, "Public Speaking," Online at Monticello.org (Charlottesville, VA).

5. "*New York Times*, "On This Day," December 5, 1923 (The New York Times Company, 2010).

6. *State of the Union Addresses and Messages*, The American Presidency Project, John Wooley and Gerard Peters, eds.

7. "Madison Debates," August 24, 1787, The Avalon Project (Lillian Goldman Law Library, Yale Law School, 2008).

8. Alexander Hamilton, *The Federalist* No. 77, April 4, 1788, The Avalon Project (Lillian Goldman Law Library, Yale Law School, 2008).

9. James L. Sundquist, *The Decline and Resurgence of Congress* (Brookings Institution, Washington, D.C., 1981), p. 39.

Chapter 9

1. *McGrain* v. *Daugherty*, 273 U.S. 135 (1927).

2. St. Clair's Defeat, as it came to be known, represents the single greatest defeat suffered by the U.S. army at the hands of Native Americans, greatly surpassing the casualties in Custer's defeat eighty-five years later at Little Big Horn.

3. *Annals of Congress*, March 27, 1792 (Gales and Seaton, Washington, D.C., 1849), p. 492.

4. *Ibid.*

5. George Washington to James Madison, May 5, 1783; Mark J. Rozell, et al. eds., *George Washington and the Origins of the American Presidency* (Praeger Publishing, Westport, CT, 2000), p. 146.

6. John P. Foley, ed., *The Jefferson Cyclopedia* (Funk & Wagnals Company, New York, 1900), p. 179.

7. *Ibid.*

8. Thomas Jefferson Randolph, ed., *Memoirs, Correspondence and Private Papers of Thomas Jefferson*, vol. iv (Henry Colburn and Richard Bentley, London, 1829), p. 476.

9. *Annals of Congress*, January 24, 1794 (Gales and Seaton, Washington, D.C., 1855), p. 38. A week earlier, on January 17, a motion was passed "directing" Secretary of State Edmund Randolph to provide the requested documents. On January 24, that motion was amended by addressing it to the President. The amendment also substituted "requested" for "directed."

10. Harold C. Syrett, ed., " Opinion on Communicating to the Senate the Dispatches of Gouvenor Morris" (Jan. 28, 1794), *Papers of Alexander Hamilton* (Columbia University Press, New York, 1969), pp. 666–667.

11. "From George Washington to the United States Senate," February 26, 1794. *Founders Online* National Archives, www.founders.archive.gov/Washington [Original source:

Christine Steinberg, ed., *The Papers of George Washington,* Presidential Series, vol. 15 (University of Virginia Press, Charlottesville, 2009), p. 284. Even as to the documents that were turned over to the Senate, Washington emphasized that "the nature of them manifests the propriety of their being received as confidential."

12. Edmund Randolph to George Washington, January 20, 1794. *Founders Online* National Archives, www.founders.archive.gov/Washington [Original source: Christine Steinberg, ed., *The Papers of George Washington,* Presidential Series, vol. 15 (University of Virginia Press, Charlottesville, 2009), pp. 92–94.

13. *Annals of Congress.* March 2, 1796 (Gales and Seaton, Washington, D.C., 1855), pp. 400–401.

14. *Ibid.,* at 424 (March 7, 1796).

15. *Ibid.,* at 612–613 (March 24, 1776).

16. President George Washington Message to the House of Representatives of the United States, March 30, 1796. Online by John Wolley and Gerhard Peters, *The American Presidency Project,* www.presidency.ucsb.edu.

17. *Annals of Congress,* April 6, 1796 (Gales and Seaton, Washington, D.C., 1855), pp. 771–772.

18. *Ibid.,* at 1296.

19. *United States* v. *Richard M. Nixon,* 418 U.S. 683 (1974).

Chapter 10

1. James Gregory Bradsher, "An Administrative History of the Disposal of Federal Records, *Provenance, Journal of the Society of Georgia Archivists* 3, no. 2 (January, 1985), p. 17 n. 3.

2. Attorney General's Comm. On Administrative Procedure, Report, "Administrative Procedure in Government Agencies," S. Doc. No. 8, 77th Cong. 1st Sess. 243 (1941).

3. *Ibid.,* at 25.

4. Senate Comm. On the Judiciary, " Report on the Administrative Procedure Act," S. Rep. No. 752, 79th Cong. 2d Sess. 17–18 (1946).

5. House Comm. On the Judiciary, "Report on the Administrative Procedure Act," H.R. Rep. No. 1980, 79th Cong., 2d Sess. 17–18 (1946).

6. S. Rep. No. 88–1219, 88th Cong. 2d Sess., July 23, 1964, p. 3.

7. President Barrack H. Obama, "Memorandum for the Heads of Departments and Agencies " (The White House, January 21, 2009).

8. Quoted in *Arizona Republic* (June 27, 1966).

9. Thomas Blanton, ed., *Freedom of Information at 40,* July 4, 2006, The National Security Archive (George Washington University, Washington, D.C.).

10. "White House Opposition Stalls Information Bill," *Washington Star,* August 9, 1965.

11. Memorandum of Robert Kitner, June 24, 1966 (The White House).

12. Lyndon B. Johnson, Statement by the President Upon Signing the "Freedom of Information Act," July 4, 1966 (San Antonia, Texas); Online by Gerhard Peters and John T. Woolley, *The American Presidency Project,* www.presidency.ucsb.edu.

13. Memorandum from Attorney General John Ashcroft for Heads of Federal Departments and Agencies: Freedom of Information Act, October 12, 2001, at www.doi.gov/foia/foia.pdf.

14. Memorandum from President Barack Obama for Heads of Executive Departments and Agencies: Freedom of Information Act, January 2, 2009 at www.whitehouse.gov/the_press_office/Freedom of Information Act/.

15. *Frankel* v. *SEC,* 460 F.2d 813, 816 (2d Cir. 1972), *cert. denied* 93 S. Ct. 125 (1972).

16. PBS Newsletter, "The RUNDOWN," Ted Bridis, Associated Press (March 18, 2015).

17. 88 Stat. 1695, 44 U.S.C.§ 2111.

18. 44 U.S.C. §2204(c)(2).

19. President Barack Obama, Executive Order 13489, Sec. 2(a) (January 21, 2009).

20. 69 Stat. 695, 44 U.S.C. §2112.

Chapter 11

1. J.R. Wiggins, *Freedom or Secrecy*, rev. ed. (Oxford University Press, New York, 1964), p. 95.

2. J.G. Randall, *Constitutional Problems Under Lincoln*, rev. ed., Peter Smith (Gloucester, Massachusetts, 1963), p. 508.

3. Abraham Lincoln, Second Inaugural Address (March 4, 1865). Online by John Wolley and Gerhard Peters, *The American Presidency Project*, www.presidency.ucsb.edu.

4. Among the first of those orders was General Order No. 35, issued by the Army's Adjutant General's Office on April 12, 1869. The order provided that "Commanding officers of troops occupying regular forts ... will permit no photographic or other views of the same to be taken without the permission of the War Department." Arvin S. Quist, Oakridge Classification Associates (Oak Ridge, TN, 2020), p. 19.

5. 52 18 U.S.C. § 795 *et seq.*

6. Freedom of Information Act, 5 U.S.C. §552(b)(1).

7. Final Report of Committee on Classified Information (Nov. 8, 1956), U.S. Dept. of Defense.

8. *Ibid.*

9. *See* Cong. Rec. Senate, vol. 152, Pt. 15 (September 28, 2006), p. 20384.

10. "Address by Herbert Brownell, Jr., Attorney of the United States," Associated Press Managing Editors Association (Chicago, IL, Nov. 6, 1953).

11. Kenneth D. Mayer, *With The Stroke Of A Pen* (Princeton University Press, 2001), p 146.

12. President Jimmy Carter, Executive Order 12065, §3-303 (The White House, June 28, 1978).

13. Department of Justice "Overview of Executive Order 12356," FOIA Update, vol. III, no. 3 (January 1, 1982).

14. President Barack H. Obama, "Memorandum of May 27, 2009—Classified Information and Controlled Unclassified Information," 74 Federal Register 26277, June 1, 2009.

15. President Barack H. Obama, Executive Order 13526 (The White House, December 29, 2009).

16. *Ibid.*, at §1.1(b).

17. *Ibid.*, at §1.1(c).

Bibliography

Records of Official Proceedings

Annals of Congress, 1789–1824. Washington, D.C.: Gales & Seaton, 1834. Online: "A Century of Lawmaking for a New Nation: U.S. Congressional Documents and Debates, 1774–1875."

The Congressional Globe, 1833–1873. Washington, D.C.: Blair & Rives. Online: "A Century of Lawmaking for a New Nation: U.S. Congressional Documents and Debates, 1774–1875."

Congressional Record. Washington, D.C. Online: http//www.congress.gov.

Elliot, Jonathan, ed. *Debates in the Several State Conventions on the Adoption of the Federal Constitution*. Washington, D.C., 1836. Online: "A Century of Lawmaking for a New Nation: U.S. Congressional Documents and Debates, 1774–1875."

Farrand, Max, ed. *The Records of the Federal Convention of 1787*. New Haven: Yale University Press 1911. Online: "A Century of Lawmaking for a New Nation: U.S. Congressional Documents and Debates, 1774–1875."

Journal of the House of Representatives, Executive Journal of the Senate, and *Legislative Journal of the Senate*. Washington, D.C. Online: "A Century of Lawmaking for a New Nation: U.S. Congressional Documents and Debates, 1774–1875."

Journals of the Continental Congress, 1774–1789. Washington, D.C.: GPO, 1904–1937. Online: HATHI TRUST Digital Library.

Register of Debates in Congress, 1825–1837. Washington, D.C.: Gales & Seaton, 1825–1837. Online: "A Century of Lawmaking for a New Nation: U.S. Congressional Documents and Debates, 1774–1875."

Rives, J., ed. *Abridgement of the Debates of Congress from 1789 to 1856*. New York: D. Appleton and Co., 1858. Online: HATHI TRUST Digital Library; archive.org/details/abridgmentofdebates.

Secret Journals of the Continental Congress. Boston: Thomas B. Wait, 1821. Online: HATHI Trust Digital Library; archive.org/details/secretjournals.

Books and Journals

Abbot, William, ed. *The Papers of George Washington: Confederation Series 329*. Charlottesville: University of Virginia Press, 1997.

Adams, Charles, ed. *The Works of John Adams*. Boston: Little, Brown and Co., 1856. Online: http://oll.libertyfund.org.

Adams, John. *Adams Family Papers: An Electronic Archive*. Massachusetts Historical Society. Online: http://www.masshist.org.

Adolphus, John. *The History of England from the Accession to the Decease of King George the Third*. London: A.E. Mallett, 1841.

Alexander, John. *The Selling of the Constitution: A History of News Coverage*. Madison: Madison House, 1990.

Bibliography

Boyd, Julian B. *Anglo-American Union: Joseph Galloway's Plan to Preserve the British Empire, 1774–1778.* New York: Octagon Books, 1970.

Bradsher, James. *Provenance.* "Journal of the Society of Georgia Archivists vol. 2. no. 2. 1985. Online: http://digitalcommons.kennesaw.edu/provenance/vol3/iss2/.

Brown, Anthony, and Charles MacDonald, eds. *The Secret History of the Atomic Bomb.* New York: Dial Press, 1977.

Burnett, Edmund, ed. *Letters of Members of the Continental Congress.* Washington, D.C.: Carnegie Institute, 1921.

Burns, James. *Transforming Leadership.* New York: Grove Press, 2003.

Butterfield, L.H., ed. *The Papers, Diary, and Autobiography of John Adams.* Cambridge: Harvard University Press, 1961. Founders Online: National Archives: http://founders.archives.gov/documents/Adams

Byrd, Robert. *The Senate 1789–1989: Addresses on the History of the United States Senate.* Washington, D.C.: GPO, 1988.

Clayton, Joseph, ed. "The American Lawyer." New York: Corporation Legal Manual Company, 1907.

Conway, Moncure. *Omitted Chapters of History Disclosed in the Life and Papers of Edmund Randolph.* New York: G.P. Putnam's Sons, 1889.

Cramnick, Isaac, ed. *The Portable Edmund Burke.* New York: Penguin Classics, 1999.

Cullen, Charles, ed. *The Papers of Thomas Jefferson.* Princeton: Princeton University Press, 1990.

Cushing, Harry, ed. *The Writings of Samuel Adams.* New York: G.P. Putnam's Sons, 1907.

Farrand, Max. *The Framing of the Constitution of the United States.* New Haven: Yale University Press, 1913.

Farrand, Max, ed. *The Fathers of the Constitution, a Chronicle of the Establishment of the Union.* New Haven: Yale University Press, 1921.

Federico, Joseph, and Matthew McHenry. *Galloway Township.* Charleston, SC: Arcadia Publishing, 2011.

Fisher, Louis. *Presidential Spending Power.* Princeton: Princeton University Press, 1975.

Fitzpatrick, John, ed. *The Writings of George Washington.* Washington, D.C.: GPO, 1933.

Foley, John, ed. *The Jefferson Cyclopedia.* New York: Funk & Wagnals Co., 1900.

Force, Peter. *American Archives, Fifth Series.* Washington, D.C.: M. St. Clair Clarke and Peter Force, 1848–1853.

Ford, Paul, ed. *The Works of Thomas Jefferson.* New York: G.P. Putnam's Sons, 1904.

Ford, Worthington, ed. *Some Papers Laid Before the Continental Congress.* Washington, D.C.: GPO, 1905.

Forman, S. *Political Activities of Philip Freneau.* Baltimore: Johns Hopkins University Press, 1902.

Franklin, Benjamin, and William T. Franklin ed. *Memoirs of the Life and Writings of Benjamin Franklin.* London: Printed for Henry Colburn, 1818.

Gay, Sidney, ed. *American Statesman: James Madison.* Boston: Houghton, Mifflin and Co., 1899.

Gilpin, Henry, ed. *The Papers of James Madison.* Washington, D.C.: Langtree & O'Sullivan, 1840.

Gordy, John. *A History of Political Parties in the United States.* New York: Henry Holt and Co., 1900.

Groves, Leslie. *It Can Now Be Told: The Story of the Manhattan Project.* New York: Da Capo Press, 1962.

Hall, John. *The Port Folio.* Philadelphia: Harrison Hall, 1824.

Hamilton, Alexander, et al. "The Federalist Papers." The Avalon Project, Yale Law School. Online: http// http://avalon.law.yale.edu

Hamilton, John, ed. *The Works of Alexander Hamilton.* New York: Charles S. Francis & Co., 1851.

Harley, Lewis. *The Life of Charles Thomson.* Philadelphia: George W. Jacobs and Company, 1900.

Hoffmann, Daniel. *Governmental Secrecy and the Founding Fathers: A Study in Constitutional Controls.* Westwood, CT: Greenwood Press, 1981.

Holmes, Jerry, ed. *Thomas Jefferson: A Chronology of His Thoughts*. Lanham, MD: Rowman & Littlefield, 2002.

Hudson, James, ed. *Supplement to Max Farrand's The Records of the Federal Constitution of 1787*. New Haven: Yale University Press, 1987.

Hunt, Gaillard, ed. *The Writings of James Madison*. New York: G.P. Putnam's Sons, 1904.

Irving, Washington. *The Life of George Washington*. New York: Cosimo Classics, 2005.

Jackaway, Gwenyth. *Media at War: Radio Challenges to the Newspapers*. Westport, CT: Praeger Publishers, 1995.

Jackson, Donald, and Dorothy Twohig, eds. *The Diaries of George Washington, July 1786– December 1789*. Charlottesville: University of Virginia Press, 1979.

John, Richard. *Spreading the News: The American Postal System From Franklin to Morse*. Cambridge: Harvard University Press, 1995.

Kaminski, John. *Secrecy and the Constitutional Convention*. Madison: University of Wisconsin Press, 2005.

Kaminski, John, and Gaspare Saladino, eds. *Commentaries on the Constitution, Public and Private*. Madison: State Historical Society of Wisconsin, 1981.

Kaminski, John, and Gaspare Saladino, eds. *The Documentary History of the Ratification of the Constitution*. Madison: State Historical Society of Wisconsin, 1995.

Kaminski, John, and Jill McCaughan, eds. *A Great and Good Man: George Washington in the Eyes of His Contemporaries*. Lanham, MD: Rowman & Littlefield, 1989.

Kidd, Thomas. *Patrick Henry: First Among Patriots*. New York: Basic Books, 2011.

King, Charles, ed. *The Life and Correspondence of Rufus King*. New York: G.P. Putnam's Sons, 1894.

Klarman, Michael, ed. *The Framers' Coup: The Making of the United States Constitution*. New York: Oxford University Press, 2016.

Langguth, A.J. *Patriots*. New York: Simon and Shuster, 1988.

Lieber, Francis. *On Civil Liberty and Self-Government*. Philadelphia: Lippincott, Grambo and Co., 1888.

Lloyd, Gordon, ed. *James Madison's Notes of Debates in the Federal Convention of 1787*. Ashland, OH: Ashbrook Center, Ashland University, 2014.

MacDonagh, Michael. *The Book of Parliament*. London: Isbister and Co., 1897.

Madison, James. *Notes on the Debate in the Federal Convention of 1787*, Galliard Hunt, ed. Oxford: Oxford University Press, 1920. The Avalon Project, Yale Law School. Online: http// http://avalon.law.yale.edu

Marshall, John. *The Life of George Washington, Commander in Chief of the American Forces*. Philadelphia: C. P. Wayne, 1805.

Massey, William. *A History of England During the Reign of George the Third*. London: John W. Parker and Son, 1858.

Mattern, David, ed. *The Papers of James Madison*. Charlottesville: University of Virginia Press, 1991.

Mcclay, Edgar, ed. *Journal of William Mcclay*. New York: D. Appleton and Company, 1890.

McPherson, Elizabeth. *Quarterly Journal of Speech*. Vol. 28, Issue 2. 1948. Online: Taylor and Francis Online, 2009.

McRee, Griffith, ed. *Life and Correspondence of James Iredell*. New York: D. Appleton and Company, 1857.

Milkis, Sydney. *The American Presidency: Origins and Development*. Washington, D.C.: CQ Press, 2016.

Morton, Joseph. *Shapers of The Great Debate at The Constitutional Convention of 1787*. Westport, CT: Greenwood Press, 2006.

"The 9/11 Commission Report: Final Report of the National Commission on Terrorist Attacks Upon the United States." Washington, D.C.: GPO, 2004.

Palmer, William, ed. *Calendar of Virginia State Papers and Other Manuscripts*. Richmond: H.W. Flournoy, 1890.

Parsons, Lynn. *John Quincy Adams*. Lanham, MD: Rowman & Littlefield, 1998.

Peeks, George, ed. *The Political Writings of John Adams*. Indianapolis, IN: Hackett Publishing, 2003.

Pfister, Jude. *Charting an American an American Republic: The Origins and Writing of the Federalist Papers.* Jefferson, NC: McFarland, 2016.

Pitt, William. *Celebrated Speeches of CHATAM, BURKE, AND ERSKINE.* Philadelphia: E.C. & J. Biddle, 1845. Online: HAITHI TRUST Digital Library.

Randolph, Thomas, ed. *Memoirs, Correspondence and Private Papers of Thomas Jefferson.* London: Henry Colburn and Richard Bentley, 1829.

Rozell, Mark, and William Pederson, eds. *George Washington and the Origins of the American Presidency.* Westport, CT: Praeger Publishing, 2000.

Rutland, Robert. *The Ordeal of the Constitution: The Antifederalists and the Ratification Struggles of 1777–1788.* Norman: University of Oklahoma Press, 1966.

Rutland, Robert, and Charles F. Hobson, eds. *The Papers of James Madison.* Charlottesville: University of Virginia Press, 1977.

Smith, Paul H., ed. *Letters of Delegates to Congress, 1774–1789.* Washington, D.C.: Library of Congress, 1976–2000. Online: http://www.loc.gov

Sparks, Jared. *The North America Review* (Hilliard, Metcalf & Co., 1827).

Sparks, Jared. *The Writings of George Washington.* Boston: Russell, Odiorne and Metcalf, 1835.

Storing, Herbert, ed. *The Complete Anti-Federalist.* Chicago: University of Chicago Press, 1981.

Sundquist, James. *The Decline and Resurgence of Congress.* Washington, D.C.: Brookings Institution, 1981.

Swanstrom, Roy. *A Dissertation on the First Fourteen Years of the Upper Legislative Branch.* Washington, D.C.: GPO, 1988.

Swift, Elaine. *The Making of an American Senate: Reconstitutive Change in Congress, 1787–1841.* Ann Arbor: University of Michigan Press, 1996.

Syrett, Harold, ed. *Papers of Alexander Hamilton.* New York: Columbia University Press, 1969.

Tansill, Charles, ed. *Documents Illustrative of the Formation of the Union of the American States.* Washington, D.C.: GPO, 1927.

Toqueville, Alexis de. *Democracy in America.* London: Saunders and Otley, 1835.

Tyler, Lyon, ed. *William and Mary College Quarterly Historical Magazine.* Richmond, VA: Whitted & Shepperson, 1912.

Tyler, Moses. *Patrick Henry.* Boston: Houghton, Mifflin and Co., 1899.

Vile, John. *The Constitutional Convention of 1787: A Comprehensive Encyclopedia of America's Founding.* Santa Barbara, CA: ABC-CLIO, Inc., 2005.

Warren, Charles. *The Making of the Constitution.* Boston: Little, Brown & Co., 1937.

Wood, Gordon. *The Creation of the American Republic, 1776–1787.* Chapel Hill: University of North Carolina Press, 1969.

Worthington, R., ed. *Letters and Other Writings of James Madison.* New York: J.B. Lippincott and Co., Published by Order of Congress, 1884.

Index